Teaching Five to Eight Year-Olds

THEORY AND PRACTICE IN EDUCATION
General Editor: Dennis Child

Teaching
Five to Eight Year-Olds

Maurice Chazan, Alice Laing
and Gillian Harper

Basil Blackwell

First published 1987

Basil Blackwell Ltd
108 Cowley Road, Oxford, OX4 1JF, UK

Basil Blackwell Inc.
432 Park Avenue South, Suite 1503
New York, NY 10016, USA

British Library Cataloguing in Publication Data

Chazan, Maurice
  Teaching five to eight year–olds.
  (Theory and practice in education).
  1. Education, Primary   2 Teaching
  I. Title   II. Laing, Alice F.
  III. Harper, G. C.   IV. Series
  372.11'02   LB1507

  ISBN 0–631–14004–2
  ISBN 0–631–14005–0 Pbk

Library of Congress Cataloging in Publication Data

Chazan, Maurice.
  Teaching five to eight year-olds.
  (Theory and practice in education; 5)
  Bibliography: p.
  Includes indexes.
  1. Education, Primary—Great Britain. 2. Child
development—Great Britain. I. Laing, Alice F.
II. Harper, G. C. (Gillian C.) III. Title. IV. Series.
LB1507.C43   1987   372'.241'0941   87–11499
ISBN 0–631–14004–2
ISBN 0–631–14005–0 (pbk.)

Typeset in 10 on 11½pt Sabon
by Cambrian Typesetters, Frimley, Camberley, Surrey
Printed in Great Britain

Contents

Editor's Preface

Very few, if any, educational problems are straightforward enough to have simple answers. Therefore, in so complex a human activity as educating, it should be no surprise that yet another series can still have a vital and significant contribution to make to our understanding of educational problems. Theorists and practitioners in the many developing interests in education quite properly continue to want to share their views and findings with others.

Theory and Practice in Education attempts to present, in a readable form, a range of issues which need to be considered by serving and student teachers in their roles as practitioners. Wherever formal, organized learning exists in our schools and colleges, there will always be questions relating, for example, to the effectiveness of teaching and children's learning, the preparation and adequacy of what is taught, the processes of assessment and evaluation, the sensitive problems of accountability, the preparation of children for 'life' and the monitoring of innovations.

The formal education of children between five and eight years of age has been an essential part of the education of all children in Britain for many years. Indeed, there are strong arguments being presented for the age of compulsory schooling to be lowered further. But despite its long history, teachers (and parents) continue to question the appropriateness of their teaching techniques, what should be taught and how best to engage the intellect and interest of the young. Teachers worry about the ways in which play, language and cognition, emotional and social development should become significant aspects of educational regimes.

It is timely that Maurice Chazan, Alice Laing and Gillian Harper have brought together in one volume a wealth of their experience and research literature in order to address the essential problems associated with the education of the five to eight age group. All three authors are well known in their different fields and it makes particular sense for them to come together in one volume. The wealth of material makes the book suitable for student and teacher alike and I feel confident that the reader will find not only topics of personal concern, but an abundance of references to further reading which should satisfy those who need to probe more deeply.

Leeds   *Dennis Child*

Acknowledgements

The authors would like to thank Mr W. T. Littlewood, Lecturer in Education at the University College of Swansea, for his helpful comments on chapter 5 (Helping Language Growth); also Mrs Christine Williams and Mrs Jill Edwards for secretarial assistance. The authors and publishers are grateful to Gardner Press Inc. for permission to reproduce the figure on p. 59.

1

The Early School Years:
An Introduction

When, in the seventeenth and eighteenth centuries, new ideas on the nature of education emerged, the focus of this discussion concerned to a large extent the early years of childhood. Thus Comenius, a practical German visionary, wrote on the education of pre-school children and produced, as well as textbooks for school-age pupils, an illustrated encyclopaedia, *Orbis Pictus* (*The World in Pictures*). This was published in the 1650s and was aimed at introducing young children, through illustration, to all he thought anyone needed to know. The *Orbis Pictus* may not now seem to be a great contribution to early education, despite its popularity for nearly two hundred years, but it did show that information could be presented to young children in such a way as to be attractive and meaningful to them and this realization was important. In the present century, Bruner (1960) has written that 'any subject can be taught effectively to any child at any stage of development' and this surely reflects the basic concept underlying Comenius' achievement. Both in their different ways are stressing, as so many educators have done, that the way in which a topic is presented is of major importance and that apparently complex knowledge is often based on simple principles.

Early education, therefore, places the learner at the centre of the educative process and not the subject to be taught. It is seen as being child-centred. The universality of this belief can be illustrated by the current concern in the Soviet Union regarding the admission of children to school at six years of age instead of seven (Shaw, 1984). Soviet teachers were warned that existing curricula and methods would not be suitable for these younger children and new approaches based on play and games would have to be implemented. Young children, therefore, are not only seen as being at the centre of any educational programme but it is also assumed that they learn in a rather different way from older children — through play;

through activity; through their own self-generated discovery. An understanding of the nature of children's development in all aspects is, therefore, necessary in order to appreciate what can be offered as education to young children.

EDUCATION AND CHILD DEVELOPMENT

So what do we mean when we use the term 'education' in relation to children aged five to eight years? Does 'education' begin when children enter formal schooling, or is school entry only part of a wider educative process? Clearly the latter viewpoint is nearer the truth of the matter than the former, for children by the age of five years have learned a wide range of skills with a speed and an efficiency which formal schooling fails to emulate. Indeed, some consider school entry to be an interruption in the proper education of the young. Furthermore, success in the formal education system owes a great deal to what has happened to children before they enter it.

In its widest sense education could be considered as the provision of appropriate learning experience to encourage optimum development, whether inside or outside the formal school system. Stonier (1982) has forecast, how accurately no one knows, that in the twenty-first century there will be a switch in what is taught inside and what is taught outside school at present, so that children will then be acquiring literacy and numeracy in their home from computers while school will offer the opportunities for social interaction that might otherwise be missed. In the meantime the emphasis seems to be more on harmonizing the experiences offered to young children inside and outside of school, rather than seeing them as complementary. Cleave et al. (1982), for example, considering the transition from home to school, or from pre-school to school, would wish that such a change 'is sufficient to be stimulating but not so drastic as to cause shock'.

To decide what are 'appropriate' learning experiences, both at five years of age and in the immediately following years, requires a considerable knowledge of child development and this is the concern of much of the present volume. However, it may be appropriate at this point to give an overview of development in these years in order to provide some sort of framework for what is to come.

The years from five to eight do not span dramatic changes in any aspect of development, whether physical, cognitive, social, emotional, moral or aesthetic. There is no sudden spurt in physical growth or in the acquisition of much-valued skills such as walking or talking. But changes there are, most of them with considerable significance for children's future progress.

Physical Development

Of course, during the years in question children grow steadily but the velocity of that growth is slow in comparison with both the very early years of infancy and the later adolescent years (Tanner, 1962). A steady yearly increment in height and weight is common to both boys and girls. The development of the cells within the brain, however, adds considerably to its weight (Tanner, 1984) and the years from birth to seven, when ninety per cent of the adult weight of the brain has been achieved, are clearly important. Presumably children's developing physical prowess and co-ordination enable them to respond to, or to create, experiences which stimulate brain-cell growth, and school entry is likely to make a significant contribution to the range of experiences available to them.

School entry may also lead to the identification of developmental problems in this area, especially if children have not attended any pre-school provision. Marked differences in gross motor-skill ability or slowness to develop fine motor co-ordination can be identified and monitored by teachers, as can difficulties in hearing or vision. Children at home, in a one-to-one situation with adults who know them well, may not be recognized as having any hearing or vision impairment, just as they may not be seen to have co-ordination problems if they have seldom had the opportunity to display fine, 'table top' skills.

Cognitive Development

For Erikson (1950), the school years prior to adolescence are a time when children demonstrate industry and initiative by becoming 'eager and absorbed units in a productive situation'. This part of their 'entrance to life' demands that they demonstrate competence in the skills they have acquired and add to these, thereby increasing their autonomy and their status. If they do not meet the challenges of this period in their development, their failure leads, Erikson believes, to a persisting sense of inferiority. Primary school should maximize children's sense of their own competence, a difficult requirement when children vary so much at five years of age in what they have experienced, however well they have been helped to interpret their experiences and their personal endowment.

Cognitive skills are not only very varied, covering as they do intellectual, linguistic, perceptual and memory abilities, but they reflect children's developmental history. They may mature in an orderly way but their potential will be developed only with adequate and relevant stimulation. Between five and seven years of age, for example, children build on their acquired conceptualization of their world by being much more selective in what they attend to and by being able to sort and classify their experiences more rapdily and more efficiently (Mussen et al., 1979). The acquisition of the skill of reading is a case in point. If their pre-school experience has not encouraged the necessary preliminary categorization of their environment, or has not given them sufficient richness of language to appreciate similarities and differences in this categorization, they cannot easily move on to the more selective approach. Teachers see them as lacking in attention or responding to inappropriate cues, when perhaps the trouble lies in some lag in their cognitive development.

The years from five to eight also lead in to what Piaget, the great Genevan writer, believed to be a major change in children's understanding of their world in all its aspects. His views have become somewhat controversial and will be discussed at greater length later in this book. Whether or not one agrees with him, it is certainly true that children at eight years of age are very different in their outlook from what they were at five, showing a degree of understanding, competence and self-reliance which adults do not always fully appreciate.

Social Development

For many parents the main concern at school entry is whether their child will be able to adjust to all the new social relationships which being with different adults and a large group of children involves. Indeed, the major benefit seen by many parents to accrue from sending children to pre-school groups of one kind or another is that attendance will promote social adjustment (Haystead et al., 1980), an opinion which is shared by nursery staff (Taylor et al., 1972). Class teachers at the primary stage also stress social development, along with emotional/personal development (Ashton et al., 1975). The older, more experienced teachers in Ashton's study were found to prefer 'a socially oriented concept of education concerned with equipping the child, both personally and practically, to fit into society'.

First schools seem, therefore, to have an expressed commitment to moving children from the stage of seeing others as being there largely to help them achieve their goals to that of realizing the benefits and satisfactions arising from co-operation and the offering of help.

Social development is not just concerned with interactional skills, important though these are. It also involves the growing recognition of the behaviour, values and motives which have societal approval and the building of children's self-concepts. School is not the sole agent of such development, of course. Parents, other relatives, neighbours, peers and fellow pupils all play their part. But school provides many opportunities for guidance, through discussion of its own mores as well as of those in a wider society, and teachers make many references to children's abilities, attributes and skills, sometimes favourable and sometimes not. Staines (1958) found in his study that the infant school teachers made more remarks relating to children's self-concept than did the junior school teachers. Their comments were more often positive than negative but, as with with junior teachers, the thrust of the comments was towards performance and status. It is difficult to say what effect these comments have, both on the children towards whom they are directed and on those who do not receive them very often. The fact that teachers are highly important adults to young children must lend their comments significance and these opinions may well be incorporated in the children's self-picture. Positive evaluations may be helpful in encouraging children to make a more constructive appraisal of their behaviour and their impact on others than they have achieved so far. But children who seldom receive any favourable attention, or those who receive mainly derogatory comments, may come to accept the low standing or ineffectiveness in school that seems to be implied in their case.

Emotional Development

As with physical development, the years from five to eight are not normally seen as full of dramatic change in emotional development. Freud (see Hall, 1954), for example, saw them as calmer years compared to what has gone before and what is to come at adolescence; Gesell and Ilg (1965) discuss them as 'the stable years of childhood'. Children in this age group are not, however, without their problems. Some of these problems may have persisted from earlier years (Richman et al., 1982); some may be exacerbated by school entry (Cleave et al., 1982); some may emerge when children face challenges which they find difficulty in meeting (Webb, 1969). Teachers can do a great deal to smooth the way for children at school entry, as Cleave and her colleagues have pointed out, and can also give specific help to children who are showing particular difficulties in adjustment (Chazan et al., 1983).

Many children of this age are faced with more than one transition, for they may again change schools at seven years of age. Although they are by now more mature, entry to junior school may also present them with problems, especially if its organization and methods are different. For example, the traditional age of entry to junior school occurs at a time when, although reading skills are beginning to be firmly established, about half of the children (Pringle et al., 1966; Goodacre, 1967) still need a considerable amount of help. Children in their first junior year may feel intimidated or inadequate and may find the control exercised by junior class teachers (Galton et al., 1980) a very new experience.

It is not surprising, therefore, that Gesell and Ilg (1965) also comment, 'Perhaps we have exaggerated the perturbation of adolescence and also the steadiness and stability of childhood. More goes on than frankly meets the eye between five and the teens'. Children's growing maturity still leaves them vulnerable to fears, anxieties, worries and frustrations and they will react to these in many different ways. The suggestion in the Plowden Report (Central Advisory Council for Education (CAC), 1967) that the first school should span the years from five to eight was partly made on the basis of children's emotional development, although cognitive and social considerations also played an important part.

Moral Development

It has already been noted that the years in question see a change in how children view the world and their place in it. They lose their highly subjective viewpoint and begin to become not only more objective but also more realistic. The line between fantasy and reality becomes clearer as does the distinction between truth and falsehood. Other people and their concerns enter into the taking of decisions or the carrying out of planned actions although, even at eight years of age, children may still reject rational explanations and prefer immediate or selfish satisfactions. Piaget (1932) equated middle childhood with the development of understanding of equality and justice, while Kohlberg (1964) would see these years as moving the child from a naive hedonism towards a conventional approach to moral problems, with adult judgements being presumed correct and adult disapproval being avoided. Where precisely children will be in these stages depends not only on their age but, as in so many other developmental aspects, on their personal attributes and experiences. When eight-year-old children were asked (Ungoed-Thomas, 1978) about situations in which they felt uncertain, unhappy or aggrieved, what frequently puzzled and disturbed them were the differences in treatment by adults of children in the same home, school or street. While they may be intuitively recognizing that adults do have different standards and lack consistency, they may also be revealing their own inability to deal with all the nuances to be considered before judgements can be made.

The infant school years also see children becoming aware of rules in the games they play. These rules, however, are not seen as flexible and capable of adaptation so that the game may be played to everyone's advantage but rather they are accepted rigidly even though insistence on them may disrupt the activity. Children are thus insisting at their own level on the unquestioning obedience which they believe adults expect of them. After seven years of age this inflexibility begins to be tempered and modifications may be allowed in order to retain and consolidate co-operation with others.

Downey and Kelly (1978) suggest that the first school can help children's moral development by confronting them with problematic situations which are in conflict with their present moral beliefs but not too much in conflict. If the situations have been well chosen so as not to be too far in advance of the children's level of development, they argue that they will be challenged to think in a more complex manner.

Aesthetic Development

Finally comes the most difficult aspect of all. Aesthetic judgements in adults do not always appear to be based on any cumulative and widening understanding but often seem to reflect instead individual prejudices or unthinking conformity.

Everyone would surely wish for children that they should come to appreciate beauty in whatever form it is found and should enjoy the tremendous feelings of satisfaction arising from creating for themselves something which is worthwhile to them. As so often in education, the difficulty, especially with young children, is for the teacher to know when to step in and when to step back. It is frighteningly easy to impose adult conventions on children's productions and to reward the expected rather than the original response to literary, musical, artistic or dramatic experiences. Conversely, it is also easy not to realize when help and guidance are required if children are to develop aesthetically.

The extent to which children's response to school can be transformed by sensitive teaching is recorded by Sybil Marshall (1963) in her account of her own work in a small village school. Most teachers, however, could not sustain her approach or might feel that it laid too much stress on certain aspects of aesthetic development, leaving insufficient time for other aspects. However, all teachers should appreciate the importance of the provision of adequate time, proper tools and appropriate materials and be willing to encourage individual effort and satisfaction by interested discussion and well-organized displays. With children under the age of nine years it is particularly difficult to know whether any attempt should be made to provide direct adult instruction in their aesthetic productions. Eysenck (1972) would seem to argue that what teachers do up to the age of eight or nine years has little effect on children's aesthetic preferences but there is really no firm evidence that controlling tightly what children do in art, music, drama and so on, as opposed to allowing them free rein to do what they want, helps or hinders aesthetic development. Certainly very different productions emerge.

This brief overview of child development has been undertaken for two purposes: first, to provide a framework for the discussion of the education of young children; and second, to introduce some aspects which will be covered more fully later. In a book of this size, selection is inevitable. However, at the end of the book there are suggestions for further reading on child development. Another point needs to be made with regard to this overview. Although each aspect of development has been identified separately from the others, in reality each is very much interrelated with the others. Children's physical development affects their social, emotional and cognitive development; moral, social, emotional and cognitive development cannot be separated; and aesthetic development permeates the whole of children's well-being. Indeed the reality of the situation is even wider than this, for children do not exist in a vacuum and can only be understood as part of a family, a neighbourhood, a school, a society.

At the beginning of the chapter the point was made that early education should be child-centred. If this means that teachers should consider the level of development of children, then such a view must be endorsed. Sometimes, however, child-centred education is seen as child-regulated education. Claims are made that teacher direction can only be damaging, as it prevents children's free response to their environment and such freedom is seen as essential if individual potential is not to be distorted. A balanced view would suggest that it may be appropriate for children aged five to eight years to be offered a classroom approach which does not swing either to the extreme of regarding teachers as interfering in natural development if they construct educational programmes, or to the other extreme of seeing teachers as the sole arbitrators both of the educational programmes offered and how they are to be experienced. Teaching young children does not call for a *laissez-faire* approach or for an authoritarian, inflexible one. If young children are to extract as much as possible from their time in school, what is offered to them must be carefully structured so as to give them opportunities for developing in all aspects, opportunities which are attractive and meaningful to them and which also accommodate individual needs, preferences and styles of learning.

TEACHING YOUNG CHILDREN

Teachers of young children have, therefore, a difficult role to fill. Some of the difficulty arises from conflicting views of their original function (see Blyth, 1965). While for some, Froebel for example, teaching was likened to gardening, with the teacher's task being to provide the optimum growing conditions in which children might flourish as individuals in their own right, to others (for example in the monitorial system) the challenge was to provide education for all so as to improve minds and bodies and raise standards of living and civic responsibilities. Once elementary education for all was established in the twentieth century in this country, the latter objectives appeared to have been realized, although concern is still expressed by some critics over standards of literacy and numeracy (see, for example, Cox and Dyson, 1971). It became possible, however, to shift the emphasis in early education in the direction that pioneer writers, like Froebel (see Lawrence, 1952), had visualized and to advocate the pre-eminence of the individual as the determiner of his or her own learning. Teaching as instruction became unacceptable. Yet, at the back of their minds, teachers of young children still acknowledge their responsibilities with regard to literacy and numeracy and strive to reach certain standards of competence in these areas before children move up to the next stage. There may, therefore, be a degree of incompatibility between what teachers would like to do and what they feel they should be doing. It may be worthwhile to look more closely at the role of the teacher in today's infant or first schools.

Teachers in loco parentis?

No one would wish for teachers of young children who do not have affection and concern for their pupils; neither would anyone wish these teachers to be only kindly and loving, adept with the scissors and the paint pot. The growing realization since the 1960s onwards of the importance of the experiences offered to children in their early years has made it more than ever necessary that teachers at this stage must be very highly skilled. Yet they can never be the 'experts' about individual children that the children's own parents are (Newson, 1976; DES, 1978b). Sheer weight of numbers prevents this. Parents also will tend to see their own child in the best light; teachers bring objectivity to bear on children's progress and behaviour.

It is no part of the school, therefore, to lay claim to sole understanding of its pupils. Its efforts should not be seen as counteracting parental practices or in any way implying that these are deficient. If the school is to succeed in its aims, it must accept the variations in experience which young children bring with them to school. Pre-school provision can help some children whose experiences would otherwise be very limited but the extent to which this can be done is again partly determined by the degree of involvement of the parents. Pre-school programmes in America were shown to be effective (Bronfenbrenner, 1974; Weikart et al., 1978) when they were well-structured, efficiently taught and, above all, carried out with full parental co-operation.

So much more of children's time is spent at home than at school in the first eight years of life that it is not surprising that Tizard and Hughes (1984) claim that the opportunities for language development, for example, are much richer there than in nursery groups. The latter could never emulate the one-to-one relationship which is the norm at home. But the professional expertise of the teacher can develop that language by appropriate stimulation (Tough, 1973a; 1977a). A partnership between home and school is therefore essential. Teachers cannot 'stand in' for parents but in association with parents can help to provide a much more rounded and balanced view of children and their developmental needs than either could have on their own.

Teachers as Programme Planners?

Just how structured should the experiences offered in the first school be? The most skilled infant teachers are probably unaware of the extent to which they are selecting appropriate experiences and activities for their pupils. They see learning as being generated by the children themselves, as indeed it often is. Yet such learning would not occur if individual needs had not been carefully identified and catered for. The experiences and activities, also, need to be not just appropriate to the children's needs but productive in themselves of further learning. Good teaching requires careful planning and to that extent is inevitably 'structured'.

The adverse reaction displayed by some teachers of young children to structured programmes (see for instance Quigley, 1971) stems, probably, from their dislike of direct teacher instruction. Programmes like the various Distar kits, published by SRA and based on the work of Bereiter and Engelmann (1966), are sometimes viewed with suspicion as potential threats to the more intuitive response to children's needs which is preferred in this country. It may be that these programmes do not fully allow for individual variations in progress and even smack somewhat of 'drill' but they nevertheless provide useful clues as to how progress can best be encouraged and maintained. They provide 'entry' information so that children are always working at the right level, they are attractively produced and they incorporate 'testing' procedures so that teacher and learner know what has been accomplished. If teachers can achieve these objectives within their own planning, they can reap the benefit of adjusting the content to suit their pupil's needs. An absence of such structure would not allow freedom to the pupils but, rather, disorganized licence or frustration because of inappropriate provision.

Paradoxical though it may appear, teachers need to structure their work to foster flexibility. Individual variations can be accommodated more easily when the sequence of learning experiences has been carefully considered. It would seem, therefore, that a major requirement for teachers in the first school is to organize a programme of educational experiences, carefully related to each other but still amenable to change or extension as individual learning patterns require.

Teachers as Observers?

To allow for individual variations in the pace or depth of the learning experiences offered is clearly to accept a child-centred approach. However, those supporting such an approach might argue that for it to be truly child-centred children should themselves select the learning experiences rather than have them selected for them. This argument is based on the belief that children will find experiences productive of learning if they are personally involved in them and if they are relevant to their needs. Children, it is maintained, are the best judges of the experiences they require. There is considerable weight in this argument but it is clear that the experiences offered must at some point have been selected by the teacher. Only a certain amount of material or books, for example, can be displayed at any one time. How far children are able to develop the work they have selected will also depend on the teacher's ability to bring in the necessary further resources where appropriate. To provide the most fruitful experiences and to encourage children to explore and discover for themselves can only be successfully accomplished on the basis of careful observation of the children concerned over a period of time. Teachers must therefore be observers in order to provide the structured framework for learning which has already been discussed.

Moreover, the study of individual behaviour, whether in motor or social or intellectual activities, enables teachers to recognize children with special educational needs. That teachers are well placed to do so has already been noted, as slow or inappropriate development may not be noticed until the children in question are seen alongside a number of their peers. Again this topic will be looked at in more detail later. For the moment, however, it may be enough to say that time spent carefully watching one child's functioning over a number of different tasks and noting down the details of his or her behaviour is certainly not time wasted. It is not only children with learning difficulties of some kind who need careful monitoring. Very quiet children, over-active children, very bright children and those with particular talents in art or music or movement are also amongst those who should be carefully observed. In the hurly-burly of the classroom, especially in the first year of formal schooling, it is only too easy to find all the time available goes in organization and immediate management with observation being neglected.

Merely to watch children, although interesting, is not enough. The observations need to be translated into records which delineate children's capabilities and progress. In the final chapter in this book more will be said about record-keeping and the extent of detailed observation required to provide information which benefits the pupils and the teachers who come into contact with them. Observation needs to be translated into records and records into programmes for the process to be complete and for education to be really child-centred.

THE AIMS OF EDUCATION IN THE FIRST SCHOOL

Much has been said here about child-centred education. However, as was pointed out at the beginning of the chapter, while all might agree on the importance of developing individual potential, there is not necessarily agreement on how this might be attempted. The extent to which teachers should participate in children's activities, for example, can cause arguments in staffrooms. If the aims of education for young children are examined, the division of opinion becomes clear.

Research in this area (Ashton et al., 1975) has revealed that teachers in primary schools are broadly and fairly evenly divided into two groups with regard to the aims they subscribe to and the concomitant attitudes and methods they adopt. While both groups fully support the importance of individual development, they differ in the nature of the individual characteristics to be developed. The difference between the two groups is highlighted in descriptions of the type of pupil each would ideally like to see emerge from the educational system. One group of teachers, according to Ashton and her colleagues, subscribe to 'societal' aims, emphasizing that children should be encouraged towards as high levels of attainment in the three Rs as possible, should be good listeners, able to concentrate and should work industriously and conscientiously. For this group of teachers the ultimate aim is that children be enabled 'to join the adult society effectively and harmoniously' – hence the use of 'societal' to distinguish this group. The other group of teachers were seen as being 'individualistic' in their aims. Their ideal pupils would be encouraged to think for themselves, to be able to plan for themselves how they would use their time and to set their own objectives, recognizing their personal strengths and limitations. Ultimately these teachers would wish their pupils to be able to take up an 'autonomous role' in society.

The research in question has, therefore, revealed interesting contrasts in opinion as to how individual potential should be developed and these clearly lead to different pedagogical approaches. The amount of teacher-direction of activities, for example, will not be the same, different levels of noise in classrooms will be tolerated and varying expectations of acceptable work will be held. To indicate differences in this way is not to imply that 'individualistic' teachers do not hold any 'societal' views and vice versa. It is likely that both groups would willingly acquiesce in the value of each other's beliefs. It is more a question of differences of emphasis than conflicting viewpoints.

To try to relate teachers' views on the aims of education to their teaching style is not an easy task. For one thing, teachers may change their style according to the circumstances in which they are teaching, taking into consideration the age of the children, the size of the class or group, the topic being taught, the ethos of the school and so on. Nevertheless their preferred 'style', that which they would ideally like to adopt, might well reflect their underlying concept of how they would like to see children develop.

Various writers (for example, Bennett, 1976; Galton et al., 1980) have tried to classify teaching styles, although not always very successfully. Bennett's (1976) grouping into formal, informal and 'mixed' styles was straightforward but somewhat arbitrary and though he claimed that these differences in style were related to differences in pupil progress, his conclusions were challenged by those who disagreed with his grouping in the first place.

The four different styles identified by Galton et al. (1980) are very much more complex. They are based on careful analysis of observed differences in teacher–pupil interaction, class organization and preferred classroom routines, providing totally different groupings from that of Bennett. In fact Galton et al. claim that there is 'a lack of congruence' between the styles they delineate and 'those aspects of curricular and organizational strategy reflecting either a 'traditional' or a 'progressive' approach' (p. 141). They point out that if child-centred education is to be interpreted as 'leading the child from behind', there appears to be little evidence from actual research observation that this occurs in *any* of the primary classrooms they studied. Instead they found that individualization of questioning most often occurred in a whole-class teaching organization and individualization of work was realized when the children were in groups. 'The setting is socialized in this sense but the work is individualized' (p. 159). Even so, those teachers who most often made use of groups (and hence worked with the individuals in these groups) also 'emphasized "telling" and task supervision' (p. 159) more than teachers with different styles of teaching. It is small wonder that the researchers say the relationship between teaching style and classroom organization is confused.

Presumably aims must influence curriculum content but this is such a large topic that only selected aspects will be considered later in this volume. Current pressure, however, appears to be applied towards making curricular objectives far more visible than they have been in the education of young children (see, for example, Richards, 1982). For this to happen staff need to work towards agreement on what these objectives should be, a process which ought to provide useful guidelines not a straitjacket, and leave plenty of scope for the individual response of teachers and children alike. Teachers demonstrate their professionalism by the extent of their ability to establish teaching goals, while at the same time enabling individual children to extract as much from their educational experiences as possible. Tamburrini (1982) has argued for 'a synchrony between children's intentions and the educational dialogues a teacher initiates' at the pre-school (three to five years) stage. For children in the five to eight years age-range, the desired synchrony has to be between teachers' intentions, as well as children's intentions, and the whole educational programme offered.

SOME FUTURE TRENDS IN THE EDUCATION OF FIVE TO EIGHT YEAR-OLDS

New Methodology

The growing realization of the benefits accruing, by way of sequencing and consistency, from the move towards a degree of consensus in curriculum content has already been indicated. So also has the change in the teacher's role from the management of learning situations to an active participation in them in order to maximize their cognitive possibilities. The teacher's part in the full assessment and monitoring of children's progress is yet another of the trends noted. All of these make for changes in the education of young children which are already evident in some schools and which, it can be predicted, will probably be universally adopted in the future. Were these changes to be implemented for all children in the first school, however, much would still remain to be done before any claim could be made that educational parity had been achieved for every child. Teaching skills and experience, resources and, above all, the children's home environment will continue to favour some children while disadvantaging others.

Van der Eyken (1982) asserts also, more than a little pessimistically, that 'the wider objectives of educational policy have their roots in policies other than education' and that 'the life that three-to-eight year-olds lead in Europe in the Eighties will very largely be decided by factors outside the field either of the family or the school' (p. 85). Financial constraints or the threat of nuclear warfare illustrate at very different levels what is implied by these statements. Yet for teachers to appraise constantly how effective they are being, to be willing to change their approach if need be and to acquire new skills can only mean that, in school anyway, young children are being offered experiences which are as appropriate as possible to their current needs.

New Learning Experiences

The need for teachers to adapt to changing circumstances is exemplified in the introduction of one or more microcomputers into all primary schools in this country. Probably pupils have responded to the learning opportunities which micros offer more enthusiastically than their teachers! However, in-service courses, resource centres, advisory teachers and commercial publishers are all endeavouring to offer help and guidance (Dodds, 1984). The potential for interactive learning offered by computers is only just beginning to be realized and teachers are still coming to terms with the implications for a wide variety of subjects and intellectual ability levels. Indeed, there is at the moment no means of knowing whether computers call upon the same cognitive skills as teacher-centred education or whether they tap intellectual abilities infrequently used in book-based learning. It would seem quite likely that different skills are required. For example, pupils regarded by their schools today as having learning difficulties seem to be as skilful as anyone else in playing computer-based games. Interactive programmes may be able to accommodate many more learning styles than can any one teacher with his or her own teaching approach. And, of course, innovations in hardware and improved software are constantly appearing. Teachers can only try to appreciate the level of sophistication which their pupils will reach in the area (Jones, 1984). There is no question, as yet, of teachers passing on knowledge acquired from greater experience or more advanced understanding, for even very young children may exhibit a confidence and a competence which their teachers cannot emulate. Pupils and teachers working together as learners may well become the typical approach in computer-based activities.

Information technology is not just an additional topic in the curriculum or an aid to acquiring conventional skills more efficiently. A range of applications – from using the computer to assist learning through to using it to promote understanding and process information – has to be covered in a pupil's school career (Hubbard, 1984). Acquaintance with this range of applications has to begin as soon as possible, for only then will pupils be able to build on the use of the computer for simple instruction in order to develop a wider grasp of concepts, arising perhaps from simulation experiences, and a facility in developing and using data bases (Rushby, 1979; Obrist, 1983). The necessity for a good foundation to be laid in the primary school is reflected in the comment, 'All pupils leaving the school gate for the last time are walking towards computers, not leaving them behind' (Roberts and Ewan, 1984, p. 85).

New Relationships

Of the many trends observable in present-day education two can be singled out for consideration with regard to young children. The first of these is the benefit for all involved that results from deliberate structuring of co-operation between parents and teachers. Children's progress in reading can be taken as an interesting example here. Different points of view have been expressed by teachers on parental involvement in reading tuition. Some believe that parents do hear their children read; others argue that many homes are devoid of reading material; some feel that any practice in reading is useful; others fear that parents may have a different, if not wrong, approach which would simply confuse children. Research has shown (Hannon and Cuckle, 1984) that, in a sample of six to seven year-olds and their teachers, the children claimed that they did read at home. However, their teachers were very vague about the nature of this reading and, on the whole, had given little advice or support. Where an organized programme of reading instruction has been worked out between parents and teachers, the findings indicate improved performance overall (Tizard et al., 1982). All of the parents in this research study co-operated, even those who themselves, for a variety of reasons, found reading difficult. Similar comments have been made by others concerned in various schemes to promote parental involvement (for example, Trickey and Crispin, 1982; Andrew and Provis, 1983; Topping, 1984, 1985).

The second trend, the implications of which have yet to be fully realized, is the thrust towards fully integrating children with special educational needs into ordinary schools. More will be said of this in chapter 8 but, for the moment, this move can be used to illustrate the necessity of increasing contact with those outside of the immediate school staff who are concerned about young children and their development. Not only parents have a contribution to make. Social, medical, therapeutic and psychological services should also have more frequent access to first schools so that a full range of expertise can be applied as appropriate to individual learning difficulties. In the early years, schools should serve the whole of the community and also involve it. The support services should not just be called upon in a crisis but should be working along with teachers, helping them to develop suitable programmes or modify existing ones.

It can be seen, therefore, that while the traditional concerns of teachers of young children remain, new responsibilities, with all their opportunities, are in evidence. It is surely a gross under-estimation of what is a very challenging job to say that one is 'just an infant teacher'.

In this introductory chapter, many points have been raised which will be taken further in subsequent chapters. Chapters 2 and 3 will look at the curriculum in more detail, while chapters 4 and 5 consider the traditional concerns of education for young children, play and language development. Chapters 6 and 7 discuss cognitive growth and emotional and social development. The final three chapters look at children who find learning difficult for whatever reason; at ways of working with parents and others; and at how the transition from the first stage of education to the next can be most smoothly accomplished. Suggestions for further reading to deepen and widen these topics will be found towards the end of the book.

2

Classroom Concerns

INTRODUCTION

Over the last ten to twenty years the curriculum has attracted increasing attention in educational debate and discussions at all levels of schooling. Since the late 1970s, for example, both the Department of Education and Science (DES) and Her Majesty's Inspectorate (HMI) have been responsible for a rapidly growing number of guidelines, frameworks and discussion documents concerned with every aspect of curriculum planning and organization for the five- to sixteen-year-old age-group. HMI have also conducted two large-scale surveys at primary (DES, 1978a) and first school (DES, 1982a) level, which are useful in illustrating how curriculum theory is translated into practice in the classroom. Concurrent with these official inquiries there have been several other investigations which have also focused on the pedagogical dimension of the curriculum.

Two investigations which are of particular interest to teachers of young children are Bassey's 1978 survey of 900 primary teachers in Nottinghamshire and the ORACLE research (Galton et al., 1980; Galton and Simon, 1980; Simon and Willcocks, 1981), which looked at primary teaching in Leicestershire. The latter, being based on classroom observation rather than interview data, perhaps offers a more accurate insight into the curriculum in action than Bassey's survey. Using evidence from investigations such as these this chapter will examine differing views of curricula for young children together with the variety of organizational patterns which derive from them. Specific areas of the curriculum, such as creative activities and environmental studies, will be considered in more detail in the next chapter.

VIEWS OF THE CURRICULUM

The curriculum at the secondary level of schooling is generally seen as a collection of subjects, as a glance at any timetable in a comprehensive school will confirm. The school day usually consists of a series of discrete forty-five-minute units labelled 'history', 'English', 'physics' or 'mathematics'. Lower down the age-range, in junior or middle school, although some subject disciplines such as mathematics or English are still identifiable, the remainder of the curriculum is likely to be far less differentiated, incorporating broad areas of learning and experience such as environmental studies or art and craft. The daily pattern for still younger children, those in infant and first schools, is likely to bear no resemblance at all to the subject-oriented curriculum of secondary schools and shows even less differentiation than is found in junior or middle schools. It may be that the only fixed points on the timetable of these youngest children will be any activity that involves use of the Hall, such as PE or Assembly.

This general lack of recognizable subject labels in the timetable of first schools can be ascribed to two important factors. To begin with, many first school teachers feel that these adult classifications of areas of knowledge are an inappropriate means of structuring young children's activities since they do not correspond to the ways in which they experience the world. The second reason is organizational rather than curricular, in that individual groups of children will often be engaged simultaneously in a variety of activities at any one time. As this is very difficult to present in conventional terms on a timetable, teachers often resort to using very general categories such as 'activity periods'. This is not to say that 'history', 'geography', or any other part of the subject disciplines have no part to play in the early years curriculum but that they are more likely to be approached through a common theme or topic which attempts to integrate them rather than to differentiate between them.

On what, then, is the first school curriculum based? How is it organized? How does it link up with curricula at later stages of schooling? The curriculum can be defined and described in many different ways, most of which will succeed in giving only a partial view of what is an extremely complex topic. It is not the intention here to try and remedy this state of affairs by embarking on an all-embracing discussion of curricular matters but, rather, to concentrate on the framework of current educational thinking within which teachers are expected to operate the curriculum and how in fact this is translated into classroom practice. For while the debate continues about who defines the curriculum and in what way, it is individual teachers who have the responsibility of meeting the needs of children in the classroom by making the curriculum work.

The Progressive Movement – Fact or Fancy?

The 1960s were years of great optimism and pride in the primary education system of this country. The Plowden Report (CAC, 1967) had set the seal of approval on many of the 'newer' ways of educating young children, such as learning through play, discovery methods and flexible organization. Infant and first schools particularly were held to be in the vanguard of much innovation by advocates of 'open' education. Galton et al. (1980) attempt a thumbnail sketch of the ideal Plowden-type teacher and his or her class, where all the children are actively engaged in exploration and discovery and the teacher moves around consulting, guiding and stimulating individuals or occasionally, where convenient, groups of children who are at similar developmental stages. She or he has intimate knowledge of the physical, intellectual and social level of each child and knows, therefore, when and how best to stimulate and intervene with each one. There is little differentiation of subjects and little whole-class teaching.

The 'quickening trend' which the Plowden Report endorsed was towards increased pupil autonomy and responsibility for what and how they learned within an informal and flexible organizational framework. This had been interpreted as complete abdication of teacher control by some contemporary critics, some of whom went so far as to try to blame the student unrest of the period upon informal primary education (Cox and Dyson, 1969). The almost immediate conservative backlash, which began in 1969 with the Black Papers (Cox and Dyson, 1971) and reached a peak in the mid-1970s at the time of the William Tyndale affair, centred around falling standards in reading and English which, according to the critics, were the direct result of children being given too much freedom in the early years of schooling. The detractors of progressive schooling attracted a great deal of media attention, making vociferous demands for the preservation of standards and a return to the structured teaching of basic skills.

The picture of primary schooling they painted was one of extreme permissiveness, bordering on anarchy, in which teachers did little except to provide a stimulating environment. Bennett's (1976) controversial study of teaching styles was used as supporting evidence by the 'back to basics' movement, as it appeared to show the superiority of traditional teaching methods over more informal ones. Evidence of a very different kind came from official sources: the results of two surveys conducted in the mid- and late seventies by HMI in primary and first schools (DES, 1978a; 1982a) showed that far from needing to return to basics, schools had in fact never moved away from them. The survey of primary schools (DES, 1978a), which looked at a national sample of seven, nine and eleven year-olds, reported that teachers worked hard to make pupils well-behaved, literate and numerate and that children were, on the whole, introduced to a wide range of knowledge and skills. Standards in reading were not falling; the results of tests on eleven year-olds showed a steady improvement since 1955. Indeed, the evidence from the survey showed that far from schools spending too little time on the basic skills of literacy and numeracy, they may have been spending too much at the expense of other areas of the curriculum, such as science and creative activities.

Other studies (Bassey, 1978; Galton and Simon, 1980; Simon and Willcocks, 1981) certainly seem to confirm that in the majority of primary schools the so-called primary 'revolution' never took place and that concern about the basics was misplaced as they have consistently received top priority. Both Richards (1981) and Alexander (1984) argue that this is because the primary curriculum, despite the rhetoric of 'child-centredness', remains essentially that of the old elementary schools with their utilitarian emphasis on the three Rs.

Alexander points out that both the elementary tradition, based on the inculcation of essential knowledge, and the progressive tradition, concerned with individual growth and autonomy, have a long history stretching back, on the one hand, to narrowly conceived Victorian criteria of utility and, on the other, to the influence of idealists such as Montessori and Froebel. Golby (1982) would add a third, more recent tradition which he labels 'technological', stressing the utilitarian values associated with science and technology. He finds it paradoxical, not that two such traditions should co-exist in early education but that teachers should so wholeheartedly espouse the language and ideals of the progressive tradition across the entire range of the curriculum. Their practice meanwhile, he argues, continues to be dominated by formal teaching of the basic skills, very much in the elementary tradition, and teachers seem to have very little awareness of the inconsistency of their position. It would be interesting to consider the validity of this argument in the light of empirical evidence from surveys and classroom research.

The Curriculum in Practice

Two recent surveys (Bassey, 1978; DES, 1982a) have looked specifically at the curriculum and classroom organization of first schools, as opposed to the wider age-range covered by HMI's Primary Survey (DES, 1978a) and the ORACLE research (Galton et al., 1980).

Bassey's (1978) survey   Bassey was interested in finding out as much as possible about how teachers teach at primary level, from the broad sweep of their curricular activities down to minute details concerning their organization of time, pupils and resources. Altogether 900 primary teachers (of whom approximately one-third were infant teachers) were interviewed, using a comprehensive questionnaire concerning every aspect of their classroom teaching. Whilst bearing in mind some of the difficulties of validity arising from interview data and the geographical narrowness of the sample (three towns in Nottinghamshire), the survey does record the varieties of practice commonly found in infant classrooms. Bassey, together with other commentators (Simon, 1981; Alexander, 1984), remarks upon the difficulty of analysing the infant school curriculum, partly because of the flexibility of its organization but also because of the refusal of teachers to define or classify it in the usual subject terms. He used the category 'activity time' to cover individual and group work across most of the curriculum areas (but excluding music, PE, TV and class story or discussion, presumably as these are generally whole-class lessons) and found that the teachers in the sample spent just over half their weekly time in this way. The remainder of their time was divided roughly between class talk, play time (outside), assembly, PE, administration and 'other'.

By a series of further questions Bassey tried to tease out what were the curricular requirements of teachers within 'activity time'. The large majority of the teachers, between eighty and ninety per cent of the sample, depending on the age of the child, expected all children to do some writing and mathematics on at least four days in the week and to have the opportunity to chat individually every day. Three-quarters of the sample also expected children to read aloud to an adult on at least three days a week. In mathematics children spent the majority of their time working individually and in a group with home-made work cards, examples written in their books and with mathematical apparatus and games. Oral number work with the teacher was mainly conducted in small groups, although some teachers occasionally extended this to the whole-class group. What is surprising is that very few teachers (twelve per cent) used commercially produced work cards or kits on a regular basis and the same was true of published language material. It would be interesting to see whether the recent proliferation of infant mathematics and language kits, considering the wide publicity they have received, has made any appreciable difference in the intervening ten years since these data were gathered.

Topic work was wide ranging, with over 400 topics mentioned that were either on-going or planned, each type usually lasting for half a term. There was a fairly even balance between areas of interest chosen by children and those introduced by the teacher. In over seventy per cent of the classrooms, resources such as paints, collage materials, small bricks, home corner and dressing up materials were always available, but in less than half were water, sand, clay and woodwork similarly available. Music lessons were mainly devoted to singing (seventy-one per cent), although half the teachers engaged in music making with their class, using rhythmic percussion.

With the exception of mathematics (on which children spent between fifteen and forty-five minutes a day depending on age), none of the questions asked about specific time requirements. It is difficult to know why this information was not obtained as no reasons are given in the survey. Without more details, however, it is not easy to discover whether in this sample the curriculum was heavily weighted in favour of the basic skills or not. Certainly from the information given it would seem, not surprisingly, that language and mathematics activities were far more structured and planned than other areas of the curriculum. In topic work, for example, although some teachers tried to achieve a balance between historical, geographical, scientific and everyday interests, over half the teachers could give no indication at all of the topics that might be covered in the following two terms. While allowing for the fact that one of the joys of teaching young children is the immediacy and spontaneity with which new interests can be pursued, there does seem to be a case for identifying topics which are appropriate for a particular class, with a view to the skills and knowledge that might be included and the availability of local resources.

DES (1982a) survey   This last point is reiterated by HMI in their survey of first schools, which was based on material gathered by observation and questionnaire. While applauding the efforts of individual teachers in particular schools, HMI were generally unhappy about the lack of planning and of guidelines for the pursuit of geographical, historical and scientific concepts through topic work. They commented frequently about the lack of development and co-ordination that could ensure 'a gradual and steady growth of skills and understanding'. As a consequence they felt that much of the topic work they had seen was too often superficial, fragmented and insufficiently followed through. The Primary Survey (DES, 1978a) had also commented somewhat unfavourably about topic work, pointing out that it did not always match children's capabilities, particularly in the case of younger and more able children. Some of the topic work they found to be repetitive rather than stretching. Concern was also expressed in the 1982 survey about religious education, art and craft and music, which were seen as being underdeveloped and used in a very limited way in many schools.

Turning to the skills of literacy and numeracy, HMI felt that most children made a satisfactory start and achieved a reasonable level of attainment early on, but considered that the development of extended skills and their application in suitable contexts was much neglected. Older children in particular were spending too much time on practising isolated examples rather than using them in a variety of circumstances.

On the basis of the evidence from these surveys the depressing picture painted by Alexander (1984) of a narrow first school curriculum, little changed in its priorities and composition since Victorian times, does seem to be exaggerated. However, it is precisely in the areas beyond the 'basic skills' that HMI feel there is room for improvement in terms of planning, development and follow through. (Alexander points out that HMI themselves could be accused of having a limited view of education, as they make no mention of dance, drama, health education or any issues concerned with social and personal development in their curriculum framework.) It is also worth pointing out that the demands that are being made upon first school teachers have increased markedly since the publication of these two surveys. The last few years have seen the introduction of computers into most classrooms and teachers are now being urged to include design and technology in the curriculum alongside the more usual craft activities. The 1981 Education Act has also made it much more likely that some of the children formerly educated in special schools will be integrated into ordinary classes, sometimes without ancillary help or specialist training for the class teacher. Such specialized curriculum require- ments demand a great deal from teachers who have always regarded themselves as 'generalists' and have serious implications for both initial and in-service teacher education.

CLASSROOM ORGANIZATION AND TEACHING METHODS

The Plowden Model

While the impact of the Plowden Report (CAC, 1967) on curricular content may have been muted, nevertheless it has had, over the years, a marked influence upon classroom organization in the primary sector, particularly in the early school years. The entire thrust of the Report, according to Galton et al. (1980), stresses the uniqueness of each child and points towards the individualization of the educational process as the 'essential principle on which all educational strategy and tactics must be based'. Above all else it is this principle of individualized learning which has had a dramatic effect upon the teaching of young children. It led, first of all, to unstreamed classes throughout most of the primary sector and encouraged the adoption of more flexible teaching arrangements, as whole-class teaching was abandoned in favour of a more personal approach. The move away from class teaching and towards more flexible group work may also have been hastened by the increasing tendency to place several age-groups in one class, as falling rolls in the primary sector affected the viability of single-age classes.

How exactly did the Plowden Committee propose that this process of individualization of teaching and learning might be achieved and how is this reflected in the current practice of teachers? The Committee advocated the use of areas outside the classroom, such as corridors and foyers, in order to free more space for individual work. It was envisaged that teachers might work in pairs, possibly in linked classrooms with shared facilities, so as to cater more usefully for individual needs. Children should have the freedom to visit other classrooms to use particular resources or equipment and to consult with teachers who might have specialist knowledge. Many of the new schools built from the 1950s onwards were, of course, much more 'open' in their design than their prewar counterparts and offered teachers greater opportunities for flexible teaching arrangements because of this.

Turning to the all-important question of how teachers might organize and manage teaching and learning activities in the classroom, the Plowden Committee was faced with an immediate problem. If all children were taught on an individual basis they would only receive seven or eight minutes a day of the teacher's attention, which is hardly sufficient. It was therefore recommended that for expedience teachers should group together children who were roughly at the same stage, although the Committee was careful to point out the dangers of such groups always being based on ability as this would correspond to 'streaming' – a practice to which they were utterly opposed. However, co-operative group work, whether based on interest, ability or friendship, was recognized as important by the Plowden Committee for a number of reasons. It was thought that working in groups would encourage the socialization process, as children learned to get along with one another and became aware of strengths and limitations both within themselves and others. Educationally it was thought children would benefit from having to articulate their ideas clearly to their peers, thus learning through teaching. Group work would enthuse the apathetic, encourage the timid and stretch the ablest and was held to be of particular importance for problem-solving in mathematics and science.

While stressing the desirability of individual work and agreeing upon the necessity and advantages of group work, the Plowden Report did not summarily dismiss class teaching but saw its use mainly as a device to develop and maintain class unity, through discussion of on-going topic work, for example. Its proposal, then, was for a very fluid system of classroom organization, calling for a high degree of managerial skill on the teacher's part, in which children moved from class to group to individual work throughout the day, according to the kinds of activity in which they were engaged.

The Reality in the Classroom

Evidence indicates that the practices of the ideal Plowden-type teacher and his or her class are most closely realized in the classrooms of first and infant schools. Only four per cent of teachers in Bassey's study (1978), for example, claimed to use whole-class teaching in activity time. The majority (seventy-five per cent) favoured a mixture of individual and group work, with decisions about activities being made either by teacher or child. In effect, this rarely meant that children were allowed to do exactly what they liked when they liked. The examples of organizational patterns given by Bassey clearly indicate a high degree of teacher control over the content of the activities on offer.

Many of the illustrative examples are modifications of the 'integrated day' organization, in which the teacher assigns a series of tasks for the day or the week and the children are free to choose the order in which each activity is tackled and how long to spend on them, but not to opt out of any. As each task is completed, children mark them off on either a class or personal record sheet. Interestingly, all the classes operating an integrated day were either vertically grouped (containing all age-groups) or transitionally grouped (containing two age-groups). The other common organizational pattern was 'rotating group work', in which teachers set up three or four activities and the children rotate around them in groups during the day. Once the required tasks are completed to the teacher's satisfaction, children are usually allowed to choose their own activity. However, studies of junior age children and their teachers have found that this particular organizational style has a number of problems associated with it. Of all the different teaching styles categorized by Galton et al. (1980) during the ORACLE survey, the 'rotating changers' had most difficulty sustaining motivation in the children, who were easily distracted and did not work as consistently as children taught by other methods. Furthermore, the general movement from activity to activity increased the likelihood of discipline problems. When tested in the basic skills children in these classes did not improve as much as those in classes where teachers operated different systems.

Certainly some of these problems are likely to be exacerbated with younger children, if such things as change-over times are rigidly adhered to. Children who work slowly, for example, may become frustrated at never being able to complete a piece of work satisfactorily. Even experienced teachers are likely to find that managing the simultaneous movement of diverse groups of small children several times a day is an exercise fraught with difficulty.

HMI in their 1982 First School Survey give scant attention to questions of classroom organization and teaching methods, devoting only two pages (from a total of sixty) to examples, mainly of good practice. The typically cautious wording used in the report makes it difficult to assess exactly what kinds of teaching and organization were in operation in the sixteen first schools which met with unqualified approval. According to HMI all the staff in these schools provided a good balance between active learning and formal teaching and between teacher-initiated and child-initiated activities, but what constitutes a 'good balance' is never explicitly defined. Similarly, the teachers in these schools used a combination of individual, group and class teaching but details concerning when and how and in what proportions are lacking. Large numbers of classes in the remaining sixty-four schools are criticized for over-directing children's work, particularly in the area of basic skills where repetitive practice predominated. A small group of schools (number unspecified) are taken to task for their over-use of class teaching which resulted in children at either end of the ability range being given unsuitable work and decreased the time available for younger children to play with materials such as sand and water. HMI echoed the recommendations of the Plowden Report when identifying the most appropriate uses of class teaching as introducing and following up topic work or enthusing the class group through story, discussion and music. However, HMI were also critical of classes where individual work was over-done as this prevented children from learning from each other and allowed the teacher insufficient time to discuss problems in any depth or engage in worthwhile conversations.

The ORACLE research (Galton et al., 1980) revealed that much so-called group work in junior schools was in fact nothing of the kind, as the children, although seated in groups, were all engaged in individual tasks. This may well be the case in first schools, as the increasing use of commercially produced language and mathematics schemes, such as Ginn 360 or SMPG, encourages teachers to guide individual children at their own pace through a lengthy series of work books and cards. If used exclusively, such schemes preclude activities such as class discussions or, among older children, attempts at group problem-solving, both thought to be especially valuable in promoting the development of mathematical concepts (DES, 1978a, 1982a).

Over-reliance on an individual approach also creates management problems for teachers. The ORACLE survey (Galton et al., 1980) found that teachers categorized as 'individual monitors' because of their high levels of one-to-one interaction with pupils were largely didactic in their approach and very rarely had time to ask probing or open-ended questions. The high level of individualized work generated a great deal of marking and the teachers' role seemed to be mainly managerial, since they moved individuals from task to task as each assignment was completed. In terms of success in the basic skills, the 'individual monitors' were almost as poorly rated as the 'rotational changers'. Paradoxically, it seems that the individualization of learning advocated by the Plowden Committee cannot be easily implemented by using the activity/discovery methods they favoured, for in order to overcome the managerial problems created by an individual system teachers resort to formal didactic methods.

Twenty years later one of the lasting legacies of the Plowden Report has been the move towards greater individualization of learning in classrooms but for social, pedagogical and managerial reasons it is not an approach that should be pursued at the expense of all others. In the ideal classroom, then as now, teachers should be offering a judicious mix of individual, group and class teaching and learning experiences throughout the day.

Questions of Balance

The key concept in any planning exercise for the first school classroom would appear to be that of balance. First school teachers are urged to provide a 'broad and balanced curriculum' (DES, 1982a), which means going beyond the 'skills and frills' model of basics in the morning and 'all the rest' in the afternoon. They have also to find a balance between individual, group and class teaching methods; between didactic and discovery-based approaches to learning; and between sedentary and more active tasks. Dowling and Dauncey (1984) point out that 'output needs to be balanced to input' – children need a variety of direct experiences to act both as stimuli and as the bases for their learning.

In terms of what is included in the curriculum it makes more sense for teachers to take a longer view, say half-termly, than to concentrate on daily activities. Attempts to cram the entire range of curricular activities into each day result in an unnecessarily fragmented and unsatisfying experience for teachers and children alike. It is often the case that in classes where children have to complete several assignments in the basic skills before being allowed a choice of activities, slower children may never get beyond the first task and suffer a narrow and frustrating curriculum as a consequence. There is no empirical evidence to show that children who are expected to complete a piece of written work as well as a mathematics task, and who are heard to read every day, progress any better than children who work on a more flexible basis.

Many assignments and activities would benefit from a more sustained effort of learning, perhaps lasting over several days, if the maximum benefit is to be obtained from them. It may be, for example, that lack of space precludes a great deal of practical mathematical equipment from being permanently available. It makes more sense to have several days set aside largely for mathematical problem-solving, with different groups having extended use of the apparatus, rather than continually dragging it in and out of stockrooms as groups or individuals require it. The same system might operate with art and craft activities where it is not easy to provide a wide range of materials in the classroom all at the same time. In this case, creative activity over several weeks might be devoted to exploring thoroughly the possibilities of a particular medium such as clay or a process such as print making. Similarly with topics and themes; during one term the emphasis may be historical or environmental, while the following term the slant may be towards science and technology. Operating this kind of planning means that as one particular aspect of the curriculum is concentrated upon in turn at the expense of others, curricular balance will not be achieved daily or even weekly but only over a much longer period. The varying emphases may mean that a balance may only be struck at the end of a school year, but given that this approach allows and encourages children to persist and concentrate on an activity/topic for an extended period of time, the benefits should outweigh the disadvantages.

Group Work

When considering the deployment of class groups and individual teaching methods, decisions need to be based on how appropriate they are to particular activities and to the age of the children involved, rather than on a belief in the overriding supremacy of one method over another (DES, 1982a). (Teachers who team teach in open-plan situations will have to take into consideration the problem of implementing a mixed approach when working alongside other members of staff.) Certain lessons usually timetabled in the hall, such as PE, drama, movement, dance and music, are nearly always whole-class activities, mainly because of the difficulties of arranging them any other way. Teachers also use class teaching for stories, poetry and discussions; for introducing, planning and reviewing work; and for children to share their discoveries and experiences with the class. For older children, these 'coming together' times might be at the beginning of the day to introduce and plan work, and at the end to discuss progress and/or share individual and group experiences with the rest of the children. These class times may need to be more frequent with very young children who are unused to classroom routines and who need the sense of security provided by regular attention from and contact with a teacher. Many teachers find a 'wave' model useful, in which children are gathered together at regular intervals during the morning and afternoon sessions for a chat and, perhaps, a story before being dispersed to begin a new set of activities or complete ones already started. As the children become more self-reliant and their capacity for working independently increases, then the period of time between such gatherings can be extended.

How and when children are grouped will depend largely on the purpose of the activity and the developing abilities of the children to benefit from certain kinds of group work. Sometimes teachers may wish to group children according to ability. Such groups may cut across the ability levels, so that the less able children are stimulated and helped by the more able, or be groups of children of similar ability levels, in order to make more economical use of teaching time when introducing a new area in mathematics, for instance. Interest groups often develop with older children in creative or topic work when they can usefully pursue and develop a common interest over a period of days or weeks. At other times, allowing children to sit in friendship groups can add to the happy atmosphere in a classroom, providing that children do not take advantage of this and become silly and disruptive.

More problematic is arranging children in groups to work co-operatively on a task or activity. This can be difficult to organize successfully, especially if the children concerned have little practice in collaborating and are unsure about what is expected of them. Teachers can begin introducing children to the idea of sharing a task as early as the reception class, initially by encouraging children to work in pairs. For instance, two children could be given a large sheet of paper on which to produce a joint picture. The teacher decides upon the subject-matter and allocates parts of it to each child. Other examples might include a joint venture in construction using Lego or junk materials, or a simple measuring task such as how many jumps on the spot can be achieved in one minute using a sand timer. Older children who have developed some skills in working together can be assigned a task and guided through the process of discussing how best to tackle it, deciding upon roles and responsibilities and reporting back upon completion, doing as much as possible by themselves. At first children may find this way of working difficult and will consistently look to the teacher for directions and solutions. Teachers will have to curb their natural tendencies to intervene, supply 'right' answers and generally dominate the proceedings by over-enthusiastic prompting or questioning.

Although collaborative group work is recognized as having value and special significance for many areas of the curriculum, HMI (DES, 1982) specifically mention its importance for problem-solving in mathematics and for integrated topic work, including aspects of history, geography and science. It was rarely found in any of the junior schools studied by Galton et al. (1980). Much of what teachers, in their study, called group work was an organiz-ational rather than a pedagogical strategy – the children were sitting in groups although working individually. Whether this was the result of teachers' reluctance to employ collaborative learning methods because of difficulties of organization or of control is not made clear. Neither is it easy to ascertain whether this pattern is repeated in the first school. This seems likely, however, given that many of the younger children will only just have reached the stage where they can play together co-operatively.

Individual and Class Activities

Children working individually really only pose a problem if the entire class is working in this way at once, a situation that calls for a great deal of teacher attention. The constant demands for attention do not allow for any extended, uninterrupted exchanges with children and teachers often find themselves trying to cope with several different children and activities at once, doing justice to none. This dilemma can often be solved by balancing a teacher-intensive activity, such as introducing children to individual 'sentence-makers', against a variety of activities that children can organize and accomplish on their own, such as completing a model from the previous day, continuing with some project work or finishing a page in a work book. Having dealt successfully with some of the children, the teacher can leave them and turn his or her attention to the other children, perhaps organizing some group activities or seeing to individual children with problems.

With young children it is also important to bear in mind that they do not find it easy to sit still for long periods of time and attempts to make them do so are likely to result in disruption. Obviously, children will have to learn to sit still for increasingly longer periods as they move through their school career but there is little to be gained from enforcing this too early for too long. If teachers strike a balance between sedentary table-top tasks and more active tasks, such as large-scale construction or painting, the problems of control are likely to be lessened.

Children need as well to be introduced to a greater variety of direct experiences than can be easily provided within the classroom by one teacher. Visits out of school can act as an exciting stimulus to project work of all kinds and are likely to be remembered for far longer than many other parts of the curriculum. Such trips do not have to be elaborate, and are most likely in the first instance to be within the immediate vicinity of school. They should be a regular part of the work of the school, not a once-a-year treat. Their purposes can be many and varied: to collect insect or plant material for detailed study back in the classroom; to carry out a traffic survey; to examine the building materials of local shops and houses; or to look at the stained glass in a local church. However, the overall aim should be to provide children with rich and vivid first-hand experiences, to act either as a starting point or as a development of classroom-based learning. Visitors to the school can serve a similar purpose, perhaps enthusing the children with a demonstration of a particular skill or craft, such as spinning or weaving. Local services, such as the police and fire brigade, can often be prevailed upon to provide demonstrations involving police horses and dogs or fire engines and fire-fighting equipment, the immediacy and excitement of which will outlast any number of books or films on the same subject.

The role of teachers in the first school is clearly a complex one. There are many competing demands on their time, energy, ingenuity and organizational skills if the needs of their pupils are to be met. This chapter has looked at various recommendations as to how classrooms and curricula might be organized and at how samples of teachers have in fact tackled these tasks. It has also attempted to show how various forms of organization can be used to the benefit of pupils and teachers. The next chapter outlines the content of the programme which should be made available to the children, whichever form of classroom organization is adopted.

3

Approaches to the Curriculum

This chapter will look at individual areas of curriculum. However, it is beyond its scope to do more than examine briefly some of the most important issues relating to these areas. Wherever possible, teachers who wish to explore further will be referred to sources providing more detailed and specific information. There are numerous ways of classifying the areas within the first school curriculum and the use of a particular subject-title is not meant to imply that this is how it should appear on the timetable. Indeed, a study of the variety of nomenclature used to described the areas of the early curriculum could justifiably constitute a separate chapter.

BASIC COMMUNICATION SKILLS

Reading

Most teachers are aware of the crucial importance of well-developed language and communication skills for every child's later learning. It is, therefore, not surprising that the teaching of reading receives highest priority in the curricula of first schools. It is important to remember, however, that the acquisition of reading skills forms only a part of children's overall language development and should not be seen in isolation from the other linguistic skills of talking, listening and writing. McInnes (1973) specifically warns against the dangers of teaching reading as a bundle of isolated skills, related neither to the general fabric of the curriculum nor to the on-going development of thought and language in the child. That advances in the understanding of the processes involved in reading over the past twenty years have been closely linked with changes in ideas about language and thinking serves only to emphasize this point. The implications of these developments are of particular relevance to the early stages of reading and how teachers introduce children to the printed word.

Prior to the 1960s, as Donaldson and Reid (1985) point out, the prevailing view of the reading process was that it was primarily a matter of word recognition. Children were taught to read by learning one word at a time, either phonically or by 'look and say' methods, and later were expected to string them together to form sentences. Research in the field of psycholinguistics during the late sixties and seventies added greatly to the knowledge of how children learn to read. Young readers were considered to be engaged in a 'psycholinguistic guessing game' (Goodman, 1967) as they formed hypotheses and predictions about how a sentence might unfold based on their knowledge of syntax and their grasp of its meaning. This view holds that reading involves the construction of meaning from text (Donaldson and Reid, 1985). In other words, children will try to make sense of what they read using what knowledge they have of grammar and vocabulary.

The majority of children who arrive at school with well-developed skills in spoken language will be able to use their linguistic knowledge to good effect when learning to read. This is not always fully appreciated, as Smith (1971) points out:

> Two things are surprising about the skills and knowledge that a child brings with him when he is about to read: the sheer quantity and complexity of his ability and the small credit he is usually given. (p. 61)

However, although children may come to school with a great deal of implicit knowledge about oral language they may know little of the nature and purposes of written language (Donaldson and Reid, 1985). Children need to come to understand that writing carries messages and that, although there is a great deal of correspondence between speech and writing, written language is more than just speech written down. Accordingly children's introduction to print should not be through single words in isolation but through examples of real written language in phrases and sentences, as these carry understandable messages. Donaldson and Reid (1985) feel that the one exception to this rule is what they term 'public print', such things as notices, street signs, labels, advertisements and bus destinations. Many of these single words, for instance 'beans', 'entrance', 'car park', are closely related to the objects or places they label and often form the child's earliest links between speech and print.

If children are to capitalize on what linguistic experience they already possess, then books and early reading material will have to be carefully selected to match and build upon their current understanding and expectations of sentence structure. This rules out many of the early readers in some of the older reading schemes which, either because of their severely restricted vocabulary and/or adherence to phonetically regular words, were forced into using almost nonsensical constructions that children may never have encountered in spoken language. Most teachers will be aware of the kind of stilted language which occurs nowhere else but in basic readers: 'Oh, Tip, oh, look, look, look. Nip is up, up, up', etc., etc. A much better introduction to print is through any of the widely available, simple picture story books which have an enjoyable and meaningful storyline and are colourful and well illustrated.

Children's growing awareness of what Clay (1972) terms 'conceptions of print' can be fostered by a wide range of language experience work, when sentences constructed by the children are written down for them by the teacher. Such an approach not only ensures syntax of an appropriate level but also gives a good illustration of the left to right praxis of print and of word boundaries and structure. Individual and class books 'written' by the children themselves can become a focus of interest and discussion for the whole class and may become the children's earliest 'reading books'. Using this broad framework for teaching reading does not preclude using any of the earlier methods. As Southgate et al. (1981) point out, it is rather a question of emphasis. They insist that having a large sight vocabulary of words, the meanings of which are understood, and a knowledge of common phonic rules are still the basis from which a child comprehends a text. However, care should be taken in attempting to develop reading skills in children who may have had little experience of books and have only poorly developed concepts of what reading is about. This point is underlined by HMI, who commented in their five to nine survey (DES, 1982a) that in almost all schools the youngest children were introduced too quickly to published reading schemes and phonic practice.

The 1982 survey also drew attention to the widespread lack of guidelines for the extension and development of reading skills, leading in many cases to an unduly prolonged concentration on basic reading schemes. Some of the findings of the recent research project mentioned above (Southgate et al., 1981), aimed at extending the reading of seven to nine year-olds, are useful in this context. They make a number of suggestions and recommendations which would require some teachers to make major modifications to their existing practices. First, they suggest a drastic reduction of time spent in the practice of hearing large numbers of individual children read every day. Such sessions, they point out, are invariably short and subject to constant interruptions so that little effective teaching help can be given, a view with which HMI heartily concur. An alternative and more effective practice, they suggest, is to spend longer periods (fifteen to twenty minutes) with individual children at less frequent intervals (perhaps every three weeks). These longer periods could be used for much more than merely listening to the child read and might include discussions about interesting books, carrying out a miscue analysis, checking comprehension, or planning reading activities for the next few weeks. Second, they suggest introducing periods of uninterrupted silent reading when children are encouraged to read for progressively longer periods from books of their own choice.

Fluent voluntary reading, adopted as a habit in early childhood, should have a beneficial effect on functional reading by extending vocabulary and improving reading skills. Teachers should use these times to read books of their own choice, to demonstrate to the class that reading is a valued and enjoyable activity for adults too. Time for these strategies could be found if, for example, children were helped to be more self-reliant when attempting to spell words for themselves. Southgate et al. found that teachers spent a disproportionate amount of time in supplying children with individual spellings. Lastly, they offer guidelines for initiating and practising study skills useful for topic work, as locating and extracting information from non-fiction books are difficult and complex tasks for seven and eight year-olds.

Schools can obviously foster children's interest in books and reading by various means. It is essential that children should have access to appropriately stocked class and school libraries, in which books are attractively displayed and classified in a fashion easily understood by the children. Schools can also organize book-selling schemes through various book clubs, or even set up their own book shop. Local booksellers will often supply a range of books on a 'sale or return' basis. Some local authorities have implemented schemes encouraging parents to take an interest in their children's reading along the lines of the Belfield Project (Jackson and Hannon, 1981) or the Haringey Scheme (Tizard et al., 1982). See chapter 9 for a further discussion of co-operation between home and school over reading.

Writing

Children's earliest experiences of writing in school usually involve watching the teacher write down their name, or a short sentence, and then being helped to trace carefully over the letters. Experience of this kind needs to be backed up with regular practice of patterns and individual letter formation if children are to achieve reasonable standards of legibility. Their spelling, vocabulary, syntax and punctuation require similar attention if they are to communicate and express themselves effectively in writing. HMI (DES, 1982a) point out that such achievements are unlikely to be found in schools where children spend most of their time involved with exercises from text books or commercially produced assignment cards, many of which involve little more than copying and occupy the children rather than stretch them.

A much better approach is to introduce children to varieties of writing for different purposes and different audiences, arising from their experiences both in and out of school. Examples are: factual writing such as recording observations in science or recipes for cooking; personal writing in diaries; letters to friends; items for class books; and imaginative writing in stories and poetry. Older children could keep records, with comments, on the books they have read, or perhaps write and illustrate a simple story for nursery children. Teachers can help by ensuring that children have sufficient first-hand experiences of visual or oral stimulation to animate and inspire their efforts. Group and class discussions can often be valuable in this respect and will be discussed in the next section.

Talking and Listening

The central importance of spoken language for early reading development has already been touched upon (see, also, chapter 5), and few teachers need convincing of the important contribution of talk to learning across the curriculum. Most teachers offer valuable daily opportunities for chats and discussions but often these occur when the whole class group is gathered together, which means that many children either do not get a chance to contribute or feel inhibited by such large numbers. Children of all ages need occasions when they can talk and discuss things in the more intimate setting of a small group, as it is through talk that children develop and clarify their own ideas and learn to take account of the views of others. Often new information and vocabulary are acquired which help in organizing and expressing thoughts (Winchester, 1985). Teachers might set specific assignments which require children to talk with their peers for real purposes, such as solving a problem in mathematics/science/computer programmes/ environmental studies or recording and reporting back on an out-of-school visit using a variety of media. Exploratory talk between children in small groups can only too easily be inhibited or dominated by the teacher, who should provide support and guidance while being sensitive to the effect which he or she may be having on the process.

Reading and telling stories figure prominently and are often a daily occurrence. Care has to be taken when choosing stories for mixed-age groups and classes to ensure that the content and language are suitable for all. It may be better in some cases to have separate story times for older and younger children if this can be arranged, and also to vary their timing from the usual last half-hour of the day so that children come to them fresh and alert.

Language Work in Multilingual Schools

There are many areas of the country in which schools have a multilingual population of children where English is not the first language of the home. A language census taken in ILEA in 1983 recorded 50,000 children whose home language was not English, and within this group 147 different languages were represented. In that authority the number of children whose mother-tongue is not English is rising, as only 11 per cent of fifteen year olds were in this category compared with 20.8 per cent of five year olds (ILEA, 1985).

It is of great importance that all children learn to speak, write and read English fluently. In schools with substantial numbers from non-English-speaking backgrounds there will usually be arrangements for giving extra help in language work (see chapter 5). Many primary schools now employ teachers with TEFL qualifications, either on a full-time or part-time basis, to organize this type of work. A more contentious issue is whether children whose first language is not English should be given the opportunity to develop their command of their mother-tongue in school time. At present this is rarely done, mainly because of the practical problems posed by having many languages and children scattered across schools but also because many parents prefer to keep the teaching of the mother-tongue within the ethnic community where it forms part of the whole cultural and religious heritage of the children.

Having children from different linguistic and cultural backgrounds within the same class can add richness and diversity not just to language work but also to the entire curriculum and 'should be regarded as an opportunity not a problem' (ILEA, 1984, 1985). One approach which has been used successfully with children of all ages in the first school has been to encourage parents to come into school and tell traditional stories and folk tales, both in the mother-tongue and in translations. These can later be turned into simple books illustrated by the children themselves and given captions in the original tongue and English. If mounted on card and laminated, a collection of home-made books like this could form the nucleus of a multilingual library. This approach also signals to children that the school respects and takes a serious interest in their home language and culture.

MATHEMATICS

In their 1982 survey of first schools, HMI were particularly critical of the way mathematics was taught. In four-fifths of the schools mathematical skills were practised in isolation, relating neither to practical experience nor to other areas of the curriculum. Most of the work was based on self-contained, commercially produced schemes or graded school-made work cards consisting, in the main, of abstract computation. This criticism was made of work for younger as well as older children, with only six schools attempting systematically to introduce mathematical language and concepts in an interesting way through play and everyday experiences. Since many early mathematical concepts can be developed from children's play, failure to do so represents a lost opportunity. Concepts such as conservation of number, matching, sorting and ordering arise quite naturally in much domestic and constructional play. For instance, laying the table, matching clothes to the size of the dolls or putting away dressing up clothes by placing each garment on a separate hanger, all help to establish ideas of one-to-one correspondence and ordering by size.

Over-concentration on practising the four rules means that a great deal of work in mathematics will be book-based and formal, thus reducing the chances children might have for applying mathematical skills to solving problems, either individually or in small groups. The Cockcroft Committee (DES, 1982b) saw the ability to solve problems as being at the heart of mathematics. The Committee asserted that 'the idea of investigation is fundamental both for the study of mathematics itself and also in understanding the ways in which mathematics can be used to extend knowledge and solve problems in many fields' (para. 250). Unfortunately, a large proportion of the software in mathematics is little more than prettily packaged computation exercises, usually to be completed in isolation on an individual basis. Using a more open-ended approach, such as a language like LOGO, is likely to promote far more discussion, group work and problem-solving, particularly if used in conjunction with a floor turtle.

For very young children, devising simple instructions for a programmable mechanical toy such as 'Big Trak' can act as a valuable introduction to spatial concepts, programming skills and group problem-solving exercises. Once children have practised simple backward, forward and turning manoeuvres, a small group could be given the task of devising an obstacle course and negotiating the toy through it. The group could then demonstrate and explain to the rest of the class how they solved the problems involved, which should give rise to much valuable discussion and, perhaps, alternative solutions. Mathematical thinking in this context is likely to be more meaningful and enjoyable than the completion of arid exercises which are often no more than time-filling. Class discussion can and ought to be a stimulating part of mathematics, giving older children a chance to 'reflect upon and discuss the methods they use to obtain the answers' (ILEA, 1985), but may be under-utilized if too much reliance is placed on the individualized work-card approach.

Taking every opportunity to link mathematics with other areas of the curriculum will also ensure that skills are used in a practical and meaningful context. All kinds of measurement will be useful in the topic work of older children, whether they are marking out the length of Noah's Ark in the playground, taking a traffic census or calculating the distance a snail will travel in a day. Estimation – an under-valued skill – can be usefully introduced and practised in this kind of work. Pictorial representation, through graphs and charts, can be undertaken with the youngest children and can be used in any number of situations from recording weather to birthdays in the year. Some topics may themselves arise out of mathematical activities, such as work on shape for instance. Children could explore the incidence of particular shapes both in nature and in the built environment, as well as through PE, drama, art and music.

As is pointed out in *Primary Practice* (Schools Council, 1983), the major difficulty arising from cross-curricular work is likely to be how best teachers can observe and record the mathematical progress of children when they are using these skills in other areas. But mathematics is one of the few areas of the curriculum where there is at least a large measure of agreement about the kinds of progress to look for.

ENVIRONMENTAL STUDIES (INCLUDING SCIENCE, HISTORY AND GEOGRAPHY)

While recognizing that science, history and geography each has a distinctive contribution to make to children's developing understanding of the environment (both local and more distant), it is usual in the first school for them to be integrated into a theme or topic which will often draw upon other areas of the curriculum – such as language work, art and craft or mathematics. Teachers must realize, however, that it is not always possible or even desirable, to pursue environmental topics in which all three elements are equally represented, for some topics will offer more scope for scientific exploration, while others may have more of an historical or geographical bias. Although children recognize no subject boundaries, it is important that teachers are aware of the important skills and concepts associated with each of these subjects in order to appreciate the most fruitful opportunities for investigation in any topic and in which direction they might most usefully be pursued. For this reason each subject will be considered separately.

Science

Since the early sixties there have been at least half a dozen projects aimed at developing and producing curricular materials for teachers to encourage and support scientific activities with young children (Kerr and Engel, 1980). The two most widely known projects, *With Objectives in Mind: Guide to Science 5–13* (Ennever and Harlen, 1972) and *Learning through Science: Formulating a School Policy* (Richards et al., 1980), both written for the Schools Council, lay emphasis on developing the processes of science. In other words, the researchers believed it to be more important to develop skills such as observation, questioning, problem-solving and critical reasoning than to concentrate on the content of what is to be learned. This emphasis on 'doing' science has an immediate appeal to teachers of young children, rooted as it is in direct concrete experience – but the process approach is not without its critics.

Kerr and Engel (1980), for example, complain that over-reliance on processes means that the content of early science is left almost completely to chance, which in turn places a tremendous strain on any teachers who lack background or experience of science. However, while earlier projects concentrated almost entirely on producing guidelines for teachers, *Learning Through Science*, although still very much process-biased, does give more practical help in the form of twelve packs of pupil materials, each based on a particular theme and containing a full set of notes for the teacher. The twelve topics chosen were included because teachers felt they represented the major underlying themes that should be looked at during children's primary school years.

With young children a good starting-point might be themselves, and could include, for example, investigations of their senses and their importance in actively exploring the environment. The link with the environment might be through a 'sensory walk' taken both inside and outside the school building, where children make a record (in words or pictures) of the things of interest that they can see, touch, smell and hear. Wax crayon rubbings are a good way of keeping a record of different textures and children can also collect small items such as leaves, twigs or pebbles which can be sorted into sets for more detailed observation back in the classroom. Using the same categories of sight, hearing and so on, a large class-record can be made of all the things children have observed, heard, smelled and touched which can be discussed and perhaps reclassified using categories suggested by the children, for example into loud noises and quiet noises, pleasant and unpleasant smells, large and small objects, or rough and smooth textures. Later walks might focus children's attention upon one particular sense. On a 'visual' walk, for example, groups of children could be given different tasks – some looking up, perhaps using binoculars, and some looking down on the ground, with hand lenses. Such direct experiences will furnish teachers and children with a wealth of material upon which to base very worthwhile topics.

There are very many other environmental topics such as weather and seasonal changes, the cycle of animal and plant life and moving things, all of which offer teachers and children great scope for scientific explorations.

History

Teachers may, at times, have shied away from introducing historical material to young children, partly because they believe that the passage of time is a difficult concept for them to grasp and partly because of the 'old fashioned view that history is all facts and dates' (Blyth, 1979). As a consequence, Blyth argues, children's introduction to history may be very haphazard, arising incidentally from stories and myths or perhaps from historic state occasions such as the opening of Parliament or a royal wedding. There are several drawbacks to this kind of patchy approach. It is difficult to ensure continuity or progression from year to year for, unless very careful records are kept, content is likely to be repeated. From the children's point of view, they may end up confusing myth and reality, or, more seriously, the topics may not relate to their own experience and may preclude them from undertaking any activity of their own.

How, then, can history be incorporated into the curriculum in such a way as to avoid these pitfalls? Jahoda (1963) believes that children's supposed difficulty with chronology can be overcome if the problem is tackled in the right way. Children as young as five, he argues, are beginning to order events into 'earlier' and 'later' and can understand the concepts of yesterday, today and tomorrow. History should begin with the children themselves in the present and work backwards through the immediate past of their family and locality, broadening out in the later years of first school to the more distant past, perhaps looking at children in Victorian times. Children should be encouraged to use a tape recorder to question older relatives about their memories of childhood and the area in which they lived; they could bring in artefacts from home or make a collection of old photographs of their family. All of these could be related to a simple time-line on the classroom wall. Blyth (1979) points out that although such a scheme may seem parochial, it offers scope for discussion and activity related to the children's own knowledge, whilst laying a foundation for the development of local and national themes in later schooling. Furthermore, it is easy for links to be made between family history, artefacts, local history and visits to nearby places of interest.

Geography

In their 1982 survey HMI comment that although most schools

included elementary geographical skills and concepts in their curriculum, there was little appreciation of the range of appropriate activities for younger children, particularly in the introduction of map work.

As with historical material the obvious starting point is the child and his familiar environment. Blyth (1984) suggests that five year olds can be introduced to routes and distances through suitable stories. Simple picture stories, such as 'Rosie's Walk' or 'Bears in the Night', centre around short journeys that can be illustrated diagramatically by the teacher, using arrows and landmarks on a large sheet of paper of on the blackboard. Most classes will have access to road and railway layouts, sand, bricks and construction sets, all of which can be used to represent the local area or to illustrate a walk to the local shops taken by the children. Children could also make simple picture plans of their own homes and gardens.

Seven and eight year-olds could be asked to make 'memory maps' of the school or their journey to school using words and pictures. This is an activity that can usefully be undertaken by pairs of children so that they can remind each other of the things they may have forgotten. Children will quickly discover that their memory is not always reliable, and they can be encouraged to go and look carefully in order to complete and verify their maps and plans. Use could also be made of aerial photographs of the school and a group of children could, perhaps, make a model of their 'journey to school' map. Field-work is essential with younger and older children, both local work on shops, streets and traffic, and also occasional distant visits, using maps to indicate the route from school.

The study of more distant lands can be introduced to older children to help them acquire some familiarity with globes or maps of the world. Multicultural schools have a distinct advantage here in that the children themselves are a living link with distant countries. Such a link offers young children the possibility of adopting a concrete approach to work on India, for example, through an examination of saris, jewellery and foodstuffs. There is the possibility of bringing in language and drama through Indian folk tales and stories, and also RE, through the differing religious festivals of the Hindu and Moslem communities. All these elements can be used in ways that promote insight into people's behaviour and can form an important part of social education.

EXPRESSIVE AND CREATIVE ARTS (INCLUDING PHYSICAL EDUCATION)

Art and craft, music, movement and drama, dance and physical education all make a special contribution to the development of imagination, creativity, feeling and practical skills in children (Schools Council, 1983). As well as enjoying rightful places of their own in the first school curriculum, they can be of immense value in other areas of work, acting as stimuli or offering children the chance to communicate and record their responses to their own experiences in a variety of ways.

That the expressive and creative arts offer many possibilities for personal and social development should not be overlooked, as they often involve elements of self-discipline and co-operation, as well as nurturing children's growing awareness of differing values and attitudes. Evidence from surveys (DES 1982a; ILEA, 1985) showed that work in these areas is among the most difficult to plan, provide and assess, and that greater use should be made of specialist teachers in helping school staff to draw up guidelines to assist their efforts in this direction.

Art and Craft

That art and craft play an important part in the life of first schools is evident from the abundant variety of work displayed in foyers, classrooms and corridors. Carefully arranged displays can do much to stimulate children's aesthetic awareness, as well as demonstrating the value that is placed upon their efforts. Teachers can use displays as a means of introducing art forms and artefacts from other cultures so that children become aware of traditions other than that of Western Europe with its emphasis on painting. It is picture-making, needless to say, that dominates the first school curriculum (DES, 1982a), albeit using a great variety of materials including chalk, pencil, paint, ink, felt pens and pastels, and processes such as rubbings, wax resist, graffito, painting and collage. Throughout their early years children need help in developing control over their materials and in acquiring higher levels of skill and co-ordination, as they quickly become frustrated if poorly chosen materials or inability in a particular skill thwart their efforts.

From an early age, children need to develop not just manipulative skills but the ability to look carefully at objects, both natural and man-made. Drawing from direct observation gives children valuable practice in examining details of form, colour and texture. Accurate observations are of value in themselves but are also essential ingredients of mathematics and environmental studies, and will often promote discussions requiring new and descriptive vocabulary. It is also true that much imaginative and reflective work can grow out of direct observation, as children will have a greater store of images to call upon and combine in new ways.

Greater opportunities for three-dimensional work are often afforded to younger children, who may regularly make models using junk, plasticine, clay, lego and wood. However, there should be development of this early work throughout the first school. For example, there is scope for introducing older children to the idea of designing and making things that work, such as a car that moves. Materials can be expensive, but parents and local tradespeople can often be prevailed on to provide a regular supply of offcuts of wood and scrap of all kind, such as polystyrene packaging. Discarded clocks, watches and other mechanical items (like typewriters) can often be dismantled to provide an interesting supply of components for children's constructions.

Crafts such as weaving, sewing and printing can be explored at many levels of sophistication and can often be linked with other areas of the curriculum. For example, during an environmental studies project, a visit might be made to a nineteenth-century weaving shop. Schools in rural areas may be able to call upon local crafts people to demonstrate all the processes of turning raw fleece into a finished knitted or woven garment; perhaps some processes can be attempted by the children themselves. There are also packs of resource materials available which allow exploration of the traditional arts and crafts of other cultures, linked to an account of the historical background of the land and people.

Music

No one could doubt that young children derive much pleasure and satisfaction both from listening to music and participating in musical activities. Children of nursery and reception age are introduced to nursery rhymes concurrently with more modern songs originating from all parts of the world. They should have the chance to experiment with sounds and investigate the noises made by different instruments, such as a collection of percussion instruments of European, African and Asian origin.

Teachers can explore rhythm, with children using their bodies as instruments – clapping, tapping and finger snapping to the pattern of their names or simple rhymes. The whole-class group can make contributions to building up quite complex rhythmic patterns to accompany well-known songs. Later children can be introduced to the idea of pitch, leading to the development of simple melodies and older children can be encouraged to learn an instrument, such as a recorder or melodica. Music is often the central focus of school concerts, festivals and carol services, where a successful performance is dependent not only on children's musical ability but on attributes such as self-confidence, co-operation and discipline.

One of the major problems with music education in the first school is that too few teachers feel sufficiently confident to teach music beyond simple singing lessons, so that the brunt of children's musical education falls upon one or two teachers who can themselves play an instrument, or who are music specialists. This can lead to musical activities becoming isolated from the rest of the curriculum, with little or no integration into any associated areas, and also to performance being emphasized at the expense of creativity (ILEA, 1985). One solution to such a situation would be for music specialists, in conjunction with class teachers, to draw up guidelines for a planned programme of activities. The scheme should cover the entire age-range, be linked to other areas of the curriculum and be capable of implementation by non-specialist teachers. A possible starting-point for a coherent programme such as this is to be found in *The Arts in Schools: Principles, Practice and Provision* (Gulbenkian Foundation, 1982).

Drama, Movement and Dance

Drama, movement and dance are often linked with music, but the links with other curricular areas are less frequently exploited (DES, 1982a). It may be, as with music, that there are not enough teachers with specialist knowledge or confidence in these areas, so that between the extremes of a weekly schools radio broadcast, such as 'Time to Move', and the full-blown production of a school Christmas play, there is little development or coherence.

Most young children revel in dramatic play of all kinds and many will be encouraged to express themselves in this way by using well-equipped school dressing-up facilities and home corners. This kind of sociodramatic play is an excellent base from which teachers can extend and develop drama in the classroom. (See chapter 4 for a discussion of the value and uses of sociodramatic play.) Beginning with the simple dramatization of nursery rhymes and action rhymes, teachers can try out simple mimes to well-known stories such as the 'Three Bears'. As children gain in confidence they can be encouraged to add spontaneous dialogue, but it is better to forego costume at this stage as it often interferes with the flow of the plot. Simple dramatizations can often be included in class assemblies to illustrate a particular topic or story.

Some authorities employ specialist dance and drama teachers, who work on a peripatetic basis visiting schools in rotation, perhaps once or twice a week for a term. Where they work closely with the class teacher the curriculum itself can be a source of inspiration for dance and drama sessions and these in turn become a resource of ideas for the class teacher to draw on and develop in the future. Alternatively, local theatres often have drama groups attached to them which work exclusively in schools and which can be booked to run a series of workshops for young children over a term or a year. Often they will offer sessions dealing with specific skills, such as simple puppet-making and the production of puppet plays.

Physical Education

Children between the ages of five and eight years make a great deal of progress in developing and refining skills of co-ordination, manipulation and muscular control and often tackle new skills with evident enthusiasm. As Sleap (1983) points out, psychologists such as Piaget, Bruner and Gagné have all emphasized the value of sensory-motor integration in the process of human development. He asserts that improvements in motor skills not only provide obvious physical advantages but have been closely associated with increases in self-confidence, self-esteem, security and other personal constructs (Zaichkowsky et al., 1980).

Physical education often suffers similar problems to those of music, dance and drama, in that teachers may lack confidence and there may be no specialist in the school to offer support and guidance. Where teachers lack knowledge and remain unconvinced of the value of physical education it is all too easy to abandon some PE periods because the children are engaged in 'more important' work. It is equally easy for PE to become merely a slightly more organized way of children letting off steam than playtime, with little attempt being made to relate the lessons to the rest of the curriculum or to provide any kind of progression and continuity.

Staff need to believe in the importance of PE, to understand more about it and to have a good appreciation of children's capacities if they are to enthuse them and advance their development (ILEA, 1985). Any school lacking a specialist should not hesitate to call in the PE advisory teacher if teachers feel unsure about the content of a suitable physical education programme. Some LEAs have drawn up guidelines concerning the different aspects of PE, and these could serve as a basis for discussion among non-specialists uncertain of their role.

Most schools nowadays have access to a good-size hall and an adequate range of large and small apparatus, although some of the heavier items are not always suitable for young children. Even though the weather in Britain is unpredictable, HMI (DES, 1982a) were concerned that teachers did not make full use of outdoor space and suggested they should consider more outdoor work in fine days in winter as well as summer.

RELIGIOUS AND MORAL EDUCATION

Whether or not children are being educated in classes drawn from a variety of ethnic backgrounds, Britain is and will continue to be an ethnically diverse society and it is against this background that schools and teachers must plan religious education. The Swann Report (DES, 1985) stressed that religious education should be based on

> a non-denominational and undogmatic approach, as the only means of enabling all pupils, from whatever religious background, to understand the nature of religious belief, the religious dimension of human experience and the plurality of faith in contemporary Britain. (p. 518)

Evidence from the HMI 1982 survey indicated that few schools had a planned programme for religious education. A common approach was to tell Bible stories (often in a random order) which were sometimes linked to assemblies and major Christian festivals. If a balanced programme is to be provided for all children, teachers need to meet and discuss important areas to be explored with the aim of producing a detailed programme of work. The LEA agreed syllabus can often serve as a basis for such a discussion.

It is important to develop close links with other curricular areas such as art, music, environmental studies and language as they will all contribute to children's growing understanding of the place of religion in the community. Religious education offers one important avenue through which the self-concept of young children can be developed and where the foundations of attitudes, such as tolerance, are laid down. Schools with a multicultural intake will be able to take advantage of the different experiences and viewpoints offered by children and parents whose faiths are other than Christian. Where this is not the case, special efforts will have to be made to ensure that children are made aware that not everyone shares the Christian faith and beliefs.

Assemblies, particularly if they are led by the children, can often serve as a valuable focus for the religious and moral themes being pursued in the classroom. They can include songs, prayers and stories written and performed by the children, as well as drama and art work. Parents, too, might be invited to special assemblies such as Harvest Thanksgiving, or could participate on a regular basis in class assemblies. In a similar way festivals can be both a starting-point and a focus for a lot of interesting work.

Moral education rarely appears on the timetables of first schools because so much of it is implicit in the everyday teaching of young children, in which great importance is attached to their social and personal development. Teachers should be aware of the stages of moral development, however, and provide a sympathetic role-model to help children towards an understanding of the conventions and systems of the society in which they live.

It is not possible within the scope of a single chapter to deal fully with the curriculum of the first school. All that can be done is to alert teachers to the contribution which various curricular areas can make to children's development. It must be emphasized again that the separate identification of specific areas within the curriculum is used here mainly for ease in discussion. Teachers need to be aware of the various areas if they are to ensure their adequate representation in the educational experiences made available to young children and to encourage the participation of their pupils in a full and rewarding programme. To the children, however, the curriculum provides their whole school experience, and as such is far more than an introduction to specific subjects or topics at certain times. The curriculum should offer them opportunities to learn, to explore, to discover, to wonder, to create and to begin to understand in a climate of support and mutual respect.

4

Play and Learning

We know that play – in the sense of 'messing about' either with material objects or with other children and of creating fantasies – is vital to children's learning and therefore vital in school. Adults who criticise teachers for allowing children to play are unaware that play is the principal means of learning in early childhood.

Plowden Report

We have described play as an all encompassing activity of central importance to the infant school. Its significance is as a vehicle for all aspects of young children's learning, development and motivation

Manning and Sharp,
Structuring Play in the Early Years at School

These ideas of play and learning, voiced by the Plowden Committee in 1967 and more recently by the researchers carrying out a Schools Council project, are now so widely accepted by infant and nursery teachers that they would scarcely raise an eyebrow in any staffroom. Certainly the nursery day is premised almost exclusively on the assumption that children learn best through play, so that no distinction is made between 'work' and 'play'. Indeed, it is possible for nursery teachers, by recourse to a number of theories of play, to justify the inclusion of almost any kind of play activity in the nursery curriculum in terms of its value in promoting the intellectual, linguistic or emotional development of the child (Coleman, 1967; Garvey, 1977; Tizard and Harvey, 1977; Sutton-Smith, 1979; Sylva et al., 1980).

But what of first schools? It seems to be the case that the primacy of play as a learning-medium dwindles as the child progresses through the educational system. Reception classes, for example, will amost always contain sand and water trays, some kind of domestic/dressing-up corner and a variety of structured playthings such as Lego or jigsaws. The use of these items is likely to be governed by the teacher and by the amount of space available; both time and space for play are unlikely to be as generous in quantity as in the nursery situation. After the reception class both the opportunity and materials for certain kinds of play generally diminish. Very few classes of eight year-olds, for example, will have a sand-tray or a Wendy house, although they may still have access to board games and constructional toys. Some teachers of older children will have made rigid demarcations between work and play to the extent that play, far from being a medium of learning, is seen as something that actively interferes with learning and is relegated to the edges of the school day to be indulged in when work is completed. Thus, for many children, the place of play in the school curriculum changes rapidly during the first four years from being accepted as the means of learning everything in the nursery to being considered as the means of learning very little at the end of first school. It has become a peripheral activity, despite the recognition of its importance in child development and learning.

Since children (and adults) of all ages find play intrinsically motivating and engrossing, it should be a worthwhile exercise to examine the play of five to eight year-olds to see what could be usefully incorporated into their classroom learning environment, not as a time-filler or reward but as a valued, integral part of the curriculum. Regarding play as valuable is important, as 'playing' can easily be used as a pejorative term by teachers. Children are quick to pick up the not-so-hidden messages in teachers' attitudes towards activities considered desirable and those not so favoured. As a starting-point it might be useful to consider certain questions. What does play mean to this age-group? What kinds of play predominate and in what ways are they important for the child's development? How can this knowledge be utilized by teachers and translated into good classroom practice? This chapter will attempt to answer these questions and to look at the possibilities for using play therapeutically and as an assessment tool.

HOW PLAY CONTRIBUTES TO CHILDREN'S DEVELOPMENT

It has been said that play is as elusive as the wind and can no more be caught by theory than wind can be caught in a paper bag (Reilly,

Play as Exploratory Learning p. 58). Any discussion of play has initially to grapple with the difficulties of definition. Since 'play' encompasses such disparate activities as adolescents having a game of hockey, young children pretending to be spacemen or a toddler splashing about in the bath, this is not as easy a task as it might first appear. Attempts by psychologists to produce workable definitions often result in rendering as unrecognizable and incomprehensible behaviour which three year olds can unhesitatingly label as play. Even the most concise definition (and many of them run to several paragraphs) has about it a dull, pedantic air which fails entirely to capture the antic nature of play. For example:

> It is a voluntary activity or occupation executed within certain fixed limits of time and place, according to rules freely accepted but absolutely binding, having its aim in itself and accompanied by a feeling of joy, tension and the consciousness that it is different from ordinary life. (Bax, 1977, p. 3)

Perhaps rather than strive for tight, lucid definitions of play it may be more fruitful to inquire into some of the major theories of play and consider their contribution to classroom knowledge.

Psychoanalytic Theories

Freud studied play because he believed it revealed much about the unconscious motives and emotions of children. He was particularly concerned with symbolic (pretend) play as, in his view, it represented the fulfilment of wishes that had been in some way repressed and had little chance of being realized. After witnessing several children repeatedly acting out quite harrowing scenes in their pretend play, he came to the view that it was unlikely that this represented wish-fulfilment. This particular form of play he termed 'mastery play', as he saw it as the child's attempt to cope, through repetition, with overwhelmingly anxiety-provoking situations.

Psychologists of the psychoanalytic school will often use 'play therapy' when working with young, disturbed children. Although such children may not be able to articulate their emotional problems or anxieties, it is thought that they may reveal much about their inner conflicts in play situations. Thus, play also acts as a 'mechanism whereby children can cope with specific sources of real life tension' (Fein, 1981 p. 1108). Play therapists adopting this approach (for example, Axline, 1971) see their role as interpreting and explaining to children the meanings behind their actions, thereby helping them to come to terms with their difficulties. Other approaches have involved dramatic play or doll play which are considered to have a 'releasing' effect upon children by allowing them to express their submerged emotions, either by acting out distressing family scenes themselves or through fantasy play with dolls. In yet another method the adult remains entirely passive and allows children complete freedom to choose their own activities in a playroom well-stocked with a variety of toys. It is hoped that in this secure but permissive atmosphere children will be able to discharge their emotions through play, thus reducing their anxiety and enabling them more easily to adjust to normal social demands afterwards.

While Freud's ideas of conflict and anxiety may not be wholly acceptable to many, the value of using pretend play, both as a means of gaining insight into the problems children may be experiencing and as 'therapy', is one readily accepted by many teachers of young children, and one which will be explored in more detail later in this chapter.

Cognitive Theories of Play

While psychoanalytic theories emphasize the significance of play in children's emotional development, cognitive theorists have been more concerned with the link between play and intellectual development. Piaget, in particular, chooses to consider play in terms of its contribution to children's developing intellectual capacities and largely ignores the social or emotional benefits which it may confer. The two important processes in Piaget's model of intellectual growth are assimilation and accommodation. Assimilation involves children absorbing information from the outside world which they then modify to match up with their own experience and level of understanding. Accommodation is the complementary process when children have to alter and develop their own understanding in order to fit it to events and objects in the environment. Piaget claims that intelligent adaptation occurs when the two processes are balanced or in equilibrium.

When the process of accommodation predominates and children have to adapt to external reality, the result is imitation. Alternatively when assimilation is dominant, people and objects will be adapted to fit the child's view of the world and the result is play. According to Piaget (1951), children do not develop new concepts and skills through play, because play is a purely assimilative process during which children practise what they already know. This means that children will play at whatever activity they have just mastered. However, if they repeat an activity in order to achieve a goal then this is classed as intelligent activity in which accommodation has a part. Making the distinction between an activity that is repeated for practice (play) and one repeated in order to understand it (intelligent activity) could prove to be difficult in some instances.

In his model of cognitive development (see chapter 6), Piaget describes the form of play characteristic of each of his stages. During the sensori-motor stage (birth to two years), practice (or mastery) play of motor skills prevails, only to be overtaken by symbolic (pretend) play which appears in the second year and increases over the next three or four years. According to Piaget pretend play develops through a sequence of stages, becoming more realistic as thought becomes more logical, and declining with the appearance of games with rules at around six years of age. Piaget's scheme (see Table 1) implies that less mature forms of play are discarded as more mature forms are added, and there is some limited evidence to support this (Fein, 1981).

Piaget's view of play has been criticized on several grounds, not least of which was that his view of play was somewhat limited. It has also been argued that he saw play as an immature function, in other words, something children would 'grow out of'. If this were the case, it would raise serious doubts about the intellectual maturity of large numbers of adults who continue to play (Scrabble, golf, bridge, amateur dramatics) throughout adult life.

Another psychologist, Jerome Bruner, whose ideas of cognitive development paralleled those of Piaget to a certain extent, has also written extensively about play (see Bruner et al., 1976; Bruner,

Table 1. Piaget's model of cognitive development and types of play

Stage	Types of play
Sensori-motor period (birth–2 years)	practice play – manipulation of objects
Pre-operational period (2–7 years)	symbolic or representational play solitary pretend play sociodramatic play
Concrete operational period (7–12 years)	games with rules – concept of winning and losing established

Source: after Piaget, 1951

1981). Bruner, however, ascribes a great deal of importance to the child's social interactions, particularly with adults, in the early years. This contrasts sharply with Piaget's view of the solitary, egocentric child acting upon a world of objects. Neither is Bruner so dismissive of the role of play in acquiring new skills and concepts. He believes that one result of play is that it promotes the kind of innovative behaviour which often helps to solve problems and thus enhances problem-solving skills. Much of the support for his ideas about the role and function of play derives from recent studies of object play in young monkeys in their natural surroundings. Play among a variety of species of monkeys seems to facilitate tool-using skills, as well as aiding the learning of completely new behaviours. Bruner argues that children (and adults) are freed from the pressures of the real world when playing and this provides an excellent opportunity to try out new combinations of behaviour. It is this playful practice of assembling and re-assembling bits of behaviour into new sequences which could prove useful later in more serious contexts.

Although Bruner's theories concerning behavioural flexibility have been linked mainly with object play, other psychologists (Vygotsky, 1967; Singer, 1973; and Sutton-Smith, 1977) consider symbolic (pretend) play to be important in the development of abstract thought, divergent thinking capabilities and creativity. Smith and Simon (1984) review a large number of developmental studies which aim to demonstrate that certain kinds of play do foster problem-solving and creative skills. Taking into account that many of these studies have serious design faults, they arrive at the tentative conclusions that play experience, particularly pretend play, does confer benefits for divergent problem-solving.

It is apparent that Bruner attaches considerably more importance to the role of play than does Piaget but this is mainly attributable to differences in the way they define and categorize play. This will become clearer if we look at how Corinne Hutt (1979) attempted to classify 'all those activities of children which adults customarily term play' (see figure 1). Hutt distinguishes between three different kinds of play. First there is epistemic behaviour which includes activities concerned with the acquisition of information and knowledge. This category is further sub-divided into the components of problem solving, exploration and productive activities, examples of which are shown in figure 1. Ludic behaviour, on the other hand, refers to those playful activities which bear upon and utilize past experience and includes symbolic (pretend) play and

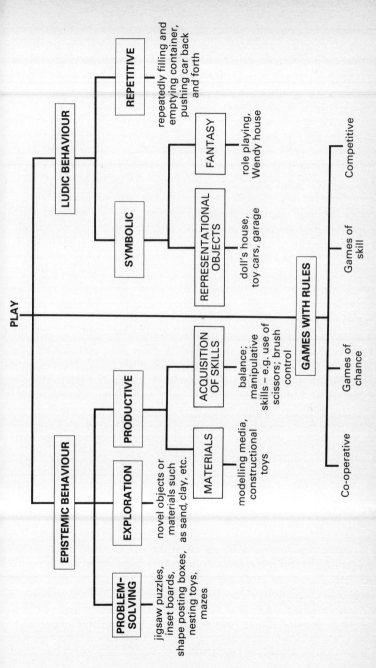

Figure 1 A classification of children's play activities (from C. Hutt, 1979)

repetitive play. 'Games with rules' seems to be a fairly straight-forward category, although the sub-divisions into co-operative, chance, skill and competitive do not seem particularly helpful as many games cut across several of these divisions. A card game such as bridge, for example, would be difficult to classify, as it is co-operative as well as competitive, and skilful with an element of chance (a more useful typology of games with rules is offered by Taylor Parker (1984), who suggests field games, floor and table games, iconic games and word games).

It is apparent that the two major categories distinguished by Hutt (those of epistemic and ludic behaviour) bring to mind Piaget's distinction between 'accommodation' and 'assimilation'. During periods of ludic activity/assimilation, the child is involved with familiar material or information and any learning is purely incidental. Epistemic/accommodative activity, on the other hand, is concerned with the active mastery of new information and skills. Whereas Piaget confines play to ludic activity (assimilation), both Bruner and Hutt have a much broader view of play which includes epistemic activities and recognizes the possible contributions of this kind of play to learning.

However, useful as these categories may be in classifying the relationships of different activities, it must be pointed out that children's play can rarely be pigeon-holed so tidily. Hutt herself points out that there is no clear-cut and dramatic transition from epistemic to ludic behaviour. A child will often alternate, for example, between serious exploration and more playful manipu-lation of an object of a toy. She describes this as a change of emphasis from 'what does this object do?' to 'what can I do with this object?'. Similarly, more complex sequences of play, such as a child making a model dinosaur out of junk and then inventing an imaginative theme around the model, contain both epistemic and ludic components.

This brief exploration of some of the major theories demonstrates how complex an activity play is, not only to define and describe but to account for in terms of its contribution to child (and adult) development. Some theorists consider its importance in terms of social and emotional gains, while others emphasize its role in learning and creativity. On what, then, can teachers base and justify decisions about the kinds of play they should be fostering, and how can these decisions be implemented within the normal classroom?

FOSTERING PLAY IN THE CLASSROOM

So far we have seen that there is evidence to support the idea that different kinds of play are predominant at different ages and stages of childhood. The two major forms of play which are associated with this age group are symbolic (pretend) play for the younger children, merging into games with rules for the older ones. (This is not to say that children of this age will concern themselves only with these particular types of play but that the proportion of time spent on them is likely to be greater than for other play activities.)

Pretend Play

Pretend play is often called by a variety of names, including fantasy or imaginative play, dramatic or sociodramatic play, symbolic play, make-believe and so on. Although Piaget has proposed that pretend play begins to wane around six years of age, most people would agree that pretend play in some form or other continues to be important throughout the infant school age range. Some psychologists take an even more extreme view and believe that the interest in pretend play continues into adolescence, where it becomes part of adolescent day-dreams (Singer, 1977).

Pretend play at infant school age can be solitary – a child on his/her own inventing stories around a doll family in a doll's house, for example – but it is much more likely to involve groups of children either constructing and playing with small worlds of their own, using Lego, wooden blocks, miniature people and cars, or dressing up and adopting roles in large-scale fantasy games. Children, given the opportunity, will use a wide range of art materials to create 'props' for their imaginative games, ranging from masks and swords to model aeroplanes, dinosaurs, robots and so on. Children obviously revel in this kind of play but is it in any sense educationally valuable? What kinds of learning does it promote?

The value of pretend play   Many of the gains claimed for pretend play have been social, which is hardly surprising in view of the fact that much of it involves groups of children playing co-operatively together. Researchers have consistently noted that the encouragement of pretend play is associated with a reduction in children's egocentricity. Rosalind Gould (1972), for example, observed that children who have learned to see the other child's point of view through make-believe games are less likely to become physically aggressive in their behaviour. Greater self-control, increased social co-operation, reduced restlessness, less disruptiveness and better concentration have all been related to extensive involvement in pretend play (Singer, 1977; Fein, 1981). Teachers would surely agree that these are attributes worth encouraging and all are prerequisites for more formal learning situations. It is impossible for a child to progress in reading, for example, unless he or she is able to sit still and concentrate for increasing periods of time.

It is more difficult to find experimental evidence which un-reservedly supports the value of pretend play in promoting cognitive skills. Experiments concerning play are notoriously difficult to design and it is easy to criticize some of them for being over-optimistic about the benefits of pretend play on the grounds that they fail to distinguish sufficiently between the effects of play and experimental effects, such as increased attention from adults.

Smith (1977, 1984) and Fein (1981) both provide detailed reviews of the many experiments concerned with both object and pretend play and their value in the promotion of cognitive skills. Most of the studies are concerned with short-term effects; none has completed long-term follow-ups, and there do not appear to have been any longitudinal studies in these areas. With all these caveats in mind, pretend play does seem to be related to an increase in divergent thinking skills (valuable for problem-solving), verbal fluency and story-telling skills.

A large-scale study in this country which looked at the spontaneous play of children in infant schools (as opposed to specifically 'set up' experimental situations) was the Schools Council Project 'Structuring of Play in the Infant/First School' which was carried out between 1974 and 1978 (see Manning and Sharp, 1977). Their study was based on the involvement and observations of hundreds of practising teachers up and down the country. They record many examples of pretend play and set out in detail the kind of motivation and learning that resulted from them. As well as the more obvious linguistic and social skills which are practised in play, they report a wealth of incidental learning such as problem-solving, transfer of knowledge and imaginative skills when making props. Pretend play often motivated children to read, research, write, draw and print, and was often the source of more long-term projects involving the entire class. The play had itself been triggered off by a variety of stimuli, varying from stories and television programmes to real-life events, such as a wedding or a trip to a building site. Throughout, the role of the teacher in observing, initiating, participating, maintaining and extending play is emphasized.

What kind of pretend play?   Pretend play, as has already been pointed out, may be on a large or small scale, involving a wide range of materials, and this distinction is a useful one to maintain in terms of play in the classroom.

Large-scale pretend play   Because this kind of pretend play by its very nature requires more space and larger numbers of children than is usual for other kinds of play, it is rare to see it extend beyond the early classes of infant schooling. Also it tends to be noisy and to involve children moving around, which can be distracting to other children in small classrooms. For these reasons many teachers adopt strategies such as using corners of the hall where classrooms open out onto them, or wide corridors directly outside the classroom, where children can be seen by the teacher but can extend and develop their play without disturbing or being disturbed by others. In summer and in good weather, it may be possible to use a verandah or enclosed area directly outside the classroom.

It has been shown (Pulaski, 1973) that younger children (four year-olds) exhibit a great variety of pretend play when given realistic objects and materials to play with, whereas the reverse is true of older children (eight year-olds) whose play themes show more diversity when the materials are less realistic. Thus, a well-stocked Wendy house with realistic contents and dressing up clothes is an appropriate way of stimulating make-believe play among nursery and reception age children. Older children might find such provision constraining and would benefit from a range of objects and materials which do not suggest specific functions because of their appearance. A fold-away screen could be used to enclose a space which, augmented by cardboard packing cases and boxes, could be turned into whatever environment children wish to create for themselves, whether it be space capsule, witch's cave, castle or boat. Similarly, while specific costumes, such as nurse, spaceman or fairy, might be popular with the youngest children, for older children much more use might be had from lengths of material (with pieces of velcro to act as fasteners attached at strategic points) and a collection of belts and headbands. Old curtains, both net and material, are very popular and lend themselves to a variety of purposes – head-dresses, cloaks, skirts and so on. Further advantages of relatively unstructured materials, such as cardboard boxes and lengths of material, are that they are readily available, cheap and easily replaced when they become dirty or worn. Access to a range of art materials (paints, crayons, glue, scissors, cardboard, paper, adhesive tape, staples, etc.) and junk (including boxes, plastic containers, beads, buttons, a variety of fabric scraps, feathers, wood shavings, wool and milk bottle tops) will greatly enhance the variety and inventiveness of children's make-believe (see Newson and Newson, 1979).

Manning and Sharp (1977) give an example of a group of children whose game of Cowboys and Indians became the starting point for a topic that extended over several weeks. The children, encouraged by the teacher's suggestion that they build a wigwam to house their game, began by researching in the library the Indian way of life. This led to days of intense constructional activity making a wigwam, totem pole, chiefs' and braves' head-dresses, axes, bows and arrows, tunics, belts and pouches. Many activities involved a great deal of co-operative effort and problem-solving in overcoming difficulties, such as how to erect both the wigwam and the totem pole and make them stable. Their teacher introduced stories about Indians, display tables were set up, and the children made-up and wrote stories which were read and painted pictures which were shown to the class. Throughout the entire period, the make-believe play about Indians continued to be elaborated and expanded upon, acting both as a stimulus for and being stimulated by feedback from all the related activities in the classroom.

Pretend play of this kind can provide the sensitive teacher with a framework around which to structure the best kind of child-centred informal learning. But children's pretend games are triggered by their imagination which needs to be fed either through direct experiences (often outside the school) or stories read aloud or presented through other media such as theatre, film or television. The teacher's role has three concurrent elements: she or he can act as a stimulator of children's imagination through the experiences she or he offers; she or he can encourage pretend play by providing opportunity, space and a range of materials; and lastly, taking her or his cue from the children, she or he can build successful learning situations onto their pretend play.

Small-scale pretend play   Many teachers, particularly of older infants, are more tolerant of small-scale pretend play because it tends to be quieter, is less demanding to terms of space and, often although not always, contains an element of skilful manipulation. At the younger end of the age group it includes playing with doll's houses, farm sets, Lego, cars, road and rail layouts, boats, play people and unstructured material such as plasticine and clay. Older children may be attracted to more sophisticated building systems (such as technical Lego and Fischer Technik, which have accessories such as wheels, cogs, axles and battery operated motors) that make working models a possibility. Such systems introduce children to problems of design and technology at an early age within the framework of play.

There is a great diversity of informal learning that has its starting point in this kind of play. Here are three brief examples of starters, which, given the children's continuing interest and support from a sympathetic teacher, are infinitely expandable in many directions.

1 Making doll's house furniture from junk introduces children to the concept of scale, gives practice in measuring and in manipulative skills and introduces new vocabulary about different items of furniture. This could lead into extending the doll family's world by making shops for them to visit or a school to attend. Perhaps a visit to the local parade of shops could be arranged to look at what they sell, how their windows are arranged, what the shop signs say and so on.

2 Play with road layouts and cars can introduce the children to rudimentary ideas of mapping. A walk around the immediate vicinity of the school could be used in an initial attempt to make a three-dimensional local layout using boxes or whatever materials are to hand to represent buildings, roads, fences, bridges and so on. This usually generates a great deal of discussion about spatial arrangements – where buildings are in relation to one another – and will necessitate further trips out to verify and extend the layout. With older children this could lead on to discussions about such matters as the relative age of the buildings (particularly if there is an old church nearby), their style and their mode of construction.

3 Constructional play of all kinds throws up problems which can themselves become starting points for new discoveries and ways of extending skills and knowledge in a meaningful context. Building with wooden bricks raises problems of stability, particularly if the building is tall or requires doors and windows. How do real builders solve these problems? Perhaps there is a building site nearby? Making model cars that run requires an understanding of

axles and, if a motor is to be added, of gears as well. Perhaps a closer examination of take-apart toy cars is needed, and how about dismantling an old clock to look at some gears? Making dolls' clothes reinforces the necessity of accurate measurement and re-closable openings. What kind of fasteners are commonly used? How can fabric be joined without sewing?

Teachers should remember that, for the youngest children, absolute accuracy of scale and representation is not important. Children see nothing odd in combining objects of varying scale in their imaginative play, so that matchbox-size cars are driven into cavernous cereal box garages and tiny dolls are fed from giant spoons. Over-insistence on accuracy by adults can ruin a child's imaginatively constructed world.

The role of the teacher   Brief mention has been made in passing of the role of the teacher in promoting pretend play. For a more detailed discussion, reference can be made to the Schools Council publication (Manning and Sharp, 1977). The key strategies which Manning and Sharp emphasize in structuring play profitably in terms of learning and development are provision and involvement. Under provision, teachers' attention is directed to the basic considerations of classroom organization necessary for the success-ful integration of play into the curriculum. It involves discussions concerning the amount of space and time to be allocated to specific forms of play and the availability and storage of materials. Teachers' attention is also drawn to the kinds of rules adopted concerning play and how these may be necessary but constraining.

The ideas put forward by Manning and Sharp about teacher involvement are somewhat more controversial in that they argue that teachers should be active participants in the range of children's play. While all infant teachers will happily join in an overtly didactic game (such as picture lotto), many stop short at the Wendy house door. It is a commonly held belief that imaginative play is the child's secret domain and that adult participation leads to adult domination which ultimately prevents children playing. This is an understandable viewpoint as the line between participation and interference is finely drawn. From their experience with teachers involved in the project, Manning and Sharp refute this, as they found that teachers who enjoyed play were welcomed by the children into their games. Their participation indicated that they valued play sufficiently to give time to it themselves. Manning and

Sharp also stress the value of observation, as they believe this to be the key to successful provision and involvement. It is only through careful observation of play episodes that the teacher can, for example, gauge when to intervene in play, either to maintain it or to extend it by providing new materials or injecting fresh ideas.

Games with Rules

According to Piaget, infant school children are at an age when games with rules begin to emerge as the form of play which will dominate the rest of childhood. It is not, of course, true to say that children below the age of five are not capable of joining in or enjoying games with rules. Bruner and Sherwood (1976) studied the simple games (mainly variations of 'Peekaboo') played by a group of mothers with their babies and discovered that, far from being passive participants, the babies learned the rules and took over the game themselves, deciding when the game should start and end and, also, who should do the hiding. However, apart from very rudimentary games with rules like these, it seems likely that five and six year-olds will need the presence of an adult in order for a game with rules to be carried to a successful conclusion. This is largely because children of this age have a very poor understanding of the need for rules and, in Piaget's terms, play 'egocentrically' with little regard for other children. Older seven and eight-year-old children have a much surer grasp of the idea of winning or losing a game and of the importance of rules but they may tend to forget specific rules and change them as they go along.

The Value of Games

There is such an enormous variety of games that it is difficult to categorize them. Some are solitary, some are played in groups or pairs and some require organized teams. They can be competitive or co-operative, indoor or outdoor, field or table, iconic or word games. They can rely on chance, strategy or physical skill, or a combination of all three. In an infant classroom, the games most commonly found are board games, word games and, more frequently nowadays, computer games. Using games as a vehicle for learning is not new, particularly at primary level, but the increasing sophistication of computer simulation games has meant that they are becoming a common teaching device throughout secondary and higher education and in business.

One of the main virtues of employing games in a learning context is that they are an excellent means of gaining and maintaining children's attention, partly because they involve children actively rather than passively and partly because they involve the emotions as well as the intellect (Strom, 1981). It is not unusual for children to become so absorbed into the world of the game that they become immune to all but the most cataclysmic of distractions. The main advantage of games is that they can be designed to offer children practice in a whole range of skills whether they be physical (for example, hand–eye co-ordination, gross motor skills), intellectual (for example, memory, planning, decision-making), or social/emotional (for example, turn-taking, co-operation, delaying gratification, handling aggression).

Strom (1981) lays emphasis on the role of games in practising decision-making skills, which he feels will be all-important in the uncertain and complex world in which today's children are growing up. In games, he says, children learn by experiencing the consequence of their actions, and games allow them safely to experiment with situations and solutions that might be too risky in the real world. This appears to be particularly true of the 'dungeons and dragons' types of game, which combine elements of fantasy and decision-making, a seemingly irresistible formula for some children, whether as a computer game ('Grandmother's Garden' and 'Dragonworld' for instance) or in book form.

What Kind of Games?

Board games and table games   For the youngest children in this age group, board games should be kept as simple as possible. Commercially produced games (such as 'Ludo' and 'Snakes and Ladders') are usually unsuitable for beginners as they take too long to complete and may have over-complicated rules. It is best at first to limit the game to two players, for if children have to wait a long time for their turn they get bored. Others will miss their turn and a few will give themselves several turns before anyone realizes. Teacher-made games are best in the early stages (and also have a lot to commend them later on), as the teacher can tailor them exactly to match the level of playing ability in the class as well as incorporating the specific skills which she or he wishes the children to practise. Using a die to move a counter along straight tracks of squares from A to B may be sufficient to start with. Each child should have his or her own track and the game can be made more interesting by racing cars along them to a garage, or having frogs hopping to a pool, etc. Later, games can be devised to include practice of number skills, such as addition and subtraction, or reading skills, such as initial sounds or blends. Although there are many software packages which include excellent examples of this kind of practice game it is important that children also continue to play them with others.

Word games   Word games, such as 'I Spy' and 'My Grandmother's Trunk', are usually games in which the whole class joins. In mixed-age-range classes, they can serve as a valuable initiation for younger children to the cognitive skills involved, providing they are helped and the game does not go on for too long.

Computer games   A number of references have already been made to these games. Great strides have been made in terms of the range of software available for this age-group, as well as in the quality both of the content and graphical reproduction. Similarly, the hardware has noticeably improved; many schools now have disc drives which cut out the frustration of waiting for programmes to load via cassette or, even worse, the programme refusing to load at all.

There are many simple game programmes available for practising skills such as spelling, simple addition, subtraction, multiplication and so on. Some of the newer programmes on the market allow teachers to insert items themselves so that within the overall game the level of difficulty or kind of problem can be matched to individual children's needs.

As fascinating as children find these games and useful though all the practice may be (not least of which we can count keyboard skills themselves), it must be remembered that there are more creative ways in which children can use computers – solving problems or designing their own graphics and programmes using 'Logo' and turtles, for instance – and also that prolonged interaction with the computer may inhibit interaction with other children. Playing games with a computer may become an all-engrossing but ultimately isolating experience.

Obviously in a busy infant classroom teachers are not always or only involved in play as they are responsible for the whole curriculum as well as teaching the specific skills involved in reading, writing and mathematics. Although these skills may be practised in play (and even be stimulated and enhanced by it), children do not pick them up by chance. Teachers will have to make their own decisions based on their own philosophy and knowledge of 'their children' about the place of play in the context of the total curriculum. Whether the time given to play is all day, part of a day or part of a week, teachers need to give as much thought to play as they do to other curricular areas and understand why they are providing such opportunities in terms of their effect on children's development.

THERAPEUTIC USES OF PLAY

Earlier in this chapter, 'play therapy' was touched upon during the discussion of psychoanalytic theories of play. Such therapies are usually based on varying interpretations of Freudian theory, not all of which stand up to close examination. Most of these therapies are very lengthy processes dependent on a one-to-one relationship between therapist and child. Thus, whatever benefits may accrue from them, it is not suggested that play therapies of this nature are suitable for use in the classroom. However, this is not to deny the therapeutic role of play for those children who are experiencing social and emotional difficulties in school. Play can also be a useful approach with young children who have problems of delayed language or learning difficulties. The remainder of this chapter will address questions of why and how teachers might use play to assist children with adjustment problems but it should be borne in mind that many of the principles outlined here will be equally effective when employed in the remediation of language or learning difficulties.

Why Use Play Approaches?

Several very good reasons can be advanced for adopting play approaches as a means of helping children with social and emotional difficulties, the most important and obvious of which will be discussed here.

First, play activities offer a rich source of social learning opportunities for children with adjustment problems. This is particularly true of pretend play and games with rules (covered in previous sections of this chapter) which are dependent for their success on sharing, co-operation and turn-taking — social skills which are often lacking in children exhibiting difficult behaviour. Through play children can learn from adults and other children alternative or more appropriate ways of responding than they may currently be using. Second, play is an enjoyable activity for adults and children alike and provides both with an unthreatening and appealing vehicle for learning. This may be important for different reasons to children displaying very varied kinds of behaviour. Aggressive children, for example, often attract a great deal of negative attention from teachers, together with exhortations to change their behaviour. Using a play approach may modify the picture they have of adults as controlling and disapproving people, and lead to more constructive and trusting relationships. For shy, withdrawn children, on the other hand, play activities are 'safe' in that they allow children to experiment with new or different behaviours without fear of failure, and the activities 'buffer' them from the consequences of the real world.

Finally, but no less importantly, teachers of young children are already familiar with the idea of structuring play activities and so, although using play therapeutically may mean altering the emphasis slightly, teachers are not required to adopt and implement a whole new repertoire of skills or practice. Indeed, the play activities suggested here should complement and enhance teachers' existing expertise in this area and can be used successfully in conjunction with any other remedial approaches a teacher may care to adopt.

Assessing the Problem

Before embarking upon any programme of activities designed to help a child with emotional and social difficulties some kind of assessment will need to be made both of the nature of these difficulties and of the context in which they occur. This assessment will entail close observation of the child in order to gain as much information as possible about the behaviour(s) it is hoped to change. Some form of general assessment ought also to be made, as it is important to view behaviour difficulties within the context of the child's overall development. It may be, for example, that weaknesses in a specific cognitive area, such a language skills, may be contributing to a child's behaviour problem and concurrent help may need to be offered to encourage language development in order to support efforts aimed directly at the behaviour difficulty itself.

In their book *Helping Young Children with Behaviour Difficulties*, Chazan et al. (1983) offer teachers practical advice, together with several checklists, to assist in the speedy and effective assessment of children prior to instituting a programme of remedial help. Part of this assessment should involve observing such children at play in order to find out what kind of games/activities interest them most and also to gauge the complexity of their play. For example, it is important to find out whether their play is repetitive and stereotyped or inventive and imaginative; whether their play episodes are of long duration or short and fragmented; whether their play is solitary, parallel or co-operative; and how language is employed throughout. Teachers should be wary of making premature judgements about the quality of children's play. Such estimations, as Tyler (1984) points out, should be based on careful observation of play in varying contexts, taking into account: the degree of concentration shown; the complexity of the sequence of elements in a play episode; the degree of social participation; the degree of symbolism incorporated; and the language content of the play. Tyler maintains that only when all these aspects have been carefully considered will teachers be in a position to intervene in children's play, and they will then be less likely to provide activities that are either too easy or unduly difficult or which fail to capture children's interests.

Choosing and Using Play Approaches

Armed with the information gained from a period of observation it should be possible to plan a range of play activities which are within the children's capabilities in order to guarantee their initial success. Gradually the activities can be made more demanding, in order to extend and develop children's repertoires with, it is hoped, subsequent benefits in other areas such as language and other cognitive skills. There is evidence (Manning et al., 1978; Chazan et al., 1983) that children experiencing behaviour difficulties of one kind or another often lack the necessary skills or knowledge to make the most of play situations. Withdrawn, shy children, for instance, may only indulge in solitary make-believe, while aggressive, over-active children may enjoy wild chasing games outdoors but avoid sedentary co-operative games. Left to their own devices children such as these may be either unable or unwilling to use opportunities for play to their best advantage. It may be vital to their future adjustment that an adult steps in and offers guidance and support, in a more structured and systematic way than may be usual with young children.

Rather than single out children with difficulties in adjustment for exclusive help and attention it is best to include them in a small group of children during the play-tutoring sessions, as it is likely that, in most cases, teachers are aiming to promote better relationships with other children. Teachers might try to have a group of no more than about six children, preferably in a quiet carpeted area of the classroom, for about twenty minutes per session on a regular basis. This can be difficult to arrange in a busy classroom but use could be made of parent helpers or NNEBs, or the headteacher might be willing to help out with the remainder of the class. It is essential to have a plan of the play activities and their sequence over a number of sessions while remaining sufficiently flexible to respond to the mood and interest of the children in the group.

Both imaginative play and games with rules offer a wide range of opportunities that can act as starting points for play-tutoring sessions. Role-playing activities, in particular, encourage children to see what it feels like to be someone else and to begin to understand more about how facial expression, bodily posture and gestures convey messages about people's emotions. Suggested activities might include simple mimes such as 'Who am I?' or 'What am I doing?' for the youngest children, leading on to acting out simple stories and rhymes, or using puppets. Small-scale toys, such as 'Lego' and play people, can be used to develop imaginative themes such as a trip to the moon or a pirate adventure. The activities need to be fun, so that, although participating and acting as role models, teachers need to beware of dominating or organizing the play too much, in case it becomes a chore and the children will not co-operate. Teachers might consider interspersing imaginative play sessions with some simple board games which are dependent upon a degree of social co-operation for their success. It is impossible to cover all the various kinds of play activities which could be used to help children overcome behavioural and emotional difficulties but reference has been made in this chapter to a number of publications which contain many useful ideas for teachers.

5

Helping Language Growth

This chapter will be mainly concerned with the growth of understanding and the increasing use of spoken language in children between five and eight years of age. With reading and writing assuming increasing importance at this age, much less attention tends to be given to oral language during this period than in the years up to five. However, the extent to which children can express themselves efficiently and understand the spoken word has a bearing on their success in beginning to master the essentials of literacy and it also affects many other aspects of development, including: adult–child and child–child interaction; the regulation of the child's own behaviour and that of others; the development of self-concept and insight into the feelings and reactions of others; memory; and the solution of problems, emotional as well as cognitive. Speech and language difficulties often need specific attention, and many children with special educational needs have associated problems of speech and language. Children's expressive and receptive language can give valuable clues to understanding their general development, and teachers' sensitive observation of children's knowledge and use of language will help them to become fully aware of their pupils' needs. It should, however, be recognized that different observers will interpret children's language in different ways and also that speech may vary considerably in different settings.

LINGUISTIC ACHIEVEMENTS IN THE FIRST FIVE YEARS

Language development is very rapid in the first five years of life and children will normally have made great strides in becoming competent in the basic uses of language by the time they enter the first school (Wells, 1985). Five year-olds will be close to mastery of the phonemic or sound system of their native language, even if there may still be difficulties in the recognition or production of some sounds – for example p/b; r/l; or s/f/th – which will usually disappear during the early years at school. By the time of formal school entry, children will have built up an impressive network of meanings, though their semantic skills will be related to their general cognitive development so that there will be a wide range of individual differences in the understanding of the meanings of language. By the age of five much progress will also have been made in sentence structure and in grasping the essential syntactical or grammatical rules of language. Most children will have quite an extensive vocabulary and will be able to use language for a variety of functions.

The uses to which young children put language have been closely studied in recent years. Halliday (1969, 1975) listed seven, somewhat overlapping, functions of language, all evident at least to some extent by the age of five:

1 instrumental – serving the function of the satisfaction of material needs ('I want')
2 regulatory – the child is aware of his/her capacity to manage or regulate the behaviour of others through language ('do as I tell you')
3 interactional – not 'one-way' as above but enabling interaction between self and others ('me and you')
4 personal – language being used as a form of the child's individuality ('here I come')
5 heuristic – helping the child to learn about things and to interact with the environment ('tell me why')
6 imaginative – children creating their own environment ('let's pretend')
7 informative/representational – enabling communication at a higher level and the expressing of propositions ('I've got something to tell you')

On the basis of her studies of three to five year-olds, Tough (1973b) maintains that all children seem to use language (a) to protect their own rights and interests, and to maintain their own comfort and pleasure; (b) to initiate and maintain relationships with others; (c) to report on present experience; and (d) to direct their own and others' actions. These functions seem to correspond largely with the first four in Halliday's list. Tough further asserts that young children from advantaged homes seem to develop a number of uses of language far more extensively than those who are disadvantaged because of limited mother–child verbal interactions: (a) to report on past experiences; (b) to collaborate towards agreed ends; (c) to extend the imaginative situation; (d) to offer explanations and justifications; (e) to consider alternative possibilities; (f) to deal with problems in the imagination and see possible solutions; and (g) to predict and plan.

Wells (1982) highlights the extent to which children differ in their language development by the age of five, when a gap of as much as three years can be found between the most and least advanced in mean length of utterance. But Wells stresses that by five nearly all children have developed mastery of the major meaning relations involved in a sentence and of the syntactic structures through which they are realized and nearly all are using language for a wide variety of functions. Normally, therefore, teachers in the first school will find that their pupils have a sufficient base of language experience to enable them to respond to the increasing scope of verbal demands of school. However, as previously mentioned, some children, particularly those with general learning difficulties or physical disabilities affecting speech and those who come from homes where there has been an impoverished language input, will have special needs in relation to their language development and will require extra attention in school. The kinds of help which may be considered appropriate for these children will be discussed later in this chapter.

MAIN CHARACTERISTICS OF LANGUAGE GROWTH FROM FIVE TO EIGHT YEARS

Language development in the years between five and eight is characterized by a growth in vocabulary; a greater understanding of more complex grammatical structures; increasing awareness of relationships, with a growing independence from the here-and-now; and a growing ability to share knowledge with others. In this development, home, school and the wider community all play their part.

Growth in Vocabulary

During their early school years children will continue to enrich their vocabulary. School will provide them with many new opportunities for expanding their knowledge of words, particularly as they begin to learn to read. Increasingly they will be asking about the meaning of new and possibly abstract words, and will be able to define words in more elaborate terms than before. By about five or six children are typically able to define concrete nouns with which they are familiar in terms of their main uses; by eight years of age they are classifying objects and defining them in terms of what they are made of, as well as shape, size and colour. Five and six year-olds may have difficulties with some relational words, for example, deep/shallow (de Villiers and de Villiers, 1979).

Greater Understanding of More Complex Grammatical Structures and Meanings

Dale (1976) points out that in the case of children older than five or six differences between the child's and the adult's use and understanding of grammar are not obvious from the spontaneous observation of free speech. However, a few difficulties are typically found in the early years at school, for example in connection with the mastery of subject–verb agreement, case endings on personal pronouns (for example, him/her confusion) and some irregular verb forms. Carol Chomsky (1969, 1972) has studied the difficulties which children between five and ten have in understanding sentences phrased in the passive rather than the active form. For example, the question, 'is the doll easy to see or hard to see?' gives rise to considerable misunderstanding. Chomsky also found that exceptions to rules – for example, sentences in which the object occurs before the subject – take some time to master.

Entwistle and Frasure (1974) note the steady increase between six and nine years in children's understanding of the structure of language as children become more sophisticated and selective in the interpretation of words and meanings. Dale (1976) highlights the variety of paths of semantic development taken by children, stressing that the achievement of full semantic competence takes many years. An awareness of individual variations and language difficulties characteristic of children in the early school years will be of considerable value to the teacher in interactions with children in the classroom.

Increasing Awareness of Relationships

De Villiers and de Villiers (1979) point out that a major development in the later pre-school and early school years comes in children's attempts to relate sentences to one another so that they can express the relationship between events; each sentence is no longer seen in isolation and the child becomes more skilled in carrying on a conversation. They note, too, that while it is usually the case that children understand any aspect of language before they actually produce it themselves, children may use language without real understanding.

The implications for teachers of a knowledge of the gradual nature of the child's increasing awareness of relationships during the early school years are: first, that they should provide a variety of opportunities and contexts for children to use language; and second, that they should not over-estimate the child's understanding of the spoken word, even on the basis of the child's own production of speech. Teachers can help children to free themselves from the restrictions of the present, to understand the concept of the future and to make use of hypothetical statements (for example, if . . . then . . .). Imaginative and symbolic play will greatly assist the teacher to encourage these advances in language use.

Increasing Ability to Share Knowledge with Others

There has been considerable controversy over the extent to which the language of children up to about seven is egocentric, in the sense that speech is used without a real social function, or as a kind of monologue where the other party to the 'conversation' is not expected to respond or even attend to the speech (Elliot, 1981). Piaget (1959) was of the opinion that dialogue involving the ability to appreciate another individual's point of view and the understanding that the views and needs of others are different from one's own does not readily occur before children reach the age of about seven (Francis, 1977). However, Vygotsky (1962) took a rather different and more positive view of egocentric speech, regarding it as an important phase in speech development which helps the child forward to verbal thought and self-regulation. Donaldson (1978) also concludes that young children are not as limited in their ability to appreciate someone else's point of view as Piaget and his colleagues have maintained.

Even if we accept that children in the early school years can genuinely share their thoughts and experiences with others to some extent and in some contexts, they do need help in developing skills of communication with others. Flavell et al. (1968), for example, found that seven to eight year-olds had considerable difficulty in communicating a very specific message to another individual behind a screen. Teachers who encourage children to work in pairs and small groups and to engage in dialogue while carrying out collaborative tasks and activities can help to foster competence in oral communication.

Influences on Language Development

Language development in the early years at school is affected by a variety of factors. Although the role of maturation cannot be neglected in considering language growth, since competence in communication is seen to increase with age, there is no doubt that children's experience in different settings – home, classroom, playground and neighbourhood – plays a very important part in expanding the use and understanding of language. The main influences involved will be discussed under the following headings, which should not be taken to indicate entirely separate categories: (a) adult care and contact; (b) socio-economic background; (c) level of cognitive functioning; (d) sex differences; (e) bilingualism; and (f) school factors.

Adult care and contact   Studies of development in the first five years of life have stressed the importance of the nature and amount of the everyday contact between the child and the main caretaker, who is usually the mother. Children brought up in a family tend to be more advanced in language than those reared in an institution, which is likely to provide less variety in its stimulation and more limited adult–child interaction, though the effects of institutional life greatly depend on the quality of care (Rutter, 1972).

Wells (1982), on the basis of an intensive study of 128 children in Bristol, found that those children whose language development was particularly rapid received significantly more verbal stimulation from adults while engaged in routine household activities than did slow developers. The fast developers also received a significantly greater number of acknowledgements of their own utterances. According to Wells, the quality of parental response at three and a half years is associated with the quality of spontaneous speech at age five, though it must be recognized that if the behaviour of parents influences the child's development, the reverse is also true – some children are easier to converse with than others. Tizard and Hughes (1984), too, underline that young children learn a great deal by being in the company of their parents and engaging in dialogue about everyday matters, pointing out that this learning occurs in a context which is very meaningful to the children. They assert that far more adult–child talk was evident in their study of four-year-old girls at home than at school, where conversations were dominated by adults to a far greater extent.

In the years between five and eight, most children will not be at home as much as before, as school and outside activities take up more of their time. Within the home, too, it is likely that children will be involved in verbal communication with other members of the family for shorter periods than when they were younger, as interests widen and other children begin to claim their attention. Nevertheless, adults in the home will continue to exercise a strong influence on children's language growth, as long as they take every opportunity for verbal interaction with a child. The nature of the emotional relationships between parents and children, as well as the extent to which there is easy communication between all members of the household, will be especially influential in promoting language competence in the child.

Socio-economic background   Over the past three or four decades an increasing interest has been taken in the relationship between socio-economic background, language and educational achievement, giving rise to empirical studies and continued controversy, still far from being resolved. It is hardly surprising that there is so much disagreement over this question, since it cannot be dissociated from general social and political considerations and since the terminology used by writers on the subject is so often vague and open to different interpretations. Concepts such as 'social class', 'disadvantage', 'language deficit' and 'language differences' are employed in many varied senses. 'Social class', for example, is a crude concept, the significance of which is rapidly changing in today's society. Social-class stereotypes may be misleading, and may lead to an under-estimation of potential and aspirations in particular sub-cultures (Roberts, 1980). 'Disadvantage' is a relative concept used to refer to a wide range of sources of deprivation suffered by families. Theories of 'language deficit', which draw attention to the gaps in mastery of language skills characteristic of children from socially disadvantaged backgrounds, are usually viewed in opposition to theories of 'language difference', which draw attention rather to the existence of many varieties of language usage among children. However, as Francis (1977) points out, difference and deficit are not mutually exclusive possibilities; they may coexist or even be interdependent.

The well-known work of Bernstein and his colleagues (see, for example, Bernstein, 1960, 1971, 1973) on the close relationship between language, thinking and behaviour in different social classes, the use of 'restricted' and 'elaborated' codes by 'lower working-class' and 'middle-class' groups respectively, and the extent to which children from different social classes differ in their readiness for the demands of the school has been variously interpreted. In his later work Bernstein himself refined his original ideas, anxious that the differences to which he had drawn attention should not be construed as language deficiencies (Bernstein, 1970). Furthermore, Bernstein and his colleagues acknowledged significant language differences within classes, reflecting differences in the quality of the home itself (Brandis and Henderson, 1970); such intra-class differences have also been stressed by Chazan et al. (1977).

The various interpretations of and challenges to the ideas of Bernstein and his team make it difficult to arrive at an agreed view of the implications of these ideas, which have certainly been stimulating and challenging. Lawton (1968) and Demaine (1980) have pointed to confusions and contradictions in Bernstein's theory. Francis (1977) prefers not to use the concept of 'restricted' and 'elaborated' codes but rather to think in terms of the individual shifting between different levels of explicitness according to the content of the conversation and the purposes it serves. Strong criticism comes from W. P. Robinson (1980), who asserts that many of the demonstrated links between socio-economic status and academic achievement have only indirect, insignificant or irrelevant associations with the language mastery of children. Robinson concludes, too, that there is no evidence for a socio-linguistic definition of 'code' which is precise enough to be applied in any worthwhile sense and that none of the relationships suggested between confinement to a restricted code and the alleged psycho-logical consequences has been confirmed.

Surveys of children in the pre-school and early school years have found differences in the measured language attainments of children from different sub-cultures. Halsey (1972) reports achievements below the norm for pre-school children living in 'educational priority areas'; and Chazan et al. (1977), in a study of 535 seven and a half year-olds from different school catchment areas, found that although children from 'settled working-class' homes did better than those from disadvantaged backgrounds, the 'settled working-class' pupils did not do as well as 'middle-class' children on a range of oral language skills. For example, the mean vocabulary age of the middle-class sample was one year above that of the 'settled working-class' children. Francis (1977), reviewing evidence on the relationship between language and social class, concludes that while there are enormous variations within social groupings, it remains true that children of the lower working class are rather less well-equipped for the demands of formal education than those of the middle class: their language learning is not as advanced, they are less likely to draw on complex and explicit forms of expression, and their vocabulary is less well suited to the needs of schooling (see also Tough, 1977b).

Francis also notes that children may use expressions in contexts and ways unfamiliar to the teachers, thus earning possible disapproval and inaccurate judgement of their abilities. W. P. Robinson (1980) lays great stress on the part played by teachers' expectations and inferences, based in part on their pupils' speech and language, in discriminatory judgements and practices in school. In his view, restricted language emerges as a consequence of experience in school rather than as a cause of it. Because of their assumptions, teachers distribute both the quantity and quality of their interactions with children unevenly. To improve the situation, Robinson calls for an increased understanding on the part of teachers of what language is and how it works; the examination of the validity of belief systems that underlie inferences about children's potential from speech and writing; and a stress on 'intra-individual' competition rather than on rivalry between individuals in the classroom.

Cognitive development   The relationship between language growth and cognitive development is a complex one. As Herriot (1971) states, some psychologists consider that thinking is dependent on language, while others maintain that language aids thinking but is not a necessary condition for thought. Wells (1979) points out that although correlations have been reported between measured intelligence and assessments of linguistic attainment the interpretation of these correlations is made difficult by the fact that most tests of intelligence require language skills. Furthermore, language and cognitive development interact to such an extent that the nature of any links found cannot be assumed; and the relationship between intelligence and language is bound to be influenced by environmental factors, including social and cultural differences in the value put upon intellectual and linguistic performance.

Teachers may well associate language ability with general learning ability and, indeed, language development will tend to be slower in children with learning difficulties and low, measured intelligence. However, children who do not seem to express themselves well orally in the early school years may not be of low intelligence; it may be that they are unduly shy or inhibited, or that they need considerable time before they feel confident enough to communicate with ease in the public setting of the classroom, or else that they have had only limited language experience at home (see pp. 91–4 for a further discussion of language difficulties).

Sex differences   No clear picture emerges from studies of sex differences in language development. McCarthy (1954), in a review of the literature, concluded that a real sex difference in language competence existed in favour of girls. Crystal (1976) supports the view that girls, on the whole, learn linguistic features in advance of boys. However, Templin (1957) and Cherry (1975) consider that sex differences in language performance have been overemphasized. Weitz (1977), too, concludes that up to the age of ten or eleven, consistent sex differences in language are rare, although throughout the school years boys outnumber girls in reading problems and speech difficulties. Archer and Lloyd (1982) conclude that the evidence for a female superiority in verbal abilities is not very convincing; studies of sex differences are contradictory and show a different picture at different ages.

Early sex differences in language development, where they have been found, have been explained in a number of ways – for example, in terms of greater mother–daughter verbal interaction or reading, as a quiet activity, being seen as a particularly appropriate pursuit for girls (Weitz, 1977). We know little about the extent to which teachers differentiate between boys and girls in their verbal interactions with their children, but Delamont (1980) argues that sex differences permeate every facet of life in schools and that these tend to reinforce rather than challenge these differences (see also chapter 7, pp. 123–5).

Bilingualism   With the recent increase in the number of immigrant children in schools in Britain, particularly in large urban areas, bilingualism has become the concern of many teachers rather than of those mainly working in schools catering for children from traditional bilingual backgrounds, as in Wales. The Bullock Report (DES, 1975) pointed out that over half the immigrant pupils in schools in Britain have a mother-tongue which is not English, and in some schools this means over seventy five per cent of the total number on roll.

Elliot (1981) stresses that there are many different kinds of bilingualism. Some children learn both languages in the home ('simultaneous bilingualism') and others learn a second language only when they go to school ('successive bilingualism'); and the home may provide very different contexts for differing children, depending on the extent to which both parents speak the two languages and the importance attached to the languages concerned. Elliot concludes that studies show that bilingual children benefit cognitively, socially and culturally from the experience of learning more than one language (see also Lambert, 1977). On the basis of a review of relevant studies, G. Saunders (1982), whose book contains much material relevant to bilingualism in children aged five to eight years, considers that among the cognitive advantages of being bilingual are: (a) an earlier and greater awareness of the fact that names are arbitrarily assigned to objects and are subject to change; (b) earlier separation of meaning from sound ('which is more like *cap – can* or *hat*?'); (c) greater adeptness at creative and divergent thinking; (d) greater social sensitivity; and (e) greater facility in concept formation.

In the course of learning to speak two languages, some linguistic interference and confusion are inevitable. MacNamara (1966), in a study of bilingualism and primary education in Ireland, suggested four sources of possible difficulties for bilingual children:

1 linguistic interference: from the first language, e.g. certain grammatical forms may persist, or certain sounds may not even be heard because they do not occur in the first language;
2 cultural interference: the second language may imply an approach to reality different from that of the first;
3 parental confusion: parents may themselves have learned the second language imperfectly and therefore provide poor models;
4 longer time needed: it takes time to learn a language and so development in two languages is necessarily slower than in one.

G. Saunders (1982) considers that most of the problems associated with bilingualism are of a social or cultural nature, that is, problems resulting from hostility felt by the majority group towards the presence of other languages and cultures, in addition to the conflict faced by children expected to cope with two cultures at the same time.

It would seem that, if a child is to learn two languages, the earlier a start is made the better. In the good home and school, mastery of two languages takes place fairly automatically in the case of able children. Lloyd (1977), in a study of bilingual first-language-Welsh children, found that on the whole a good performance in Welsh tended to accompany a similar performance in English. This finding accords with the 'threshold-level hypothesis' proposed by Cummins (1979), which suggests that children with a high threshold level of linguistic competence in their first language are in a position to attain a level in the second language sufficient to allow them to cope well with the more academic aspects of the curriculum. Conversely, children with a low threshold of competence in their first language are not likely to do well in their second. This means that children of lower general ability, resulting in some degree of language delay, may well have greater difficulties in mastering two languages than if they had to cope with only one and will need special attention. It also means, as Baetens Beardsmore (1982) points out, that it is important to provide support for minority group first languages in order to ensure that children from such groups are not handicapped educationally.

Many factors affect the provision of bilingual education (see, for example, Thomas (1986) for a discussion of the development of bilingual education in Wales), and considerable differences of opinion exist about the best ways of catering for the educational needs of bilingual or multicultural pupils (Lewis, 1981). The approaches to the language teaching of ethnic minority children has given rise to considerable controversy. While there is general agreement with the view of the Bullock Committee (DES, 1975) that schools should adopt a positive attitude to their pupils' bilingualism, views about methods of achieving acceptable standards in two languages greatly diverge. Brown (1979), on the basis of close observation of infant school children learning English as a second language, stresses the importance of tackling the educational problems of immigrant children at an early stage and advocates the need to organize specialized language groups which encourage easier communication between adult and child. The HMI survey of eighty first schools in England (DES, 1982a) found that in ten first schools with substantial numbers of ethnic-minority pupils, special help with English as a second language was given to those children who were non-English speaking or for whom English was their second language. This help was given mainly through small withdrawal groups. The DES report expressed concern that although the quality of the work in specialist language groups was usually good, in some schools containing ethnic minority children there was no evidence of constructive attempts to use the mother-tongue to ease and make more effective the transition from home to school and from the language of the home into English.

The Swann Report (DES, 1985), however, was not in favour of withdrawing ethnic minority children to language centres or even to separate units within the child's usual school. The Swann Committee saw the needs of primary school pupils in respect of English as a second language as being met within the normal classroom situation by class teachers, emphasizing that the needs of ethnic minority pupils should be met by provision within the mainstream school as part of a comprehensive programme of language education for all children. The Committee advocated that first priority in language learning by all pupils must be given to the learning of English, recognizing that their views had implications for training and staffing in mainstream schools.

As the Swann Report points out, although it should not be assumed that ethnic minority pupils will automatically have particular educational difficulties, a proportion of these pupils do underachieve in language and other basic skills. Many of these pupils, too, may be overwhelmed and bewildered when they first arrive in school and may switch off and withdraw from the situation facing them (Bowker, 1968). It is essential, therefore, that school staffs have a considered policy towards meeting the language needs of ethnic minority pupils and that teachers are appropriately prepared and supported in attempting to achieve effective language learning. Ideas and strategies for multicultural teaching and language work with immigrant children may be found in a variety of sources, for example Derrick (1966); Schools Council (1972); Ward (1977); and M. Saunders (1982).

School   The ways in which the school influences language development have been touched upon in many places in this chapter, and it will suffice to make some general observations here. A number of sources have advocated the need for more planned intervention if teachers are to make the maximum impact on their pupils' language development. The Bullock Report (DES, 1975) stresses that teachers should create situations in which children can use more elaborate forms of language and recommends that more adults should be involved in school to afford a one-to-one or one-to-two relationship with children as often as possible. Tough (1984) highlights the desirability of teachers of young children observing language behaviour closely in order to build a picture of the ability each child has in using language. The Schools Council Communication Skills in Early Childhood Project has suggested many ideas to help teachers recognize language needs and provide opportunities for constructive dialogue with children (Tough, 1977a, b). Rosen and Rosen (1973) also show vividly how teachers can encourage young children to talk, fostering social skills and verbal competence at the same time. Francis (1977) asserts that the extent to which the first school manages to bridge the gap between the mutual understanding of mother and child and the lack of a similar shared experience between teacher and child is probably very significant in relation to the child's confidence in schooling and expectations of the teacher's behaviour.

It would seem that although teachers readily recognize the importance of spoken language as a foundation for acquiring the basic skills, they do not always provide their pupils with the optimum opportunities for developing oral language skills. The HMI survey of first schools (DES, 1982a) found that only a minority of schools actively planned work to improve listening skills and that children were occasionally expected to listen for too long and so became inattentive. Toleration of excessive noise and the lack of enclosed spaces in open-plan schools tended to inhibit talking and listening. Most teachers gave high priority to telling or reading stories, which were greatly enjoyed by their pupils; but in some cases the stories lacked challenge, variety and quality. Fewer opportunities were given to listen to poetry, and five and six year-olds were only infrequently engaged in dramatic play.

In a survey of views and practices in language teaching in thirty-three primary schools, Francis (1982) found that there had been a recent strengthening of interest in the teaching of language, especially with younger children and in connection with reading. However, teachers showed only a vague and global understanding of the role of language in learning and had rarely taken up directly ideas and approaches suggested by projects on language learning and teaching. Rather, teachers focused on familiar aspects of language and materials supplied by educational publishers.

Wells (1984), in his intensive study of thirty-two children between five and seven, found that on almost every language measure infant schools provided less opportunity than the home for children to use their linguistic resources or to add to them except in very narrow areas of vocabulary. This was true irrespective of social background. For example, whereas in all homes children initiated more than half the verbal interactions, this was reduced to about fifteen per cent in the classroom; and parents extended the child's meaning in thirty-eight per cent of their utterances, as compared with fourteen per cent of utterances extended in the classroom. Children took a much more passive role at school than at home. While Wells acknowledges that a number of teachers do promote an interactional environment that is conducive to effective and creative learning, he does not think that the teachers involved in his study were, on the whole, as concerned with what the children had to contribute as requiring them to follow the adult's train of thought. This study, which comes to broadly the same conclusion as Tizard and Hughes (1984) (see p. 79 in this chapter), points to the need for a consideration of changes of classroom practice and organization likely to lead to more active language learning, though teachers can argue that interaction with a large class is very different from the interaction possible at home.

LANGUAGE GROWTH AND BASIC ATTAINMENTS

Language and Reading

The relationship between the development of oral language skills and reading attainment has received relatively little attention. Herriot (1971) asserts that a certain level of language development must be attained before the learning of reading can begin and advocates all possible use of established language skills in the teaching situation. Semantic cues can be supplied, for example, by reading aloud to the child the short story which he will subsequently have to read. Grammatical and phonological features may be highlighted visually, for example, by colour, level of print or spacing. Productivity, considered by Herriot to be the outstanding feature of language skill, may be enhanced by helping the child to use different combinations of the same letter strings in many different but correct positions. Both the Bullock Report (DES, 1975) and Crystal (1976) stress that the syntactic or grammatical features of a text should relate to the level of language ability of the child and that reading material should be linguistically meaningful and familiar.

Others suggest that, while language obviously has a bearing on the ability to learn to read, proficiency in a spoken language is not necessary for success at the initial stages in reading; some children learn to read simple sentences and stories at a very early age, when their speech is still immature (Robeck and Wilson, 1974; Francis, 1977). Francis (1974) found no correlation between the syntactic structure of children's speech and their word recognition and sentence-reading abilities up to age of seven. However, Wells (1979) found that the quality of response that a mother gives to a child's speech in the early years has a significant influence on his subsequent linguistic development, including reading attainment at ages six and seven. In his study of thirty-two children through the primary school years, Wells found a complex pattern of relationships between home environment, language development and school attainment. He places much emphasis on a child's ability to handle the 'disembedded' or 'context-independent' use of language to bring into existence experiences that are not encountered at first hand (Wells, 1984). This ability seems to be related to the parents' own frequency of reading and writing and of reading stories to their children, as well as to the amount of time children voluntarily engage in activities associated with literacy.

Language delay in young children appears to be associated with later reading difficulties. Richman et al. (1982), though underlining the complexities of the relationship between early language development and later attainments, found that children with a marked degree of reading backwardness at eight years of age had shown delays in language at three and four years. They suggest that in individual cases slow language development in young children with good general ability, as assessed by a non-verbal test, many be a precursor to specific reading difficulties later on. Rutter and Yule (1975) compared a sample of older primary school children with general reading backwardness to a sample with specific reading retardation in respect of a number of aspects of speech and language, including a history of language delay. The only feature to show a significant difference between the two groups was poor complexity of language (referring to a child's use of different parts of speech, the length of sentences and the presence of subordinate clauses), which was found more frequently in the reading backwardness group. However, it is worthy of note that in both groups a history of language delay was three times as frequent as in a general population control group.

Language and Mathematics

The Plowden Report (CAC, 1967) on primary education stressed

the need for the introduction of the appropriate language simultaneously with the provision of suitable experiences relating to
number. In supporting this view, Westwood (1979) emphasized
that in the case of less able pupils the vocabulary of early number
situations (for example, same, different, more, less, as many as)
needs to be repeated and over-learned (see also Bell, 1970;
Williams, 1970). The Cockcroft Committee (DES, 1982b), set up to
consider the teaching of mathematics, also highlighted the importance of: (a) teachers being aware of the great variety of language
which is used in connection with many of the mathematical
operations which children meet; (b) children learning that words
may be used in mathematics in a different sense from the usual; and
(c) building up reading skills in mathematics at the same time as
other reading competencies, so that the children can understand the
explanations and instructions which occur in the text-books used
(see also Choat, 1984).

Matthews (1984) discusses ways in which children can be helped
to acquire mathematical concepts in the early school years, giving
examples of conversations between teacher and pupil aimed at
giving children a better idea of, for example, number comparisons,
shapes and perspective. Williams and Somerwill (1982) have
devised a scheme to assess children's acquisition of early mathematical language through observation and questioning. The
scheme, which is intended particularly for reception classes, covers
the language of spatial awareness, number, length, weight and
shape, volume and capacity, and time.

LANGUAGE AND SOCIAL–EMOTIONAL DEVELOPMENT

Children's language skills clearly affect, at least to some extent, the
quality of their interaction with adults and other children; their
understanding of the feelings and reactions of others; the extent to
which they are able to foresee the consequences of their behaviour;
and their approach to the solution of emotional conflicts and social
problems. Herriot (1971) considers that it is perhaps in the
organization of the self-concept that language is most important,
particularly as a child matures: the way in which teachers use
language plays a crucial part in the internalization by a child of the
behaviour of others. It should be recognized, too, that not only does
language competence influence social and emotional development
but personality and temperamental characteristics may affect

language growth. Wells (1979), while acknowledging the difficulty of disentangling the relationship between language skills and personality traits, thinks it likely that the differences between the active, outgoing child and the placid, retiring child will influence many aspects of the linguistic interactions that they experience and that this in turn may have an effect on both rate and style of language learning.

The links between language delay and behaviour difficulties have been explored by Richman et al. (1982). They found a tendency at three years of age for behaviour problems to be associated with delay in articulation and the development of expressive speech, as well as for children with language delay to show a high incidence of behaviour problems. There was less of a link between language and behaviour at eight years, but Richman and her colleagues came to the conclusion that children with a marked degree of language delay at three have a high chance of later cognitive and educational deficits, possibly leading to anti-social behaviour by the age of ten or eleven.

In promoting language development during the early school years, teachers should be mindful of the ways in which language competence is related to emotional and social development. Apart from the models provided by teachers of appropriate changes in language to suit changing situations, role-playing will be found a useful way of teaching pupils the language register suitable in different contexts (Herriot, 1971).

SPEECH AND LANGUAGE DIFFICULTIES

Children with speech and language difficulties, at least of a mild nature, will be found in nearly every class of five to eight year-olds. Teachers of children in this age-group are likely to encounter immature speech and instances of stammering, as well as children with delayed or impoverished language. To a lesser extent, they will come across what may be termed language deviance, indicating a serious communication problem (see p. 93). In all these cases, they will need to consider whether the child needs some special attention, perhaps through calling for help from speech therapists or other support services. 'Speech' problems cannot easily be distinguished from 'language' problems (Crystal, 1980) but for the sake of convenience difficulties in oral expression (faulty articulation and stammering) will be dealt with here separately from difficulties relating mainly to the understanding of language.

Speech Problems

By the age of about seven, most developmental mispronunciations will have disappeared spontaneously (Butler et al., 1973), but there will still be some children who have difficulties in articulating all the sounds. Faulty articulation may be related to auditory impairment or defects of tongue, lips or teeth; cerebral palsy; intellectual retardation; or faulty models of speech at home. The overall prevalence of speech difficulties in the years five to eight is hard to estimate accurately, since different criteria of what constitutes a difficulty are adopted, and doctors, teachers and parents do not always perceive or report speech difficulties in the same terms. Morley (1972) found about four per cent of six and a half year-olds to have articulatory difficulties, while the National Child Development Study (Pringle et al., 1966) reported that a marked degree of unintelligibility in speech was ascertained at a medical examination in 76 out of 4,053 boys (1.8 per cent) and 38 out of 3,917 girls (1 per cent). Overall, in 16.2 per cent of the boys and 11.4 per cent of the girls, speech was not fully intelligible on testing. Fundudis et al. (1980) found that 133 (4 per cent) of 3,300 children in Newcastle were retarded in speech as defined by the criterion of 'failure to use three or more words strung together to make some sort of sense by the age of 36 months'. They followed up 102 of the speech retarded children at the age of seven. Excluding children with marked intellectual handicap, cerebral palsy and specific syndromes such as autism, there were 84 children who could be considered developmentally retarded in speech at that age, suggesting a population incidence of two to three per cent.

It would seem that speech retarded children are a very vulnerable group. Sheridan and Peckham (1973) found seven-year-old children with speech considered by both teachers and school doctors independently as 'unintelligible' to be particularly disadvantaged in that they tended to be poor at both reading and number, as well as showing greater emotional instability than other children. Fundudis et al. (1980) also reported that children with delayed speech at seven were significantly poorer than controls on a range of cognitive and language tests. A detailed follow-up at eleven and sixteen of the children studied by Sheridan and Peckham (1973) mentioned above showed that, with very few exceptions, they did badly at school and in society, suggesting that markedly defective speech at seven indicates the likelihood of continued backwardness in verbal communication, social maturity and scholastic attainment

(Fogelman, 1983). It is likely that children with severe speech problems will be identified at an early stage and receive appropriate attention. However, in view of the poor outlook for these children, schools, in co-operation with the support services and especially speech therapists, should ensure that they are given every possible help and support.

Children who stammer need particularly sensitive handling in the classroom. Stammering or stuttering, which affects about one per cent of primary schoolchildren (mostly boys), has not been satisfactorily explained. Of the variety of theories put forward, some emphasize factors relating to the brain and nervous system; others stress psychological experiences, for example over-pressure of some kind at home or at school. It is difficult to know to what extent teachers should call on children who stammer to express themselves publicly; it might be just as damaging to their self-esteem to ignore them altogether as to expose their difficulties to the other children. Male and Thompson (1985) consider that it is not advisable to ask children with speech disorders to read aloud in front of others in the early stages of reading until they have gained more confidence, though they might be encouraged to read in unison with others rather than be passed over. If teachers are asking questions around the class, it is suggested that they should not delay asking a child with a speech difficulty for too long to avoid tension mounting. Of course, some children want to read aloud or speak in public in spite of their speech problems and these children should be gently encouraged.

Language Delay and Difficulties

Teachers of five to eight year-olds in ordinary schools will only very rarely encounter children with severe language problems (which may be termed language deviance) related to pathological factors, such as *aphasia*, due to brain injury occurring after the acquisition of language, or *autism*, a severe condition evidenced by an unwillingness to use speech, a lack of interest in social contact and an exceptional resistance to change. These children need very specialized help, perhaps in a unit for pupils with communication difficulties. However, with the tendency to integrate children with special educational needs into the ordinary school, teachers will increasingly have to deal with pupils showing language delay associated with a moderate degree of intellectual retardation, as well as children with hearing loss. They will need to work closely with speech therapists and educational psychologists, as well as medical personnel and specialists in auditory impairment in some cases, in planning suitable language experiences for these pupils.

Many teachers, especially those working in schools admitting children from a social priority areas, will face problems associated with language improverishment resulting from inadequate verbal experience and stimulation at home in the early years. As previously mentioned, such language impoverishment can be found in children of average or high ability, who may well fail to realize their potential unless action is taken to fill the gaps in their language attainments.

Specific Help for Language Delay and Impoverishment

As Gulliford (1971) points out, teachers of children in 'the early school years emphasize that the wide range of activity and the social interaction in the classroom provide excellent opportunities for promoting language growth'. Indeed, all children at this stage will benefit from their daily experiences in class, talking about their play and other activities, listening to and discussing stories and interacting informally with other children. However, it can be argued that children with language delay or impoverishment may need more specific, planned and structured help with language.

A wide range of language schemes are now available to help children with language delay or other difficulties. Teachers of young children in Britain tend not to be happy with very structured language programmes (Quigley, 1971), but the schemes available are varied in their philosophy, content and methodology. Some are in keeping with the more traditional practices of the first school, emphasizing flexibility of approach, self-expression and incidental language enrichment in an appropriate environment; some models aim at promoting language development through the direct teaching of specific skills; some focus on instructional dialogue, with the aim of extending, expanding and elaborating the child's language through interaction with adults; while yet others adopt an eclectic approach, selecting ideas from different approaches. Examples of each type of language scheme are given in the Further Reading section at the end of this book. Not all of the works listed have been specifically written with children aged five to eight in mind, but all provide practical guidelines and useful strategies for stimulating language in the classroom.

In the past, particular attention has been given to speech and language in the first five years of life and it is true that language development is very rapid during these years, which can be regarded as an especially sensitive if not critical period for language growth. However, this chapter has shown that much can be done in the early school years to promote oral communication skills and teachers have a considerable part to play in this, not least in the case of those children who enter school with relatively poor language attainments. Teachers need to consider whether their classroom organization and teaching style are conducive to the promotion of language development. In all cases, they need to collaborate closely with parents, who have such a crucial role in the language growth of their children; and, where there is evidence of speech and language difficulties, collaboration with the support services, especially speech therapists and educational psychologists, will be beneficial. Teachers will find it stimulating, rewarding and enjoyable to plan and carry out strategies for encouraging competence in communication in their pupils.

6

Some Aspects of Cognitive Growth: Piaget and Others

Any consideration of cognitive (or intellectual) development in children aged five to eight years must take account of the work of Jean Piaget. His writings over a long life (1896–1980) have largely focused on this aspect of development, although his views have applicability to other aspects (for example, moral or social development). The classroom applications of his work were never uppermost in his mind; he saw himself as concerned mainly with how children come to understand the world about them so that they can function within it. His explanations of their development in this area have, however, clear implications for the type of educational experiences which might encourage such understanding and hence can be taken to offer guidance on the type of educational programme appropriate, especially in the early years. In America attempts have been made to provide a school programme which is completely based on Piagetian views (Kamii, 1971; Furth and Wachs, 1974) and in Britain many of the currently held beliefs as to how young children can be encouraged to acquire mathematical and scientific understanding is so based. Indeed, his contribution to the study of child development as a whole is so substantial that it is difficult even to put it into perspective.

This chapter will attempt to examine the major tenets of his theory concurrently with the views of other writers who have also considered cognitive growth in young children. It is not possible to examine his work in the detail it really deserves, and for those not familiar with his views, further reading is necessary (see, for example, Piaget and Inhelder, 1969; Richmond, 1970; Phillips, 1981). It is hoped, however, that the following discussion will clarify the main points of his theory and examine how they might influence teaching and learning in the early years. It will also compare Piaget's views on cognitive growth with those of some other writers interested in this aspect.

WHAT DOES PIAGET SAY ABOUT EARLY COGNITIVE DEVELOPMENT?

First, Piaget sees young children's understanding of any situation as qualitatively different from that of mature adults. It is not just that children's experience is more limited than that of adults and this limitation narrows the extent of their understanding. Piaget maintains, rather, that children's views of what is going on around them lack the basic rules for organizing experience which adults take for granted. To put it another way, children's thinking is highly subjective (Piaget calls it 'egocentric') as they cannot as yet achieve objectivity. Children are so involved with the trees that they are not able to step back mentally to look instead at the wood.

It is not really surprising that this should be so. Children are not born with understanding ready made; they have to construct that understanding from their experiences. They have to learn not just to say 'dog' when they see the same dog several times but also to accept that a totally different looking animal is also a 'dog'. Furthermore, they have to become able to sort out for themselves what it is that makes an animal a 'dog' and not a lamb or a wolf, so they can identify new examples of the class when they meet them. They have to come to see common qualities in their experiences and to adjust their understanding to take into consideration the new information which these experiences are constantly providing.

This new information compels them to alter and extend their existing concepts so that 'dog', for example, comes to include the notion of a poodle, an alsatian, a labrador and so on, as all having something in common which they do not share with other animals. Their concept of 'dog', moreover, enables them not merely to identify further members of the category but also to be able to react to them appropriately. They come to expect them to bark, to wag their tails if patted and so on. When children become able to anticipate what is going to happen around them, they also become able to that extent to control their environment. Objectivity then becomes possible, as they are not thrown off balance by a new experience but can see what it has in common with other similar past experiences as well as how it differs from them. They also come to realize that a dog seen from any angle and whether lying down, running or hiding, is still a dog.

Children, then, according to Piaget are actively engaged in constructing their understanding of their environment. It is from their actions and the results of their actions that they make as much sense of that environment as they can. Their interaction with the environment increases as they grow older and so do their opportunities for understanding it. As more information comes their way they absorb it and regulate their subsequent actions accordingly. Clearly, if children have to go through this process to build up simple concepts of objects, animals and so on, abstract concepts such as 'courage' or 'truth' are going to take longer to acquire. Numerical concepts may also present difficulties. Children have to learn to recognize '3' of anything, just as they had to learn to recognize what is a dog and what is not, but they have also to come to realize the relationship of '3' to other numbers and that it itself is composed of other numbers (for example, 1 + 2). Simply to be able to recite a sequence of numbers, say from 1 to 5 or 10, is not fully to understand any one of them. Piaget sees children's own actions as promoting this understanding. This is why his theory has been taken to advocate discovery and activity methods as being most likely to encourage young children's learning.

Second, Piaget asserts, if this is how young children's understanding develops, then the experiences they encounter are of crucial importance. Certainly, in the very early years, practically anything in the environment can attract children to investigate further and learn from their investigations. But if they are faced, at school for instance, with experiences beyond their current understanding, they cannot really extract from them the information which they require. At any stage in life it is confusing and frustrating to be faced with material which is far beyond one's level of understanding and the material is consequently dismissed as incomprehensible. At the same time, if the experience has nothing new in it the material may also be dismissed, this time as boring because it is already known. It would seem that the most satisfying experiences and those most productive of learning are those which are just at the edge of the learner's understanding. They contain just enough of what is new and puzzling to make the learner want to understand them but are not so new and puzzling as to make the effort to understand too demanding. Hunt (1961) refers to this as the 'matching' of the experiences provided with the learner's level of understanding.

But how can such experiences be provided in the classroom where there may be thirty or more children all with different levels of understanding? One way would be to offer such a variety of possible experiences that whatever level of understanding any child might have reached there would be something which would be appropriate for each. Presumably, too, the learner is the best judge of what could be considered appropriate. Here can be seen the justification for the child-centred approach which encourages children's self-chosen activities, as discussed in chapter 1. But it would also be extremely helpful if teachers could be given some guidance as to the general learning situations and approaches suitable for children at any particular stage in their school career. It would then be possible for them to select learning experiences particularly devised to promote cognitive development.

A third aspect of Piaget's theory concerns his descriptions of stages in intellectual development through which he believes all children pass. These stages cover the period from birth to adolescence but for the moment particular attention will be paid to five to eight year-olds. Does Piaget's account of cognitive growth in the stages relevant to this group help teachers to provide appropriate environmental stimulation? The answer to this question is in the affirmative but must be qualified for reasons which will become apparent when his account is looked at in a little more detail.

PIAGET'S DEVELOPMENTAL STAGES

The years from five to eight span the stages which Piaget calls *pre-operational* thinking and *concrete operational* thinking. By 'operational' thinking Piaget means thinking determined by the basic 'rules' which govern how the environment is organized. These rules have been gradually identified by the child from his or her experiences and enable him or her to acquire the objectivity required to cope effectively with these experiences as has already been discussed. An example might help to clarify this point.

In all his writings Piaget makes frequent reference to actual experimental situations in which children are asked to come to a decision about the nature of a display and then to explain why they have reached that decision. It is perfectly possible for teachers to replicate these situations for themselves (see Brearley and Hitchfield, 1966; Fogelman, 1970; Hughes, 1979), although finding sufficient time to do so requires ingenuity. One of the experimental situations most commonly discussed is that concerned with children's ability to maintain that a certain quantity of liquid remains the same when it is poured into a collection of differently shaped containers. Children are presented individually with two similar glasses, containing orange squash for instance, and agreement is reached that the content of both glasses is the same. The squash in one of the glasses is then poured into a tall, thin glass and the child is asked if one or other of the containers now holds more squash or whether the amount of squash is the same in both. Whatever decision the child reaches, he or she is asked to explain why he thinks this is so.

Children in the pre-operational stage in their cognitive development seem to centre on only one aspect of the problem, the rising level in the tall, thin glass which finishes up well above the level of the squash in the glass which has not been poured. They claim that there must now be more in the thin container because the level reached is higher. They fail, therefore, to take into account the different shape of the glass which is much narrower than the original. If the squash is returned to the original container, they will again agree that there is now the same amount but they do not maintain the idea of 'sameness' if the liquid is then poured either into a wide, shallow dish or into a number of smaller containers. It seems that their decisions are taken on the basis of the appearance of the squash in the new containers without bearing in mind the shape of the containers.

When children begin to wonder if they are perhaps making the wrong decision and, indeed, to realize that the level which the squash reaches may be misleading them, they begin to move into operational thinking and they change their previous decisions, asserting now the 'sameness' of the liquid whatever the container. As yet, their ability to stand back from the immediate focus of the rising liquid and to affirm that as no squash as been added or removed no real change can have occurred, depends on an actual display being presented to them. They would still have difficulty in working all this out in their heads in an abstract way with no glasses and squash to manipulate. Hence Piaget uses the term 'concrete' to describe the stage of understanding now reached. The rule which the children in the concrete operational stage have come to recognize is that unless more is added or some taken away, the quantity will remain the same. A further rule would be the realization that the quantity must be the same because if the activity were reversed and the squash returned to the original container, it would reach the level it had before and would be identical to that in the untouched glass. Clearly these are rules which have wide and useful application.

To say, therefore, that for Piaget the years from five to eight span the stages of pre-operational and concrete operational thought is both helpful and unhelpful for the teacher. It is helpful to know that, if Piaget is correctly interpreting children's performance on his experiments, children at five years may not be able to appreciate what are the vital aspects of a new situation and how they are related to one another, so that they concentrate on only one aspect (and that aspect not necessarily the most important), neglecting to consider how this aspect may be affected by others. Similarly, in their play they may concentrate only on what they are doing at that moment and not see how, by relating to what another is doing, their play could be more interesting or exciting. It is also helpful that Piaget gives an indication of the age at which their pre-operational thought is abandoned in favour of concrete operational thinking which bears a much greater resemblance to adult thought than did the previous stage. Cohen (1983) notes:

> Awareness of the inadequacy of his views and accumulated experience will slowly change the child. The dramatic changes begin to occur after the age of six. By the age of 8, the puzzles that made younger children make confusing mistakes have become simple. (p. 43)

Piaget's description is unhelpful, inasmuch as the ages tentatively associated with his stages in children's thinking are clearly averages which represent a considerable range. Some children aged seven years may be capable of using concrete operational thinking, while others of the same age may be a long way from achieving this, still in the pre-operational stage. It is not easy for teachers to distinguish between them without considerable observation and interaction. In addition, replication of Piagetian experiments has shown the same child to be at one and the same time at different levels of understanding on different tasks. There does not appear to be an 'across-the-board' move forward in thinking. Rather, less advanced thinking in some situations persists concurrently with more advanced thinking in others. Piaget and his co-workers agreed that this was so, explaining the lack of consistency in children's thinking by lack of sufficient experience or failure to extract fully from the experience all the information they might have gleaned (Inhelder et al., 1974). Whatever the explanation, retardation in some aspects of thinking co-existent with advances in others makes the teacher's attempts to 'match' the provision of experiences to children's cognitive level with any degree of precision very difficult indeed. It also calls into question one of the fundamental principles of Piaget's theory, namely the whole concept of stages in children's thinking. Before considering this point further, however, it might be useful to look at the extent to which Piaget's theory can be taken as a basis for teaching and learning.

THE PIAGET-BASED CLASSROOM

From what has been said so far, it is clear that any educational programme derived from Piagetian theory would place considerable emphasis on children's active learning. This would be especially so for children at the pre-operational stage, where their exploration and experimentation are the means of their beginning to come to terms with the environment. It is also clear that, as the next stage in cognitive development according to Piaget will be that of concrete operational thought, children will continue to need practical experience in order to progress in their acquisition of the basic 'rules' which have already been mentioned as being established at this stage. It could, therefore, be expected that a Piaget-based classroom would be especially concerned to offer a programme of activities which would encourage children to identify and develop from many examples the qualities which such examples have in common.

It is perhaps necessary to give a little more consideration to the nature of these rules in order to clarify what might be seen as programme objectives at these two stages of cognitive development.

It will be recalled that the effect of the emergence of these rules is to enable children to go beyond their own personal judgements of their experiences in order to achieve greater objectivity. The rules must, therefore, be universal, abstracted from children's understanding of many specific incidents. These experiences must be structured and elaborated by the children so that they become able to reason about them. It would seem important to help and encourage this process by providing access to experiences which would appear to be particularly conducive to the mental activity required, especially if children for whatever reason – a disadvantaged pre-school environment for instance – have not really begun to structure their experiences meaningfully. The main proponents of the Piaget-type programme for young children have been Kamii and her fellow workers and they developed their approach for young, disadvantaged children in Michigan (see, for example, Sonquist and Kamii, 1967; Kamii, 1971).

What kind of experiences would these be? Kamii (1974) argues that there is an important difference between 'discovery' and 'invention'. Children 'discover' some existing physical law, such as that a needle will sink if placed in water whereas a wooden block will float. But, she claims, they have to 'invent' the notion of specific gravity cognitively from their grasp and understanding of actual experiences of floating and sinking. They could be told about specific gravity, of course, but that would not establish the 'rule'. They have to establish that for themselves. Once established, it can be applied whenever necessary and children's thinking has obviously become more advanced in this particular area.

Children, therefore, are seen to need experiences which encourage them to *classify*, that is, group objects into different levels of categorization (e.g. apples are fruit; fruit is food); *to seriate*, that is, place objects in order from smallest to largest and to see the relationships between them; and to cope with *ideas of number*. The latter is not just the ability to count or to identify groups of the same number. In Piagetian terms, it also involves advancing from an ability to produce a one-to-one correspondence to a realization of the invariance of any quantity despite changes in the way that quantity is distributed (as in pouring the squash into a differently shaped glass). Children also need to acquire *spatial* (above, under etc.) and *temporal* (last, next etc.) *relationships*, and to *use symbols* rather than actual objects. In their dramatic play, for example, they may use a plastic block to stand for a cup so that they can have a tea party. Working with other children is also of importance as the realization that others have a different point of view helps to move children on from their own subjective, egocentric stance.

CAN COGNITIVE DEVELOPMENT BE ACCELERATED?

The next point to consider must surely be whether the provision of experiences which 'match' children's level of intellectual development and which give them the opportunity to construct basic logical 'rules' will speed up their progress through the various stages of thinking which Piaget described.

In all, Piaget outlined four stages, the first preceding the stage of pre-operational thought already discussed. This first stage was seen as a sensori-motor one (lasting until about eighteen months) during which babies begin to find out the possibilities in their surroundings by using all their senses to try to take in environmental information which might help them to understand what is going on and by developing control over their movements (such as learning to grasp, direct their hands, crawl) so as to acquire even more information. The second and third stages (pre-operational and concrete operational thought respectively) are followed by a formal operational stage when reasoning through the construction of hypotheses becomes possible. The young person (by now at the secondary stage) can mentally review possible solutions or actions, working out their consequences without necessarily having to resort to practical experimentation. Could an educational programme bring children more speedily into, say, the concrete operational or even the formal operational stage than might otherwise be the case?

It has to be said at this point that Piaget himself was very dubious both about whether this could be done and about the point of doing so. His colleagues, however, did show acceleration to be possible but only, they felt, when children were very close to moving into the next stage anyway (Inhelder et al., 1974). Where some acceleration has been achieved in other studies (see, for example, Gelman, 1969; Sheppard, 1974), the degree of success appears to depend on the level of understanding reached before the training programme is begun and the extent to which the programme encourages practical manipulation of the materials and discussion of the results (see also Anthony, 1977).

Clearly there can only be advantages in offering children, at whatever stage, an interesting programme which will challenge them without sapping their confidence and which will stress understanding not technique. Such a programme should also be suited to promoting an optimal rate of development through Piaget's stages for every child. Development, for Piaget, is much more than learning. While learning may be specific to the situation in which it occurs, development requires the integration of this learning with previous understanding (Voyat, 1974). To learn to respond appropriately to the questions in Piaget's experimental tasks does not necessarily mean that full understanding has been achieved. It is for this reason that Piaget himself viewed attempts at acceleration somewhat sceptically.

A CRITICAL LOOK AT PIAGET'S STAGE THEORY

The question of how helpful Piaget's stage theory is to the classroom teacher has already been raised, with reference to the slow and uneven development through the stages. Teachers will not find in the theory precise indications of where children should or could be in their cognitive growth. Rather they will find guidelines indicating how the quality of children's thinking can be estimated and how development in thinking can be promoted through their active participation in a range of experiences.

Central to Piaget's stage theory is that this cognitive development takes time. Recent work, however, has shown that Piaget may have over-estimated the time required. Without implementing any training programme and thereby avoiding the problem of deciding exactly what changes (if any) have taken place as a result, researchers have found that children can show understanding of some of the basic 'rules' considerably earlier than Piaget maintained they could. Bower (1974, 1977) working with young babies; Povey and Hill (1975) with two year-olds; Bryant (1974) with three to five year-olds; and Donaldson and her co-workers (1978) have all produced evidence of children displaying operational thinking while still apparently, according to Piaget, being in the pre-operational stage. All of them devised ingenious puzzles for the various groups of children, designed to tap the same areas of understanding as Piaget examined. Instead of merely replicating his experiments, however, they adapted them to make them more meaningful to the children and asked them similar questions, again trying to make the language used as natural as possible.

Thus, Donaldson (1978) reports an increase in the number of children understanding quantity when the experimental conditions were slightly changed. Instead of an adult moving an arrangement of counters so that one row occupied less space than the other, it having been clear to start with that there were the same number of counters in each row, the change was brought about by 'naughty Teddy' who came out of his box and disturbed things. The children were asked whether the upheaval he had caused had changed the number of counters in any way or if it was still the same. Some children thought the number had been reduced because the counters had been pushed closely together but more now affirmed that the number was still the same than had done when an adult brought about the change. Presumably the children viewed a change brought about by an adult as highly significant and, therefore, assumed that some alteration in quantity must have been made by such a change, whereas a displacement caused by Teddy's misbehaviour did not carry such an implication.

All the researchers mentioned above would agree that there is sufficient discrepancy between their findings and Piaget's to indicate at least some doubt with regard to his interpretations. Their findings suggest that the children's responses which Piaget believed to reveal lack of understanding may, rather, have revealed only confusion about the nature of the exercise or the questions they were being asked. Children found the Piagetian-type questions strange and often answered what they thought they were being asked rather than what they were actually asked. If this barrier was overcome many more children showed that they did understand that the number of objects had not changed just because they had been re-arranged. Similarly, they may have felt that the rising level of squash in the thin container must be affecting the situation because adults were producing this change in the appearance of the liquid and asking them about it.

The uneven nature of cognitive development, which Piaget himself recognized, and the findings of these other researchers combine to call the whole idea of Piaget's stages into question. The reality of the situation, as Flavell (1962) has pointed out, does not seem to be so tidy and pre-determined as Piaget's theory would suggest. In the present state of our knowledge, teachers might be well advised to avoid making assumptions about the ages at which reasoning and cognitive rules are accessible to children and to listen instead to what children are actually saying or watch what they are doing in order to estimate the quality of their understanding.

LANGUAGE AND THINKING

While Piaget does not underestimate the part played by language in thinking, he does not give it a position of pre-eminence, certainly not in the early years. Actions come first. It may be that as children acquire linguistic fluency they make greater use of language to increase or codify their understanding. But, as far as young children are concerned, for Piaget it is from the manipulation of objects in the environment that they begin to structure their understanding and abstract the all-important logical rules.

This viewpoint, however, overlooks the social context in which so much of early learning takes place. The work of Wells (1981) and Tizard and Hughes (1984) has shown, from analyses of what young children actually say, that their interactions with adults not only extend their experiences but also provide opportunities for clarifying their thinking, reviewing their activities and using reasoning which is not always tied to the situation then present. In their view, language is neither egocentric nor dependent on understanding; rather, it enables communication with others to take place and promotes cognitive growth.

Vygotsky (1962) and other Russian writers also stress the

importance of communication both in the transmitting of information by adults which could enhance children's understanding
and in the ordering by the children themselves of their experiences.
There is every reason to believe that the speech system – which is
formed in the process of the child's social intercourse with the adult
– is a powerful means of systematic organization of our mental
processes (Luria, 1961, p. 144). Clearly, this alternative view leaves
much more room than that of Piaget for the influence of teachers on
children's intellectual development. Discussion can lead children to
further insights; it does not just merely comment on insights
already gained.

The many functions of language and the importance of linguistic
development for educational progress are discussed above in
chapter 5. It would be appropriate here, however, to indicate the
classroom implications of theories of cognitive growth which
emphasize the role of the teacher in directing this growth, using
language, of course, as the main tool. Such an approach would be
rather different from classroom approaches based on Piaget's views
discussed earlier.

COGNITIVELY ORIENTED CLASSROOMS

In teaching approaches which are termed 'cognitively oriented', the
emphasis is placed on the direct teaching of the skills children are
expected to acquire. This is not to advocate 'drilling' of new
techniques, although some approaches have certain overtones of
children making unison responses and copying the linguistic model
offered by the teacher (Bereiter and Engelmann, 1966).

For example, Ausubel (1963), a strong advocate of the place of
verbal learning in children's cognitive growth, is certainly not
urging rote memorization of parrot-like responses. Ausubel sees a
total reliance on children's own discoveries as being an approach
which in fact limits understanding, inasmuch as it confines it to
what children can organize for themselves in concrete situations
(Francis, 1977). He maintains that teachers can extend children's
understanding and, indeed, have an obligation to do so as far as
many aspects of knowledge are concerned. 'In contrast to those
who advocate discovery methods of teaching, "open education"
and experience-based learning, Ausubel stands unashamedly for the
mastery of academic material' (Joyce and Weil, 1980, p. 76). In
order that children may achieve this mastery, teachers should plan
very carefully how the new material is to be introduced, organize its

actual presentation so that anything novel is made meaningful to the learners and provide plenty of opportunities to practise and establish this new learning. Ausubel specifically states that there is no need for 'learners to rediscover every principle in the syllabus' (1963, p. 154) in order to be able to solve problems or tackle new tasks.

All this is a long way from an insistence on 'learning by doing'. Ausubel instead stresses the importance of meaningfulness and what he calls 'belongingness' (that is, relating new material to existing knowledge or to children's usual way of understanding their environment). Children have to reflect on what is being presented to them and to make it their own; teachers have to provide the 'intellectual scaffolding' which makes it possible for them to do so.

Bloom (1976) and Gagné (1974, 1977) were also concerned about developing cognitive competence in the classroom although, again, children's own discoveries and self-chosen activities do not figure prominently. For Bloom, cognitive progress (as progress in other aspects of development) results from an interaction between the learner and the available learning environment, a view which would not be unacceptable to Piaget and his followers. However, what concerns Bloom is that the environment should be such as to promote 'mastery' in the learner. For him 'mastery' arises from careful sequencing of the various steps in the skill to be learned or of the information to be acquired. This would be, of course, the responsibility of the teacher.

That the effect of environmental experiences is a powerful one is emphasized throughout Bloom's work. The effect is also long-lasting, as it persists through all subsequent learning. 'Developments at one period are in part determined by the earlier developments and in turn influence and determine the nature of later developments' (Bloom, 1964, p. 215). Bloom advocates that the aim of the school – a new and powerful environment for young children – should be to promote 'equality of learning' by ensuring that all children, if at all possible, acquire the competencies required for adequate functioning in society. While Piaget is concerned with how children construct their understanding of their world, Bloom focuses on what they are able to do in that world. He urges teachers to make the environment as efficient a transmitter of information as they can, while bearing in mind the quality and quantity of the children's experiences outside of school, especially prior to school entry.

Gagné, too, is concerned with the promotion by the school of competence in its pupils. The latter bring to the learning situation the abilities and learning potential they possess and the level of acquisition of skills they have so far achieved. These comprise the conditions for learning within the pupils which meet with the conditions within the new learning which the teacher has control over. In order to promote learning, therefore, the teacher has to be sure that the learners have the necessary 'pre-skills' or 'pre-knowledge' on which to build. If they do not, they must acquire what is necessary before the new learning can be tackled.

Gagné (1977) shows how the learning process can be analysed to promote competence in whatever aspect of learning is being tackled, indicating at the same time the learner's part in any successful learning episode (1974). Clearly this is not a simple account of how learning takes place. In fact, to look at Gagné's work in any detail (see Bigge, 1982) makes the reader realize how naive it is to talk about 'learning' and 'the environment' as if these terms were self-explanatory.

The writers mentioned present cognitively oriented theories, inasmuch as they advocate the efficient transmission of skills and knowledge to children. They believe that only if this efficiency can be achieved will learners from very diverse backgrounds and with different abilities and aptitudes make the cognitive advances for which their proposals aim. Although they see the ability to generalize any skills taught to other appropriate situations as an essential part of the learning process, they do not postulate a gradual development of basic logical 'rules' before such generalizations can take place. Smedslund (1977) would support them in this as he can see no justification for assuming that young children lack logic. Limited experience may lead children to strange or incorrect conclusions but these errors in reasoning do not reflect an absence of reasoning. Furthermore, the views of the cognitive theorists discussed here highlight the crucial importance of the teacher's organization of the learner's environment and of the value to that learner of discussion, direction and clarification through language.

IS COMPROMISE POSSIBLE?

It surely cannot be right to dispense with either action or language as a means of developing children's understanding of their experiences. Equally, self-chosen activities are not necessarily to be seen as excluding teacher-directed activities or vice versa. Piaget certainly did not underestimate the value of language for understanding and his co-workers point out that action is not necessarily productive of that understanding: 'being cognitively active does not mean that the child merely manipulates a given type of material; he can be mentally active without physical manipulation, just as he can be mentally passive while actually manipulating objects' (Inhelder et al., 1974 p. 25). Francis (1977, p. 67) makes a similar point when she notes that 'discovery learning has sometimes been emphasized without due regard to the necessity of harnessing it to other learning or to agreed ends'.

Teachers of young children may well wish to continue with discovery methods and to stress the necessity for children to choose activities for themselves if they are fully to acquire understanding from them. They may find keeping Piagetian stages in mind helpful in selecting appropriate experiences for their pupils. What this chapter has tried to show is that there are a number of different viewpoints on how young children's cognitive development can be encouraged. Teachers have to decide on the amount of stress to place on linguistic interaction in this development, on how learning should be organized and on the extent to which they feel they can (or should) directly influence cognitive growth. What they cannot do is to ignore what these various writers have said about how children come to understand.

In this respect it might be of interest to look again at the practical advice which is being offered to teachers of children in the five- to eight-year age-range with regard to mathematics teaching. What becomes apparent is how the suggested aims encompass an understanding and appreciation of mathematical processes and logical relationships, an awareness of the relevance of mathematics to the world outside of school and a stress on the ability to talk about mathematical experiences. All of these are seen to blend into producing confidence and, presumably, competence in children in this aspect of their learning (see, for example, DES, 1979).

Similarly, in the Cockcroft Report (DES, 1982), both the importance of mathematics as a means of providing 'powerful, concise and unambiguous' communication and developing 'powers of logical thinking, accuracy and spatial awareness' are mentioned at the very beginning as being among the aims of mathematics teaching, but the weight of emphasis is placed rather more on the former than the latter as it comes first in the list of desired objectives at the primary stage:

The primary mathematics curriculum should enrich children's aesthetic and linguistic experience, provide them with the means of exploring their environment and develop their powers of logical thought, in addition to equipping them with the numerical skills which will be a powerful tool for later work and study. (DES, 1982, para. 287)

The influence of Piagetian theory can clearly be seen in this statement while the other theorists discussed in this chapter have a great deal to contribute to how skills can be efficiently and effectively acquired.

As yet we do not have much information about the effect of experiencing one type of approach in the classroom as compared with another. What information there is often tends to look at the results of specific training on Piagetian tests, as has already been mentioned (see Brainerd, 1978; Vuyk, 1981). However, in the field of compensatory education, work has been undertaken to assess the later effects of different types of programmes originally offered to pre-school children living in disadvantaged areas in the United States. For example, Weikart et al. (1978) compared their own approach, which has always drawn considerably on Piagetian theory, with a highly structured language programme, cognitively oriented and teacher-directed, and with a typical nursery pro- gramme not really based on any one particular theory. Their conclusions were that 'all were effective and none was more so than another' (p. 136). Some follow-up studies (Becker, 1978; Rhine, 1981) have found the highly structured, teacher-directed approach and one using behaviour analysis in the classroom most effective, although recent evidence does not entirely favour a highly structured approach (see Hagedorn, 1986). Other long-term follow-up results would seem to support the benefit to dis- advantaged children of any early programme which has been well thought out, efficiently taught, is of adequate duration and has the committed support of the children's parents (Lazar and Darlington, 1979).

It has to be remembered, of course, that these findings arise from work originally done with pre-school children and the programmes may have been particularly intended to extend language or build up positive attitudes both towards school and towards the child himself or herself as a learner. The results are difficult to interpret as criteria for success with regard to aspects of cognitive growth or school 'competence' are not easily specified, any more than are the reasons for any effects found (Woodhead, 1985). Firm support for any one approach rather than another cannot, therefore, be given.

CURRENT VIEWS ON COGNITIVE DEVELOPMENT

Piaget died in 1980. His contribution to our understanding of how children 'come to know' is considerable and will continue to make a lasting impact, especially as far as the education of children up to the age of eight years is concerned. Other workers will inevitably question his methods, his findings and his vision. Are there any emerging trends which can be identified as likely to be of importance in the future?

The ever-increasing emphasis being placed on the role of language in promoting understanding has already been noted and, indeed, is currently to be found in educational programmes recommended for young children. Language is not seen, however, as being solely responsible for cognitive development and this reflects the current view that it is important to keep the 'whole' child in mind and not look at any one aspect of development in isolation from others or from the total situation in which the child lives and learns (Tomlinson, 1981). Attention is being focused more and more on the 'interactive framework within which development occurs' (Geber, 1977). Thus Woodhead, in his discussion of the long-term effects of pre-school education comments that

> in order to explain the effectiveness of pre-school education we may need to look not only at the characteristics of the programme and the population to whom it was applied, but also at the social context of family and school processes both during the period of intervention and during the later stages of education. (1985, p. 141)

This current ethological view (Charlesworth, 1983) is also to be found in medicine and in conservation policies.

Turner (1984) discusses several new developments with regard to cognitive growth among which is the work of several writers who believe that such growth involves the building up of skills (for example, Fischer, 1980), an argument put forward earlier by Bruner (1973). Fischer's proposal is more complex than Bruner's as he sees a number of tiers, each containing skills at increasing levels of competence, all contributing to an hierarchical model of skill acquisition. Both, however, explain cognitive competence in terms of the extent to which skills can be acquired and then, in turn, become incorporated into yet more advanced skills.

In the early stages of acquiring any skill considerable mental application may be required. As the skill begins to become established concentration on it is somewhat lessened and spare mental capacity thereby becomes available to elaborate the skill or develop it in some way. Case (1974, 1975) has linked children's increase in understanding over the years to growth in their capacity to process information, a suggestion which would not be at variance with Fischer's work. Case would argue that young children's understanding is limited because they can only take in a certain amount of the information available to them. Therefore, any educational experiences offered to young children should not overload their ability to see clearly what these are all about or their capacity for remembering the essentials. The number of items of information presented at any one time must be kept low (Halford (1980) would suggest that children aged five to eleven years can process only up to four 'chunks' of information at any one time); plenty of opportunity for practice and review must be offered; and children's attention should be directed through discussion to the essential learning aspects in any situation.

Mention can also be made of metacognition, which Nisbet and Shucksmith (1984) define as 'the awareness of one's mental processes, the capacity to reflect on how one learns' (p. 1). They argue that insufficient attention has been paid to the actual processes of learning, since only by examining these mental processes, as best one can, can they be 'orchestrated' by the learner in such a way as to promote optimal learning. Learners are often unaware of the decisions they have taken when they tackle any learning task or those choices that they make in the course of learning. Yet these decisions affect the degree of efficiency with which they learn and how productive that learning will be. At what age children should be encouraged to consider how they are setting about learning and what help they can be offered so that they become more proficient in directing their own learning, are questions that still have to be fully investigated (Robinson, 1983). However, moves are afoot to identify appropriate teaching strategies and to consider the implications of metacognitive theories for the curriculum (for example, teaching literacy – see Olson and Torrance, 1983).

Piaget was fascinated by how children come to know and understand their world. Work in cognition now seems to be more concerned with how children, in the context of their own world, can be *helped* to learn about it. Only they can do the learning but the responsibility is with teachers to guide them towards anything that might help them. A variety of suggestions has been made as to how this might be done, including teaching approaches derived from Piagetian theory and those based on direct instruction and careful pre-planning by the adults concerned. Interestingly, attention is again being given to encouraging active participation by pupils in specifically cognitive tasks, such as those associated with Instrumental Enrichment (Feuerstein et al., 1980; Weller and Craft, 1983) or lateral thinking (de Bono, 1976). While the exercises devised by these writers are intended for use with pupils over the age of eight years, the ideas behind them have wider application.

Feuerstein (1981) acknowledges direct experience of the environment to be vital to learning in young children (indeed, it continues to be important throughout life) but he argues that it is not enough for the full development of cognition. He believes learners also need guidance from a 'mediating' adult, that is, an adult who will organize the experience and transform it to make it more meaningful than it might otherwise be and who will provide learners with the means of taking over this function for themselves. Through practising 'grouping, scheduling, linking and relating objects and events otherwise disparate' (p. 94), pupils develop a reflective attitude and a confidence in their ability to think which leads them to tackle new learning experiences with the expectation of success. The materials Feuerstein has developed (which he calls 'instruments') promote discussion and creativity as they challenge children to find out and defend their own solutions. Cognitive skills are thus taught directly, as in de Bono's approach.

This chapter has tried to offer an overview of the contribution of Jean Piaget to our understanding of children's understanding. Opinions still differ as to the extent of that contribution, with some of his proposals being challenged. Yet from his work has come much that has transformed the education of young children. It has generated a view of classroom practice in which, as Murray says,

> good schools are those which place a high instructional premium upon self-initiated and self-regulated 'discovery' learning activities in situations that demand social interaction, and a higher curricular premium on thinking and knowledge than on learning information and skills. (1980, p. 588)

His work and his approach may now appear rather dated but both have much to offer any teacher trying to provide optimal conditions for young children's cognitive growth. 'Piaget is important and irreplaceable because he asked important questions and tried to answer them' (Meadows, 1983, p. 22).

7

Promoting Emotional and Social Development

To a considerable extent child development is a continuous process, with no entirely separate or distinct stages. However, formal entry into the world of school, at about five years of age in Britain, is in a sense the beginning of a new phase of emotional and social growth. It is important for parents and teachers to recognize that children of this age have still far to go in their acquisition of emotional control and social competence, but also that they have already travelled quite a distance. Most five year-olds are able to tolerate and even enjoy the separation from home demanded by compulsory attendance at school. They are relatively self-sufficient and independent, while still showing some degree of dependability and consistency in behaviour both at home and at school. They have a certain capacity for maintaining friendships and show some sensitivity to social situations, even if they quarrel verbally more or less than before. Five year-olds have an elementary sense of shame and are more conscious than before of cultural and other differences between individuals. They can show anxiety and fears which are not always justified but typically they are developing self-assurance, confidence in others and social conformity.

   After a brief outline of different theoretical perspectives on emotional and social development, the first section of this chapter discusses the various tasks or challenges faced by children in the early school years. The part played by the school in relation to sex-role identification and cultural differences among their pupils is also considered. Behavioural difficulties at this stage do not necessarily mean that a child is disturbed but may often indicate that emotional and social development is not progressing smoothly and point to the need for the teacher to take some action. The second section of the chapter, therefore, covers teachers' perceptions of common behaviour difficulties in the classroom, understanding the causes of such difficulties and offers possible strategies for preventing and coping with them.

DIFFERING PERSPECTIVES

As already indicated in chapter 1, there is no single theoretical framework providing an agreed overall view of emotional and social development in the years from five to eight; rather, there are a variety of perspectives which in their different ways illuminate how children mature during this stage. Here the perspectives of psychoanalytical theory, social-learning approaches and inter-actional models will be discussed.

Psychoanalytical Theory

Psychoanalytical theory, based on the writings of Freud, tends to see the period between five and puberty as a latency period, when the sexual and aggressive impulses of the child are in a subdued state. As Wolff (1973) puts it: when children leave the nursery for school they experience a further transformation of their social life, diverting their energies from the intimate relationships within the family and investing them in peer relationships and learning. During latency, the erotic longings of early childhood, its jealousies and its fears, become hidden until the psychological and social changes of puberty bring them to life again. According to the Freudian view, the latency stage is less significant for the formation of personality than earlier or later periods.

Erikson (1950), however, while subscribing to Freudian teachings in a number of respects, takes a rather more realistic view and considers middle-childhood to be a most decisive stage socially – a period which involves doing things beside and with others and developing the first sense of the division of labour. Erikson attaches considerable importance to school life in children's emotional and social growth. In his view school represents a culture all by itself, with its own goals and limits, achievements and disappointments. Dangers lie ahead if the child has a sense of inadequacy and inferioirity at this stage: if children despair of their skills or their status among their contemporaries, they may be discouraged from identification with them.

Social-Learning Approaches

The work of the various learning theorists is clearly relevant to our understanding of emotional and social development, stressing as they do that the principles of learning can explain differences in children's behaviour and that this can be changed by controlling the environment, particularly by systematically rewarding behaviour regarded as desirable. Social-learning theorists such as Sears et al. (1957), Bijou and Baer (1961) and Bandura (1977) have been especially interested in the effects of child-rearing practices on aspects of development, for example dependency and aggression, emphasizing that much of a child's learning comes from observing others. The treatment of behaviour problems in children owes much to the work of the social-learning theorists and is discussed later in the chapter.

Interactional Models

Although much of Freud's work was concerned with the relationship between mother and child, until recently child development tended to be regarded as mainly a one-way process, with the child seen as more or less passively responding to the behaviour of others. Now increasing attention is being given to two-way interactive processes and to understanding how the child may be affecting the parent or teacher as well as how parent or teacher may be affecting the child. For example, a child's behavioural style may significantly influence the quality of the parent–child relationship and the consequent trend in the child's personal development (Fries and Woolf, 1953). In the school situation children's temperament and behaviour will as often determine the teachers' attitudes and behaviour towards them as the other way round. Teachers may behave very differently, for instance, if they are dealing with a quiet, introverted child rather than a noisy, outgoing pupil. Interactive processes are complex but, if learning and teaching are to be improved, it is essential to take account of all aspects of situations and relationships including the individual characteristics of both children and teachers involved (Cronbach, 1957; Tomlinson, 1981).

The perspectives described above all contribute to our understanding of how children develop emotionally and socially. Teachers of children in the early school years may well find an interactive model, which tries to take account of all the variables affecting any professional situation in which they find themselves, a most useful one. The understanding of interactional processes should lead them to a better insight into their own personalities and attitudes, as well as to a clearer recognition of the various developmental challenges that face their pupils during the period under discussion.

DEVELOPMENTAL CHALLENGES

It is useful for teachers to look at specific periods of childhood in terms of the developmental challenges or tasks which have to be faced by children during those periods. Havighurst (1972) defines developmental tasks as those which arise 'at or about a certain period in the life of the individual, successful achievement of which leads to well-being, positive adjustment and success with later tasks, while failure leads to unhappiness, disapproval by society, and difficulty with later tasks' (p. 2). During the first five years of life, children need in particular to acquire a sense of basic trust and security, derived chiefly from the mother's feelings and attitudes towards them, as well as a growing sense of independence combined with some control of self-assertiveness. They have to solve their internal conflicts in relation to their parents, and to begin to transfer some of their interests and emotional involvement to children of similar age (Erikson, 1950).

What seem to be the major developmental tasks for children aged five to eight years on the road to greater social and emotional maturity? It is not easy to answer this question in terms of this relatively short period, but the following somewhat overlapping tasks may be said to be faced by all children in the early school years:

1 learning how to behave appropriately in school;
2 learning to relate to, and interact with, peers; and
3 beginning to develop a positive self-concept as an individual and a learner.

In considering these developmental tasks we need to bear in mind that learning appropriate emotional and social behaviour involves the mastery of a number of skills, which take time to acquire. It is worthwhile considering whether we do not sometimes take these skills for granted, instead of actively helping children to master them over time.

Learning How To Behave Appropriately in School

During the early school years children have to learn how to respond appropriately in a variety of situations in school. They face the transition from home to school or from nursery group to infant school and perhaps also a change to a new school setting at the age of seven (see chapter 10). In their contacts with adults they need to be able to cope with the realities of relationships between pupils and teachers. These are different in several respects from relationships with adults in the family, being more formal and usually demanding immediate and unquestioning compliance; at the same time, children are expected not to be overawed or excessively inhibited in the presence of adults in school. In their relations with others of their own age (discussed more fully later in the chapter), children are required to learn to share what they do not want to share, to respond to teasing and even bullying without over-reacting and to behave differently in the classroom and playground.

In learning how to behave appropriately in school, young children are helped by having one familiar teacher most of the time for at least a year, though they still have to adapt to the teaching and management styles of the various teachers with whom they may come into contact. If they come from homes where there is little or no discipline, inconsistent handling or attitudes of antagonism to authority, they may have particular difficulty in adjusting to the standards of behaviour set by the school. Although the majority of children enjoy their school experiences, teachers should not underestimate the extent to which some children, whatever the nature of the home background, need help in adapting to the demands of school. In a longitudinal British study of eighty-five boys and seventy-nine girls at primary school, Moore (1966) found a surprisingly high incidence of negative attitudes to school both at six and at eight years of age, particularly among boys: a number of children experienced difficulties in connection with relationships with teachers, scholastic work, school meals and toilet accommodation. School conditions have doubtless improved in many ways since this study was carried out and, as Moore states, every child has to cope with difficulties which they need to face up to. However, teachers are likely to support Moore's plea that children's fastidiousness, personal modesty and sensitivity to the opinions of others about their appearance, behaviour and work should be respected.

Learning How To Relate to Peers

During the nursery stage (about three to five years), significant changes are seen in children's social relationships. As Bee (1975) states, not only does the amount of interaction with peers increase throughout this period but the kind of interaction changes toward more co-operative rather than parallel play (that is, when children play alongside others rather than with them). Children begin to develop reciprocal relationships and to show concern for others. The development of genuinely constructive and helpful relationships between children continues between five and eight, with an increasing tendency for the formation of relatively fixed 'pairs' and small groups or gangs of close friends which help the child to extend his social interests beyond the close confines of the family. Children learn new habits, vocabulary and ideas from their peers, with whom they may spend an increasing amount of time outside school hours; they begin to discover the many ways in which other children differ from themselves, and how to accommodate to these differences; and they become anxious to gain acceptance from other children (Strommen et al., 1977).

Group norms of behaviour begin to be important (Hartup, 1970). In the case of some children, particularly those from communities where children are exposed to street cultures from an early age, group pressures may soon lead to behaviour which is deviant from that approved by society (Trasler, 1962). Most children will feel some conflict between the values and standards of home, school and group, although only a minority will fail to resolve such conflict successfully. Children learn how to behave differently in different contexts to a surprising degree (see, also, pp. 125–6 for a discussion of attitudes to cultural differences among children).

Increasingly, pairs and groups become single-sex. Sociometric studies, which provide some indication of the degree to which children seek or avoid each other's company in class or in out-of-school situations (see Cohen and Mannion, 1981), have shown that the patterns of social relationships still tend to be rather unstable at the age of seven (Blyth, 1965). However, at about eight years of age, sociometric choices (based on questions such as 'who do you like to sit next to in class?') are largely confined to members of the same sex, at least when a public declaration of choice of partner for various activities is required. Peer acceptance and popularity seem to be associated with friendliness, sociability and extraversion. Popular children tend to be more accepting of others, brighter, and physically more robust and attractive than other children, though factors such as social class and ethnic-group membership also affect popularity (Bee, 1975; Strommen et al., 1977). Real friendship takes time to develop; only gradually over the early school years will friendship come to be based on similarities of interest and mutual attraction.

At the same time as friendly and constructive relationships with peers are developing, so are feelings of jealousy, rivalry and competition. Children between five and eight years old gradually learn to substitute verbal hostility for physical aggression and to control their feelings of antagonism towards others, to some extent at least, but this learning is not easily or rapidly accomplished. In Britain, as in the United States, schools tend to put more emphasis on the individual and on individual competition than on the group (Bronfenbrenner, 1970), so that teachers tend not to be over-concerned about the ways in which group patterns are developing in their classes. However, in recent years there has been increasing attention to the value of learning in groups (Stephens, 1974). Furthermore, teachers will find that sensitivity to the group structures in their classes will alert them to those children who are failing to make good peer relationships. Such children, who may be isolated or rejected, nearly always need help with their emotional development. Poor peer relationships have consistently been found to be related to measures of maladjustment during childhood (Evans, 1962; Hartup, 1970). In some cases, maladjustment leads to an inability to relate well to peers; in others, a failure to be accepted by other children brings feelings of inferiority and emotional upset. Whichever happens, a vicious circle soon results from which the child will find it difficult to escape. What teachers can do in these cases is obviously limited but they can try a variety of strategies to ameliorate the situation (see pp. 134–9).

Beginning To Develop a Positive Self-Concept as an Individual and Learner

It is crucial to children's development between five and eight years of age that they should begin to build a positive concept of themselves as individuals and learners. As mentioned earlier in the chapter, Erikson (1950) considered that the emotional development of children of this age may be impaired by a sense of inadequacy in coping with the tasks expected of them: if a child develops a sense of inferiority rather than industry he will lack confidence in himself and feel that he has a low status among his contemporaries.

Many factors affect the development of a child's self-concept, including cognitive and linguistic abilities, physical growth and membership of majority or minority groups. Thomas (1973) stresses that the parent–child relationship is a very important determinant of self-concept, supporting the view of Coopersmith

(1967) that self-esteem is affected by parental attitudes and behaviour as well as by the parents' own self-concepts. School experiences, however, also greatly influence the development of adequate self-concepts in children. Burns (1979, 1982) states that by the time children enter school they already have a predisposition towards achievement or failure which is related to parental interest, affection and acceptance, although their self-concepts are still susceptible to modification. Teachers and peer groups become a major source of information about the self and pupils face daily reminders of their strengths and weaknesses, potentials and limitations. It is hardly surprising that differences in self-esteem are associated with differences in scholastic attainment from an early age (McMichael, 1977), though it cannot be assumed that this association is a simple, causal one.

Teachers need to consider whether their attitudes and practices are conducive to fostering positive self-concepts in their pupils. Burns acknowledges that teachers can do much in this direction but emphasizes that each pupil should be enabled to achieve a real measure of success rather than be falsely praised for an inadequate performance. Teachers can help pupils to achieve genuine success by formulating objectives for each pupil that are potentially attainable and by helping the pupil to make progress towards that goal. Encouraging children to improve on their own previous attainments rather than to compete against others is likely to assist even those with severe learning difficulties to experience a sense of success.

While children from socially disadvantaged backgrounds or minority groups are most likely to be exposed to experiences that adversely affect the development of self-esteem, children from advantaged homes may also have to face pressures that are potentially damaging to their self-concept. Even in the early school years, children may suffer from the unrealistic expectations of their parents. For example, children of high ability sometimes come to think of themselves as failures because their achievements, although of a good standard in the eyes of the school, fall short of the parents' unrealistic expectations. Adequate communication between teachers and parents can help to avoid such situations (see chapter 9).

SEX-ROLES AND THE TEACHER

Traditional concepts and expectations in relation to the ways in which boys and girls, men and women should behave – sex-role standards or stereotypes – have been strongly challenged in recent years. Parents and teachers no longer find it easy to decide to what extent sex differentiation should be encouraged. For example, should boys be discouraged from playing with dolls, or should girls be encouraged to conduct themselves in a 'lady-like' way rather than engage in rough and aggressive games? These questions will be answered differently by different people but it has to be recognized that the traditional differentiation of sex-roles, while less rigid than in the past, is still considered important in the community at large and among children of school age. Indeed, sexual identity is established long before the age of formal school entry. In the school years, sex-role behaviours are consolidated, establishing patterns which will continue into adulthood (Kagan and Moss, 1962). Strommen et al. (1977) highlight three major factors influencing sex-role development: the shaping of children's behaviour through rewards and punishment from others; the child's identification with and imitation of sex-role models; and cognitive development. Although parents and other adults play a considerable part in the development of children's sex-role-related behaviour, peers and teachers also exert much influence during the early school years.

Between about six and eight years of age, most children have fairly fixed and even intolerant ideas about behaviour appropriate to each sex (Maccoby, 1980). Although these ideas are likely to become less rigid later on, sex-role identification is clearly important to children at this stage of their development and teachers need to be aware of this – whatever their own views on sex-role stereotyping may be. At the same time they should be aware that, apart from the models which they present to their pupils, their expectations appear to be important in influencing children's behaviour, self-concepts and school attainments (Rogers, 1982). For example, their expectations about the success of boys and girls in relation to different aspects of the curriculum are likely to be self-fulfilling. Teachers who expect girls to be better than boys in the early stages of reading but boys to be superior to girls in mathematics help these expectations to be fulfilled because they have more contact with each sex in the subject in which they are, supposedly, better (Leinhardt et al., 1979). Rogers (1982) points out that while it cannot be stated with certainty that younger pupils are more susceptible to the biasing effects of teacher attitudes towards them, it seems probable that this will be the case since they are still in the process of developing motivational styles and self-concepts.

Delamont (1980) asserts that teachers in many nursery, infant and junior schools regularly use sex and gender as an organizing principle and a management strategy within their classrooms. They may issue different instructions to boys and girls, or make statements about what boys can or cannot do (see King, 1978). Teachers differentiate between boys and girls both in teaching basic skills and in promoting social and emotional development, reinforcing quite different behaviour patterns. Delamont recognizes that pupils come to school with clearly stereotyped ideas about boys and girls which even a teacher trying to inculcate sexual equality can do little to shift. She warns that poorly planned attempts to change children's attitudes may do more harm than good, and advocates both a commitment to changing sex-role relationships in school and a skilful use of well-designed materials to achieve this end.

ATTITUDES TO CULTURAL DIFFERENCES

Differences in behaviour related to traditions, standards and models in different sub-cultures may be apparent in the case of indigenous pupils, as already noted (see p. 121). They may also be noticeable in the case of ethnic-minority children, although any real differences here may be exaggerated by stereotypes on the part of both teachers and pupils. Many teachers do not discriminate in any way between pupils from different backgrounds and as Brittan (1976) states, there are dangers in generalizing about teachers' attitudes towards ethnic-minority pupils, especially as individuals often have ambivalent feelings or ambiguous perceptions within themselves. However, the Swann Report (DES, 1985), summing up the findings of a number of relevant research studies, concluded that some teachers did have clear stereotypes of the academic and social behaviour of ethnic-minority children, although different ethnic groups were perceived quite differently. For example, attitudes towards Asian pupils were generally positive, these pupils being considered as well-behaved, polite and courteous, industrious and responsible (Bowker, 1968; Townsend and Brittan, 1972). West Indian pupils, on the other hand, were seen by many teachers as less well-motivated in school and more prone to behaviour problems than other children (Brittan, 1976; Stone, 1981).

Stereotyped and prejudiced attitudes are learned and, if they are held by adults, it is not surprising that children also have such attitudes, especially given that at the age of eight, children's concepts of religious or national groups are often vague and inaccurate. By the time children reach school, prejudiced attitudes are often already developing, and derogatory labels are being learned as well as the more accepted names of ethnic and religious groups (Strommen et al., 1977).

The Swann Report makes a number of recommendations for the improvement of attitudes, policies and practices in the education of children of ethnic-minority groups (see also Brown, 1979; M. Saunders, 1982), although it is generally acknowledged that no simple solutions exist to what are complex and deeply rooted problems. Much work remains to be done over a period of time but if teachers hold positive and unprejudiced attitudes towards children from ethnic-minority groups and treat them as equals in every way while recognizing the value of their traditions and customs, they will contribute much to the emotional and social development of all their pupils.

DEALING WITH COMMON EMOTIONAL AND BEHAVIOURAL DIFFICULTIES

Few teachers of young children will not have to deal with emotional and behavioural difficulties in the classroom, whether these are over-reactions or under-reactions. Most of these difficulties will be of short duration and without lasting significance, but even minor difficulties may be an indication that all is not well with a child's emotional and social development, and in some cases the problem will become relatively fixed over a period of months or even years, affecting emotional growth and school progress.

Teachers play an important part in preventing some behaviour difficulties ever arising. Observation of primary school teachers by Kounin (1970), for example, showed that a feature of successful classroom management was an ability to prevent disruption from occurring (see also Calderhead, 1984). With experience, most teachers learn how to handle behaviour difficulties in the classroom with some degree of effectiveness and to recognize when outside help should be called in. However, the emphasis in the past on clinical perspectives in helping children presenting behaviour problems has perhaps coloured teachers' perceptions of such problems, so that they consider them to be the province of an expert. This is certainly true in some cases but most problems arising in the classroom are not of a pathological nature, nor are they evidence that the child is 'emotionally disturbed'. Rather, in the majority of cases, behaviour problems are the result of difficulties in learning or undeveloped social skills, both of which teachers can do much to rectify. This means that every teacher needs to acquire an understanding of the possible causes of emotional or behavioural difficulties, to identify such difficulties at an early stage and to be aware of a range of strategies which may be effective in dealing with them.

Teachers' Perceptions of Behaviour Difficulties

'Severe attention-seeking both from teacher and other pupils; tends to fill a scapegoat role.'

'Sullen, withdrawn. I presume that she is very angry.'

'Constantly restless; twists about in his seat; lacks concentration; little response to correction, attends to anything but his work (this behaviour I find very irritating).'

'Too lethargic to be troublesome; sits lifelessly most of the time; spiteful to other children when he thinks he is unobserved; too timid to stand up for himself.'

'Aggressive to other children, e.g. biting. Lies immediately afterwards about such behaviour. Unable to accomplish anything as far as his school work is concerned; does not respect school property.'

These comments by infant school teachers about children causing them concern (Chazan, 1973) illustrate the kinds of problems which most teachers are likely to meet during the early school years. Surveys of children aged five to eight years have shown that such problems are surprisingly common. Chazan and Jackson (1971) asked teachers for information about the nature and extent of behaviour difficulties in a sample of 726 children aged five years to five years seven months attending schools serving different types of catchment areas. Teachers' ratings showed that as many as twenty-four per cent of the total sample displayed behaviour deviating from the norm as perceived by the school: approximately thirteen to fourteen per cent of the children appeared to need some extra attention, although only a small proportion were thought to need specialist help. Boys presented considerably more problems than the girls, especially in respect of over-activity and aggression, and significantly more children coming from 'deprived' catchment areas presented problems than those living in 'middle-class' residential areas. A repetition of the survey two years later largely confirmed the overall picture presented in the children's first year at school (Chazan and Jackson, 1974).

Hughes et al. (1979) obtained teachers' ratings of children's difficulties in a sample of 260 children in their first term at an infant school in inner London. Overall, 13 per cent were considered to have difficulty in coping with school and, according to the teachers' own descriptions, most of these children seemed to be showing some kind of emotional or behavioural disturbance. Common difficulties included lack of concentration, dependency on the teacher and problems with social relationships, and were generally more frequent amongst boys than amongst girls. Further data collected on 114 children who were still at the same school four terms later (mean age six years four months) showed that 14 per cent were having difficulty in coping with school at the time.

Davie et al. (1972) also report a similar proportion of seven-year-old children rated by their teachers as 'maladjusted' in the National Child Development Study. In the case of junior school teachers, Merrett and Wheldall (1984) found that the behaviours that caused teachers most concern were talking, non-attending, disobeying and disturbing others (including aggression). However, a large number of 'withdrawn' children were also identified by teachers. Croll and Moses (1985), in their study of 428 junior class teachers' perceptions of special needs, report 7.7 per cent of the total sample of children, that is about two children in the average class, as having behaviour problems. Most of these pupils were seen by their teachers as being behaviourally or emotionally disturbed, with about half of them posing discipline problems for the teacher. Seven to eight year-olds showed a slightly higher prevalence of behaviour problems than older children (8.2 per cent, as compared with 7.2 per cent to ten to eleven year-olds). In the Newcastle School-Based Action Project, Kolvin et al. (1981) reported a much higher number of seven to eight year-olds as having problems of some kind, as many as 27 per cent. This high figure may be due, at least in part, to the project's use of four measures as a basis for identifying children at risk of 'maladjustment' – sociometric ratings; reading retardation; the Rutter teachers' scale; and frequent absenteeism.

It is clear from all these studies that, apart from wide individual variations in the perception of emotional and behavioural problems, teachers in different schools and catchment areas may have very divergent experiences of such problems.

Persistence of Difficulties

It would seem that while many new problems arise specific to the early years in school, a sizeable proportion of children presenting difficulties at this stage have a history of behaviour disturbance going back to earlier years. Richman et al. (1982) followed up ninety-four children showing behaviour problems at three years and a control group of ninety-one children free from such problems at that age. On the basis of all the available information, the research team concluded that sixty-two per cent of the problem group still showed some degree of disturbance at eight years of age. However, twenty-two per cent of the control group, who had not presented any behaviour problems at age three, now showed some degree of disturbance. Among those who had been disturbed at three, the following variables were particularly predictive of continued problem behaviour:

1 gender: boys rather than girls;
2 degree of disturbance: moderate and severe rather than mild;
3 nature: restlessness and high activity level.

Children not disturbed at three years of age were most likely to become so if:

1 they showed *any* problem behaviour, even to a minor degree;
2 they were restless and very active;
3 the relationships in their families were disharmonious.

Both the Chazan and Jackson (1971, 1974) and the Hughes et al. (1979) surveys show that, while the overall prevalence and pattern of behaviour difficulties are similar at five years of age and at follow-up eighteen months or two years later, there were considerable changes in the individual children who were experiencing difficulties. Hughes et al. report that, although on the whole the majority of difficulties on entry were relatively short-lived, there was a substantial minority of children (between a quarter and a half on most of the items on their checklist) for whom difficulties persisted from entry to follow-up. Fogelman (1983), using National Child Development data obtained with older children (seven, eleven and sixteen years of age), similarly found that many children change positions in ratings of deviant behaviour, with only very small numbers of children remaining in 'deviant' groups (defined as the top thirteen per cent at any age in degree of deviance) at all three ages (2.28 per cent for home ratings; 2.09 per cent for school ratings).

It is possible that teachers' perceptions of and attitudes towards deviance are important factors in the continuity of at least some behaviour problems. Teachers may feel strongly about over-reacting behaviour in their pupils and their attitudes towards disruptive pupils may not easily change (Safran and Safran, 1985a, b).

Understanding Causes of Behaviour Difficulties

In the case of an isolated incident of aggressive or disruptive behaviour, or of a child bursting into tears, it is usually possible to ascertain the cause of the trouble without prolonged investigation: usually the child will be reacting to provocation of some kind or be temporarily upset because of failure at a particular task. However, in cases where the child is showing a more prolonged pattern of anti-social or withdrawn behaviour, the situation is likely to be more complex. It will often be found that such behaviour is related to a combination of factors rather than presenting evidence of a simple association between a cause and its effects. The more obvious 'precipitating' factor which appears directly related to disturbed behaviour may be less important than other 'predisposing' factors which have brought about a situation where such behaviour is likely to occur. A classroom incident, involving provocation on the part of another child or even of the teacher, may be the last straw which causes a child under strain to lose control: children in the age-group five to eight are still in the relatively early stages of acquiring self-control and a rational response to stress.

Temperamental, congenital, physical, familial and school factors may all play a part in the causation of problem behaviour. Obviously, teachers are limited in the extent to which they can do anything about many of these factors, but an understanding of the wide range of individual differences in personality among children and the sources of stress and strain affecting them will help teachers to adopt an appropriate approach to children with difficulties. Moore (1969) emphasizes that adults can help or hinder children's attempts to cope with stress. They can sometimes show children how to handle difficult situations, whereas if understanding or sympathy is lacking, the child's efforts can be undermined.

The main factors or groups of factors affecting children's emotional and social development will be discussed under the following headings: (a) temperamental characteristics; (b) congenital factors; (c) physical factors; (d) family structure and influences; and (e) school factors.

Temperamental characteristics A wide range of individual differences in temperament exists among children, differences in their basic emotional disposition and reactivity which seem to be, at least partially, inborn. Temperamental characteristics such as adaptability, intensity of reaction, quality of mood and distractibility have been observed in children at an early age and may influence the child's relationships and responses to stress. By the age of five or six, teachers will be able to identify children who seem natural 'copers' or almost always extraverted, as well as those who find life heavy-going or who are difficult to arouse. Thomas et al. (1968) and Thomas and Chess (1977) have concluded that temperamental features do play a significant role in the origin and development of behaviour problems in children. However, they did not find any specific patterns of temperament which necessarily resulted in behaviour disturbance: such disturbance was the outcome, rather, of the interaction between a child's temperamental characteristics, abilities and motives and significant features of the environment.

Children in their early years at school are under the control of the same teacher for most, if not all, of the school day. It is helpful for teachers to recognize that they are likely to get on better with some children rather than others. Occasionally there may be a clash between a teacher's own temperament and that of a pupil. Recognition of such a situation may serve to prevent conflicts arising which may lead to outbursts or withdrawal on the part of the child.

Congenital factors Congenital factors include those conditions or events, particularly brain damage, which affect the infant at the pre-natal stage or at the time of birth. Marston and Stott (1970) have suggested a neurological and probably congenital origin for what they term 'inconsequential' behaviour. 'Inconsequential' pupils, familiar to most teachers of younger pupils, are those who are easily distracted and prone to provoking or interfering with others. They are often the centre of disturbance within the classroom, playing the clown and shouting out regardless of classroom conventions; they tend not to heed correction and generally react very impulsively and foolishly. Certain kinds of behaviour, such as hyperactivity and distractibility, tend to be associated with indices of brain damage. However, the validity of these indices is not always well-established, nor is the nature of the association between brain damage and behaviour problems in children well understood (Werry, 1972; Rutter, 1977). While even slight brain damage may affect behaviour, and while the suggestion that a child may be suffering from 'minimal brain damage' may help teachers to understand certain types of reaction, such a diagnosis is unlikely to have practical implications for teachers wishing to plan intervention strategies.

Physical factors   Poor physical condition may reduce a child's resistance to stress and thus be a factor in emotional upset. Some children in their early years at school are frequently absent on account of colds, ear trouble or other ailments. While such absences may be of short duration, they may result in the child feeling unsettled at school and in a lack of continuity in school work, perhaps leading to some degree of retardation in the basic subjects. An awareness on the part of the teacher of possible difficulties arising out of frequent absences due to illness may well help to minimise the consequences of absenteeism.

Given the current tendency towards the integration of handi-capped children, teachers in ordinary schools are likely to come into contact with physically handicapped pupils more frequently than before. Children with a marked physical or sensory defect or handicap do not always present emotional or behavioural problems. However, they are usually susceptible to emotional disturbance because of their feeling of being different from others and because of the attitudes of peers and society, and possibly their parents also towards them (Thomas, 1978). Anderson (1973) reports that a significantly higher number of a sample of twenty-five physically handicapped infant school children complained of aches and pains, and showed more restlessness and poor concentration than was the case in a normal control group; disturbed behaviour shown by these children varied widely from marked aggression to almost total withdrawal. Severe physical handicap or marked visual or hearing defects in five to eight year-olds can lead to frustration, tension and moodiness. Teachers can greatly help children with physical handicaps or sensory loss to adjust to the demands of the ordinary school by having a positive attitude towards them, liaising with the home and support services and guiding the other children in their classes in ways of relating to them constructively.

Family structure and influences   Teachers readily acknowledge that the behaviour of a child in a class may be the direct result of a crisis at home, or of generally disturbed family conditions. Behaviour difficulties in middle-childhood tend to be significantly associated with methods of discipline at home and family background problems such as marital disharmony, parental separation, single parenting or parental ill-health (Rutter et al., 1970; Kolvin et al., 1977; Richman et al., 1982). Particularly vulnerable families are those children whose mothers are young or of low ability (McGee et al., 1984). Mothers of children in the five- to eight-year age-range may well have other young children and there is evidence that a high proportion of mothers who have to cope with several young children in difficult circumstances suffer from depression (Brown and Harris, 1978).

Teachers may feel they can do little towards bringing about desirable changes in their pupils' home backgrounds. To some extent they may be justified in this view, as many family and community problems are deep-rooted, requiring radical solutions. However, in the early years at school, teachers may be the first to suspect that something is amiss at home, and they are in a position to alert the appropriate support services. They can also greatly help by avoiding stereotyped attitudes towards parents and not seeking to blame parents for their children's behaviour on the basis of limited evidence. A good home–school relationship will be particularly valuable in the case of behaviour difficulties which give continued cause for concern, and its relationship is discussed in more detail in chapter 9.

School factors   Until recently, school factors have tended to be relatively underplayed in the causation of behavioural problems and indeed it can be acknowledged that primary schools – infant and first schools in particular – are usually able to offer their pupils a more secure basis and homely environment than large secondary schools. Nevertheless, the developmental tasks discussed previously may give rise to emotional difficulties. A number of studies have established an association between anti-social behaviour in middle-childhood and reading difficulties (see Chazan, 1985 for an overview of these studies). McMichael (1979) reports the existence of this association even in the case of infant school boys but suggests that the anti-social behaviour precedes rather than follows reading difficulties. The boys in McMichael's study who showed anti-social behaviour and reading difficulties at the age of six or seven appeared to have entered school with a constellation of earlier problems connected with delayed linguistic, perceptual and cognitive development, low self-esteem and anti-social behaviour. However, McMichael acknowledges that early educational problems may be sowing the seeds of later frustration, loss of self-esteem and anti-social behaviour.

When behaviour difficulties are shown in school, it is not sufficient to regard within-child factors as being of primary importance. It is always worthwhile for teaching staffs to consider whether their attitudes, classroom management practices or other within-school factors have any bearing on children's behaviour difficulties. Children in the early years at school are, for the most part, treated sensitively in the classroom. Nevertheless, they may react badly to any negative attitudes shown towards them on the part of a member of staff, which may be shown by carelessly expressed remarks relating to a child's weaknesses, social background or ethnic membership. Sometimes a reaction against an insensitive teacher may be generalized into a hostility towards school as a whole and possibly result in a refusal to attend school. When a child is emotionally upset an unsympathetic teacher can add to the disturbance felt.

Hughes et al. (1979) suggest that while some children's difficulties on starting school are related to personality and/or home background factors, the way the school intake is organized may affect the extent to which children adjust to school; this question is discussed further in chapter 10. This chapter will conclude with a consideration of school and classroom strategies for preventing and coping with behaviour difficulties.

Strategies for Preventing and Coping with Behaviour Difficulties

The vast majority of children with behaviour difficulties are dealt with in the context of their usual classroom: only the more serious and extreme cases will need to be placed elsewhere, in a special unit or a day or residential special school. Educational psychologists are increasingly endeavouring to provide help for children presenting emotional or behavioural problems in their own class or school rather than in an outside clinical setting and have expanded the use of strategies which involve working closely with teachers and parents in school. Teachers, too, accept that it is part of their responsibility to cope with the majority of pupils who have special needs, including those relating to emotional and social development. However, it would seem that teachers of young children only rarely employ carefully planned strategies in their efforts to deal with behaviour difficulties. Rather, on the whole, they tend to repeat actions or activities which they believe to be helpful, or give the children longer time to accomplish what everyone else is doing. Such procedures work in some cases, but are not always helpful (Chazan and Laing, 1985; Laing and Chazan, 1987).

Many behaviour difficulties commonly occurring in classes of five to eight year-olds can be resolved fairly easily and expeditiously but teachers, both individually and as a staff, need to consider carefully whether they ought to increase their repertoire of skills in handling children whose emotional or social development is giving cause for concern, for two main reasons. First, it can be asserted that schools have as much responsibility for promoting the emotional and social growth of their pupils as they have for fostering intellectual development and they should, therefore, have a clearly formulated policy to that end. Second, even a single pupil in an otherwise orderly class can severely disrupt the work of the class as a whole and cause the teacher much stress and anxiety. Strategies for preventing and coping with behaviour difficulties that might be considered by schools and teachers will be discussed here under four main headings (the practices of working with parents and the support services will be dealt with in chapter 9): (a) school policy and classroom management; (b) play techniques; (c) behavioural approaches; (d) problem-solving and social skills training.

School policy and classroom management   Schools catering for younger pupils do not normally have a fomal system of pastoral care, such as many secondary schools have developed. Nevertheless there are questions relating to pastoral care that infant and primary schools need to consider. Teachers feel much more secure when they can look to ready support from the headteachers, deputy head or other senior members of staff when they are faced with problems in the classroom. School staffs need to examine the support available within the school for individual members of staff, as well as: their relationships with parents and external agencies; their participation in in-service training courses; the ways in which school organization and climate might be improved; and any problems specific to the school as a part of a particular community. Educational psychologists are increasingly considering how the school as an institution needs to change to meet all the needs of its pupils (Burden, 1981; Quicke, 1982). Schools will, therefore, find most school psychological services keen to co-operate with them in discussions about possible desirable innovations in school policy and organization.

The way in which a class is managed will have a bearing on the extent to which behaviour problems will arise (Calderhead, 1984). Successful methods of class control commonly used by infant school teachers in King's (1978) study were typically 'oblique', with a preference for making requests rather than giving orders and for rewarding good behaviour rather than punishing misbehaviour evident. The teachers used eye-scanning and eye-contact as well as their voice to give the children the idea that they were aware of everything that was going on. When the teachers were asked how they dealt with the 'naughty ones', they mentioned distraction (nine per cent of the teachers); appeals (nine per cent); deprivations (seventeen per cent); isolation (twenty-nine per cent) and verbal methods (forty-one per cent). Forty-seven per cent of the teachers admitted to smacking, though they stressed the infrequency and lightness of the smacking.

Roberts (1979) stresses that the application of four general principles will help infant school teachers to avoid labelling their pupils as deviant:

1 rejection of type-casting – even if a child comes with a 'bad reputation', the teacher seeks for the child's strengths and treats a disruptive act as a matter for surprise rather than expectation;
2 soliciting of assistance – the teacher encourages peers to help a child who is failing;
3 promotion of appreciation – the teacher helps the class to accept the difficulties of a handicapped child by making use of the child's talents while playing down the difficulties;
4 promotion of tolerance – the teacher gives, for example, a very fat, clumsy child limited opportunities to demonstrate a sequence of movements in an effort to neutralize the derision of his peers, praising the strengths of his performance.

Hare and Hare (1977) provide practical advice for teachers of young children in controlling hyperactivity, helping withdrawn children, dealing with temper tantrums and managing aggressiveness and hostility; and Webb's (1969) detailed accounts of how a school dealt with a variety of cases of behaviour problems are also very illuminating. Calderhead (1984) discusses recent research and thinking on classroom management, including the ways in which primary school teachers deal with difficult pupils.

Play techniques   The ways in which play techniques can be used in the classroom to help young children with emotional and behavioural difficulties are discussed in chapter 4 above (see also Chazan et al., 1983) and will not be considered further here. These techniques are especially appropriate in the case of children of infant school age, as learning through play forms a substantial part of their daily activities.

Behavioural approaches   Behavioural approaches are seen by many psychologists as offering a concrete programme of help to children, parents and teachers. Behaviour modification strategies in the classroom encourage teachers to adopt an experimental approach to children presenting behaviour difficulties. They also demand the statement of the problem and of desired goals in precise terms and the careful planning of a programme designed to achieve the kind of change anticipated (Leach and Raybould, 1977). Strategies of this kind are particularly suitable in the case of younger children, who are likely to be more responsive than older pupils to various kinds of reward, whether these are in a tangible or verbal form, though behaviour modification programmes normally take up a great deal of the teacher's time and usually need the involvement of an educational psychologist. Merrett and Wheldall (1984) consider that most of the problems which junior school teachers find troublesome are readily amenable to remediation by behavioural methods.

Although full behaviour modification programmes are usually time-consuming, they provide a basis for close co-operation between school staff and educational psychologists in attempting to help children and teachers in as practical a way as possible. Useful ideas for classroom approaches will be found in many books and manuals now available to teachers (see section on Further Reading). Even if teachers are unwilling or unable to participate in a behaviour modification programme which seems to make excessive demands on time, most will find it helpful to consider the application of some simple general behavioural principles in their daily work, if these principles do not already guide their practice.

O'Leary and O'Leary (1977), for example, list a number of procedures which all teachers should make a part of their natural interactions with their pupils, such as (a) praising desirable behaviour; (b) ignoring minor disruptions; (c) making classroom rules clear to all children; (d) modelling desirable behaviour; (e) shaping both scholastic and social behaviour; and (f) using soft reprimands. O'Leary and O'Leary stress the value of praising behaviour incompatible with disruption, developing appropriate social behaviour to replace aggression and observing children regularly to evaluate progress with any procedure adopted. They stress the wide range of individual differences in the ease and spontaneity with which teachers relate to their pupils and the need for teachers to cultivate positive attitudes towards pupils who seem to go out of their way to incur displeasure.

Simple principles are not always consistently practised by teachers, for example giving praise as soon as possible following appropriate behaviour, smiling and mentioning the child's name when giving praise, varying the volume and intensity of voice, showing excitement when this is justified, or using concrete tokens such as stars. All too often difficult pupils receive mainly negative attention and even if they are 'on task' for some of the time, they may not gain any praise or positive reaction from the teacher for this achievement.

Problem-solving and social skills training As Spence (1983) points out, there has been a recent growth of interest in developing strategies for teaching social skills to children, particularly those who have failed to learn to interact with others in an appropriate manner. Although too little is as yet known about the efficacy of social skills training, there have been some promising approaches to improving both cognitive problem-solving and behavioural skills in children.

Spivack and Shure (1974) have pioneered useful strategies which emphasize the role of the adult in encouraging children to think up their own ideas of how to behave in specific situations; to consider alternative courses of action for themselves; and to look ahead to possible outcomes rather than to act impulsively and without consideration of the consequences of their action (see, also, Spivack et al., 1978). The basic philosophy underlying this approach is that if children's behaviour is to be changed then one must influence the thinking which controls the behaviour. Other approaches to social skills training have emphasized the behavioural rather than the cognitive aspects, aiming, for example, to increase eye contact, improve conversation skills or encourage assertiveness (Argyle, 1973; Cooke and Apolloni, 1976; Oden and Asher, 1977).

Experiments in both cognitive and behavioural social skills training have employed a variety of techniques, including modelling, role-play, simulation exercises, video feedback, stories, cartoons, games, puppets, instructions and discussion. Much more thought needs to be given to the development of social skills training but teachers may obtain ideas for developing their own programmes from a number of sources (see the section on Further Reading). Although Spivack and Shure have devised problem-solving pro-grammes for children as young as four years, much of what has been written about social skills training has been concerned with older pupils and adults, and teachers of five to eight year-olds will need to adapt many of the suggested techniques to meet the needs of this age-group.

This chapter has stressed that the school has a very important part to play in helping children to face the emotional and social challenges that are characteristic of the early school years. Schools can also do much to prevent behaviour difficulties from arising and developing. When behaviour problems requiring special attention do occur, teachers should be in a position to call upon a range of strategies and skills to enable them to provide appropriate help for children in trouble. There should be very few cases when children between five and eight years old cannot be coped with in the ordinary class, and education authorities are now thinking in terms of children of all ages receiving special help when this seems necessary, within their usual class rather than outside it. Neverthe-less, adjustment groups may have their value in catering for children too immature or too disturbed to remain in their normal class all the time. Labon (1973), Chalk (1975) and Boxall (1976) have given accounts of specially established adjustment, support or nurture groups to cater for poorly adjusted children at the primary school stage. Groups of this kind, which allow children to 'attend' on a part-time or full-time basis, aim to help the children work out their relationship problems and become more ready to face the demands of normal school life. In a study of various forms of intervention designed to help junior school children at risk of maladjustment, Kolvin et al. (1981) found that these children responded well to the regime of specially established playgroups and nurture groups. Whether five to eight year-olds are in ordinary or special classes, teachers have a key role to play in providing their emotional and social development.

8

Learning Difficulties

In every class, no matter how the allocation of pupils has been made, streamed, unstreamed or vertical grouping, there will always be those whose progress is more rapid than that of the other members and those whose progress is slower than most. These children, who are the exceptions to that which would normally be expected from any particular grouping of pupils, present difficulties to their teachers with regard to the nature and level of the programme they should be tackling and they may face further learning difficulties if they find that programme unrewarding, unstimulating or out of step with what they need. They may be very able children, slow children or children whose behaviour interferes with their learning.

The inclusion of very able children in a chapter dealing with learning difficulties may at first sight appear puzzling. It is not always the case, however, that gifted children fulfil their capabilities. As far as some gifted children are concerned, their potential is under-used and wasted; they find themselves 'able misfits' (Pringle, 1970), 'living down' to their teachers' expectations, exhibiting a variety of educational or, perhaps, behavioural difficulties. As with those whose problems in learning stem from low ability, these gifted pupils pose problems of identification and assessment, raise organizational and placement queries and create unease with regard to the suitability of the curriculum. How can teachers recognize giftedness when the children may appear to be bored, mischievous, unco-operative or even insolent? At what point do children become gifted and have they any characteristics in common? Should they be taught in a group together or even segregated into a special class or a special school? What modifications have to be made to the curriculum to satisfy their special educational needs? Similar questions could be asked about low ability pupils.

It is not the purpose of this chapter to examine exceptionality from the point of view of highly intelligent or highly creative pupils. The Schools Council Enquiry into the teaching of gifted children of primary age (Ogilvie, 1973) presents a useful overview of many of the points raised here, as do a number of other writers (for example, Vernon et al., 1977; Leyden, 1985). While in America such children have long been recognized as having special educational needs, this has not been so historically in Britain and they were excluded from consideration by the Warnock Commitee:

> we did not regard the problems of highly gifted children as falling within our remit, except insofar as these problems may result in emotional or behavioural disorders similar in effect to the problems of other children with whom we are concerned. (DES, 1978b, 1.2)

CHILDREN WITH SPECIAL EDUCATIONAL NEEDS

Who, then, are usually considered to be children with special educational needs, where do these needs originate and what educational provision will best satisfy them? Although each of these questions will be considered in turn, it should be said here that there are no clear answers to any one of them and all three are so interrelated that looking at one question in isolation is somewhat artificial. With regard to children aged five to eight years these questions pose particular problems, especially in the first two years of formal schooling. While it may be obvious in some cases that young children have special educational needs (for example, children with marked auditory or visual impairment; severe mental retardation; poorly developed speech; or extreme distractibility), there are others whose needs are not detected until they are faced with acquiring and developing reading and number skills or with having to adapt to other children and to teachers. The educational programme in the early years at school allows for wide individual interests, abilities and achievements and teachers are often reluctant to be specific about their concern over some children's progress or response to the school situation, fearing that more harm than good may be done by identifying a child as having difficulties in learning. However, they may also fear that to leave their concern unexpressed until nearing the end of the first school may be equally unhelpful for those children.

This chapter proposes to look in more detail at what special educational needs are and where children who are considered to have such needs should be educated. The teacher's role *vis-à-vis* these children will then be considered and some attention given to lack of progress in the basic skills. Finally, sources of support for teachers will be briefly considered, although these are dealt with at greater length in chapter 9.

While much of this discussion has general application whatever the age of the pupils, it should be borne in mind throughout that, first, the years from five to eight normally see a very rapid and significant growth in children's ability to cope with school-based activities; and, second, that it is in these years that children are introduced to skills which they continue to develop over the years. To falter at the first hurdle can never be an encouraging experience and, therefore, whether or not teachers formally express their worries over young children's slow or erratic progress to head-teachers or to others, they should unobtrusively do as much as they can to make the educational programme as appropriate and satisfying as possible to all those in their class.

Definition

The Warnock Report (DES, 1978b) regards children as having special educational needs if they are 'likely to require some form of special educational provision at some time during their school career' (para. 3.18). This is a broadly functional definition and a wide-ranging one, moving away from the previous concept of specific disabilities towards a concern for a substantial proportion of children who require extra help if they are to make progress in their school work. The number of children involved is estimated in the Report to be up to one in five and the help required is seen as ranging from the provision of special equipment, facilities or other resources to modifications in the curriculum – perhaps even the substitution of a different curriculum – or in the social and emotional ethos of the school. The 1981 Education Act which gave legal expression to the Warnock Report's concerns, relates special educational needs to learning difficulties, the latter implying 'greater difficulty in learning than the majority of children' of a similar age or an inability to make use of the normal educational facilities within the school. The Act further states that special provision is that which is 'additional to, or otherwise different from' normal educational provision.

By attempting to break away from the practice of placing children in categories based on a concept of 'handicap' and thence in schools specially set up to focus on each specific handicap, these new definitions create possibilities for more fruitful deliberation leading to decisions in each individual case. At the same time these definitions lack precision and, while a degree of vagueness may be helpful in achieving solutions tailored to specific needs, it can also lead to widely varying practices and a blurring of responsibilities. It also places the burden of identification very much on the shoulders of teachers as being those most likely to detect learning difficulties and to have to make some form of special provision for them, as will be discussed later in this chapter.

Sources of Learning Difficulties

There are at least three, and almost certainly more, possible ways of considering why children have difficulties in learning, none of which is ideal. In the first instance, difficulties could be seen as stemming from conditions affecting children before they are born, during birth or after birth. Thus, genetic or chromosomal abnormalities, or damage caused by maternal illness or drugs taken during pregnancy, fall into the first of these three classifications. Difficult or awkward births which lead to damage to the baby exemplify the second, while the third category is a wide, 'catch-all' one, encompassing illness, accident and all environmental adversities to which children may be exposed after birth. These may seem tidy and comprehensive categories and, indeed, they do help to distinguish conditions where the implications for many aspects of development, including educational progress, are considerable and long-lasting. The third category, post-natal conditions, is a very wide one, however, and there is the danger of regarding any identification of sources of difficulty in this area as a complete and unchangeable explanation. Indeed, it is a category where it may be more useful to realize how interrelated the various aspects of children's developments and experience are, rather than to attempt to isolate any one aspect as the major source of any lack of progress.

A second way of categorizing sources of difficulty would be to identify specific factors which can be shown to be closely related to poor educational progress. A possible list would include limited intellectual ability, social disadvantage, maladjustment, linguistic impoverishment and physical or sensory disabilities (see, for example, Gulliford, 1985; Gillham, 1986). Focusing attention on these aspects helps to alert those concerned with children with learning difficulties to sources of stress which may be affecting progress. The danger here is again that attention may be centred on only one of the possible categories, for example, social disadvantage, and all of the difficulties being displayed may be attributed to this factor alone. Teachers create an hypothesis as to the possible source of any learning difficulties but may be too easily satisfied that they have conclusively identified it. Thus, children's 'failure' in school might be attributed to their poor home conditions and these then might be seen as accounting also for their lack of communication and troublesome behaviour, without consideration being given to the effects of mild hearing loss or lack of acceptance by peers, for instance.

A third way of looking at learning difficulties is through an intensive assessment of individual children. While assessment is essential in any attempt to delineate learning difficulties sufficiently precisely for appropriate assistance or remediation to be offered, an undue concentration on within-child aspects may overlook important considerations, such as school conditions. A further problem is that detailed individual assessment may prove to be too time-consuming. To illustrate these criticisms one need only think of a teacher trying to assess the learning difficulties of a newcomer to a class of thirty children who is non-English speaking. Furthermore, as Hegarty and Lucas (1978) point out, even to know the aetiology of failure with reasonable confidence does not always help to indicate its implications for the various aspects of any educational programme.

While all three of these approaches to attempting to identify the source or sources of learning difficulties are of use of teachers, there is also a very good case to be made for any difficulties to be seen alongside the strengths which these same children have. An over-concentration on sources of difficulties may not provide teachers with all the practical information they require about pupils' present and potential functioning in the classroom. Such functioning cannot be adequately managed without very close observation of these children in all aspects of their school life and an understanding of their out-of-school life. It would seem appropriate, therefore, always to consider learning difficulties within a wide frame of reference, utilizing as much information as can be acquired with regard to the 'whole' child in his or her total environment.

When primary school teachers themselves were asked for their views on the sources of special educational needs (Croll and Moses, 1985), their explanations were found to be 'dominated by factors related to children's innate qualities' (level of intelligence for example) as far as learning difficulties were concerned, and by 'characteristics of their home and parents' in the case of behaviour difficulties. As Croll and Moses comment, 'characteristics of the school and the teacher are seen as being causally relevant to difficulties in only a small minority of the cases' (p. 47). Such views are understandable but may lead to attempts to offer help which are inadequate because they do not consider all aspects of the learning difficulties presented and the essential interrelatedness of such aspects.

In a multicultural society it is particularly important that teachers look for potential for learning in all children rather than anticipating either 'good' or 'poor' performances. Work in the 1960s showed West Indian children to be achieving less than could have been expected of them (Tomlinson, 1983), and there still remains a worrying degree of under-performance, particularly among West Indian boys. Schools have come to realize that these pupils may need different teaching approaches and that the curriculum should at all stages reflect the multicultural society which is Britain now (Williams, 1979). The fact that some ethnic groups, for example those of Asian origin, reach a relatively high educational standard in comparison to other groups (Mabey, 1981) would seem to show that they are viewed as educationally more able by schools and achieve accordingly. It cannot be denied that the first school has a vital part to play in receiving young children into what may be for them a bewildering environment in which contact with their mother-tongue would be immensely reassuring (Williams, 1984). It is, moreover, in the early years that interest in other ethnic groups can be aroused and those children in such groups can be encouraged to acquire the linguistic and behavioural skills necessary for educational progress.

Integration and Segregation

> There is hardly a personal or social problem, or any difficulty connected with learning which will not be found in an ordinary infants' school, albeit often in embryo. (Webb, 1969, p. 22)

> Special education must be understood as a social process, set within a social and political context, if the special needs of children are to be truly served. These special needs . . . are related to the public issues as to why society decides to

separate, however minimally, and in whatever way, children who are special from children who are normal. (Tomlinson, 1982, p. 182)

These quotations reflect very different viewpoints, the former that of an educationalist and the latter that of a sociologist. In addition, they are separated by fifteen years, during which time the Warnock Report and the 1981 Act appeared. Yet while one views learning difficulties rather emotively and the other strives for rationality, they are not so far apart in practice. For different reasons both are critical of the practice of moving children, especially young children, with special educational needs out of the mainstream.

Behind the arguments as to whether segregation can be justified or whether integration is feasible or effective, lie many sleeping tigers, all with tails which, if twitched, can pull the unwary into conceptual turmoil. Egalitarianism, comprehensiveness, deviance, social control and learned helplessness are only a few of the concepts in question, all of them affected by current changes in the way in which accountability, the teacher's role and children's rights are construed. Clearly, thinking about integration and segregation is not easy and only a few points for discussion can be outlined here.

In the first place, there is probably unanimity in acknowledging that, as far as possible, all children should be educated together. Such a view is now legalized in the 1981 Act: 'Where a local education authority arrange special educational provision for a child . . . it shall be the duty of the authority . . . to secure that he is educated in an ordinary school' (para. 2.2). The indicated omissions in the above quotation cover the notion of a 'statement' of special educational needs for a small number of children and the conditions which must exist in the schools to enable the authority to carry out its duty. The statement of needs is envisaged as a composite account of a child's learning difficulties (and strengths) gathered from representatives of all the services concerned – educational, medical, social, psychological – and his or her parents. It also contains the authority's proposals as to where the child can best be educated in the light of this information and is subject to regular, yearly review.

Although the format of the statement itself may be reasonably clear, the Act gives little guidance as to who should be 'statemented' and no indication as to where the resources are to be found to implement the proposed placements. The burden of identification and of provision is left with the local authorities who may or may not feel able to shoulder it in its entirety. A segregated, special form of education can be proposed if the necessary conditions for integration are lacking, these conditions being that the child's special needs can be met in the ordinary school with an efficient use of resources, without affecting adversely the education of the other pupils, and that the parents agree. Certainly, there is considerable vagueness in these stipulations which is already leading to local variations in practice.

In the second place, integration can take many forms, some of which seem very close to segregation. As Galloway and Goodwin (1979) remark, 'a child can be physically integrated into an ordinary school yet feel socially isolated'. In the Warnock Report, three forms of integration were envisaged – locational, social and functional – providing a range from mere physical proximity to complete involvement in all of the school's activities with only the minimum of extra help being required. Furthermore, the Report recognized the continued existence of a separate, special system for: children with severe and complex handicaps; those who require highly specialized teaching or equipment; those with emotional or behavioural disorders which disrupt the education of other pupils; and those who are 'more likely to thrive in the more intimate communal and educational setting of a special school' (para. 8.8). Whether support for segregated education in these cases reveals an ambivalent attitude towards integration, a realistic assessment of the practicalities of running ordinary schools or a view calculated to conserve power in the hands of the majority can be argued. Certainly the 1981 Act sees the local educational authority as ensuring that 'the child engages in the activities of the ordinary school together with children who do not have special educational needs' (para. 2.7), with the same provisos as previously indicated.

Special educational needs in young children may not present as many problems to the school as do those in older pupils. For one thing the actual school building may be easily accessible and relatively hazard-free. Again, in the first years of school children may be more concerned with their own activities and fairly indifferent to what others may or may not be able to do, unless it directly affects their own well-being. As they grow older, they become more aware of differences but at seven or eight they are often protective towards those with difficulties or perhaps even feel responsibility for them. It is also the case that differences in achievement are accepted, indeed expected. Furthermore, most children of this age require individual attention from their teachers to sort out problems they have encountered. In the early years of the first school, therefore, children with special educational needs are on the whole able to engage in the school's normal activities. As the pace of learning quickens and becomes more formalized their learning difficulties may become more marked and discussion of suitable placement, both currently and in the future, becomes pressing if their involvement in the ordinary school cannot be said to be truly adequate.

It may be possible to give only fairly general guidance on where children with special educational needs should be educated; nevertheless, there has emerged a degree of agreement on some of the conditions which make social and functional integration successful and the evidence on this area provides a third topic for discussion here. A number of these conditions are obvious, for example suitable access, equipment and toilet facilities, although the fact that they would seem to be essential does not always mean that they have been provided (see Chazan et al., 1980). In America, emphasis is laid on placing children in the 'least restrictive environment' (Public Law 94–142, 1975) by which is meant that they should be offered no more by way of separate special education than is necessary and, therefore, should not be moved out of the ordinary classroom unless it is absolutely essential for their progress.

Before decisions can be taken as to the extent of the extra help to be given, a great deal of information must be available about children's special needs and the implications of these for the educational programme and for social acceptance. Whatever the extent of the learning difficulties, whether mild, moderate or severe, full briefing of school staff, specific in-service training and adequate support are the pre-requisites of possible classroom success. Other factors which must be considered are the nature and severity of the learning difficulties. Research (Anderson, 1973; Cope and Anderson, 1975) indicates that physical handicaps, even if quite severe, do not present undue problems to schools, always assuming that any necessary structural modifications to buildings have been made. Intellectual limitations and behaviour difficulties are less easy for teachers to cope with, even at the early stages of education.

The Swansea-based study (Chazan et al., 1980) showed not only that nursery staff were identifying a fair percentage of children aged four to five years as having cognitive (particularly linguistic) and behavioural problems (approximately fourteen per cent of the total sample being placed in each of these two categories) but also that staff in the ordinary schools or classes appeared to be less successful in coping with these particular problems than with those which were predominantly the result of physical handicaps. In the Swansea research, a sub-sample of fifty-one children with special needs in ordinary nursery provision was looked at in considerable detail. The researchers judged that fifteen of these fifty-one children were 'very difficult for the teacher to cope with' (see Chazan et al., 1980, table 10.1). Of these fifteen, nine were displaying behaviour difficulties and the other six showed varying degrees of mental retardation and developmental delay.

Successful integration also depends on the attitudes of class teachers, although it may be too simple merely to state that these should be favourable. Thomas (1985) suggests that teachers' attitudes may not be as crucial with regard to a child's successful integration as the teachers' personality and professional competence. Teachers in his study who had declared themselves to be opposed to 'mainstreaming' had effectively integrated handicapped children into their classes through showing empathy, flexibility and imagination when faced with such children, these being their usual classroom characteristics. Indeed, they were frequently critical of what they were achieving and felt that their training had not helped them in this area. As Thomas points out, these particular teachers were equal to the task of integration, although they did not feel they were and often continued to remain opposed to it. Alternatively, it is possible for teachers to feel considerable goodwill towards pupils with special educational needs but to fail to realize how these needs should be met.

THE CLASS TEACHER'S RESPONSIBILITIES

Identifying Children with Special Educational Needs

While children may have difficulties in learning to walk or to talk or in any of the many other skills normally acquired in the very early years, facing up to the demands of school may lead to the first emergence of problems. Teachers, therefore, have a very important part to play in identifying and diagnosing learning difficulties in young children. They also have the advantages of seeing any one child's progress in relation to that of others of a similar age and of having access to educational, medical and psychological advice. Indeed, teachers usually can quite easily identify certain difficulties, poor speech development, anti-social behaviour or over-dependence for example. They may be less aware of sensory loss, withdrawal or even giftedness.

However, in the infant school years, what may concern the teachers may be not so much recognizing individual children's difficulties as deciding whether anything – and, if so, what – should be done about them. Teachers may, indeed, be wary of 'labelling' children (see Goodacre, 1968, for the effect of teacher expectation on the progress of disadvantaged children) and yet, without the label, there may be a tendency to shelve the problem as not being sufficiently serious or being open to alleviation through the passage of time. Lovitt (1982) suggests that labelling may be more upsetting for the adults than it is for the children concerned. Galloway and Goodwin (1979), however, incline more to the opposite point of view and see pupils accepting certain views of themselves as learners because of the labels they have been given – slow-learning, maladjusted, disruptive and so on. Labelling, in fact, may not be so important in itself as the decisions which are taken subsequently. If because children are labelled 'slow', less is expected of them than they could achieve; if children are identified as 'pilferers' and so their every move is watched with suspicion; or if they are thought of as 'a nuisance' and only their tiresome behaviour noted – then labelling is not being helpful. If, on the other hand, children are labelled 'slow' and then considerable effort is made to provide work which is suitably challenging; or they are seen as 'pilferers' but their need to acquire all sorts of bits and pieces is understood in the wider context of their whole development and environment; or the teacher really studies the whole classroom situation and its various demands on those who are 'nuisances' – then labelling could help to reduce difficulties in learning.

The need for a wide variety of information to be gathered in connection with any learning difficulties has already been noted. Research in junior classes (Croll and Moses, 1985), however, has shown that many teachers adopt a fairly restricted view in the initial identification of learning difficulties. In this study of fifty-nine primary schools in ten local authorities, teachers of children aged seven to eleven years frequently equated learning difficulties with reading difficulties. Furthermore, in most of the cases identified, as has already been said, they placed the source of the difficulties in factors associated with the children themselves. It is interesting to compare these findings with the concern expressed by Hargreaves (1980) and Galloway (1985) over the effects of seeing virtually all of the causal factors of emotional and behavioural difficulties as being in the pupils themselves or their home background. Such attribution appeared to these writers to be unhelpful, at least with the older pupils they were considering, as all efforts at remediation were thereby directed at changing the pupils and none was focused on changing the classroom or school environment. Teachers of younger children should perhaps bear in mind that, by identifying as having learning difficulties mainly those children who are making poor progress in their reading, they may be identifying the result and not the cause of the difficulties. They may also be overlooking other pupils whose reading is progressing fairly satisfactorily but who, nevertheless, have learning difficulties (as shown in withdrawn behaviour or poor number or spelling skills for instance). They should perhaps also consider to what extent the school's demands are creating the difficulties – what might be called the 'ugly sisters' syndrome. It will be recalled that there was nothing wrong with the ugly sisters' feet, except that they failed to fit into a slipper designed for someone else.

Classroom Indications of Special Education Needs

Apart from slow progress in acquiring pre-reading or early reading skills, teachers of young children should be alert to any evidence of slow or poor language development. Children who seldom speak at all, either to adults or other children; children whose articulation makes it difficult for others to follow what they are saying; children who never take part in imaginative, pretend play; and children who rely on physical demonstration rather than verbal expression to get what they want are all examples of children whose learning may well be affected by linguistic inadequacies. Others whose behaviour should alert the teacher are those who seldom settle to any sustained activity; sit apathetically looking at unfinished work; or appear too timid to co-operate with others in any way. Children who frequently destroy their own or other children's work may have problems in learning as they seem not to have adapted to classroom expectations. It is clear, therefore, that teachers should be sensitive to children's speech development, physical health and well-being, social and emotional adjustment, ability to acquire new skills and attitudes to peers, adults and school in general.

To list the various aspects which teachers of young children should consider indicates that identification is not a simple 'one-off' task. Various measures do exist to help staff, both in the pre-school years (Bate et al., 1981) and when children enter the infant school (e.g. Chazan et al., 1976, 1980). While it may be invidious to select specific measures for comment, two warrant closer examination. The Effectiveness Motivation Scale (Sharp and Stott, 1976) is concerned with competence in learning in the pre-school years and looks at how effectively children are coping with a broad range of play activities and how they interact with others. It is therefore a very practically based assessment which could be of use at the reception stage and is fairly quickly completed, as staff need only indicate the level of expertise reached by each child in the various situations. The implications of good or poor overall scores on this Scale for school progress are obvious and examination of specific ratings can show where extra help is required. With regard to somewhat older children, Lindsay (1980) has developed an Infant Rating Scale intended not so much as a predictive measure to gauge future progress – a venture which he views with suspicion (Lindsay and Wedell, 1982) – but rather as a means of helping infant school teachers to structure their own observations.

Decision-Taking

Schools are under many pressures, not the least of which is society's expectation that they should at one and the same time be the main agents both for socializing children and for disseminating knowledge, two pressures which are often in conflict (Ford et al., 1982). Particular problems arise when teachers feel that the uneasy balance between these pressures is threatened by certain pupils, either because of their unacceptable behaviour or their resistance to the acquisition of knowledge. The solution may be seen as a decision to refer the pupils in question for special education. Special educational needs are, therefore, relative rather than absolute. Thus, teachers will vary with regard to taking this decision according to a wide number of factors including their own personality, teaching experience and standards of expectation; parental pressures; the school's views on referral; availability of local authority resources; and the children concerned. While there may be guidelines as to *how* teachers should refer children, there are really none as to *when* this should be done. Additionally, while the format of the statement of needs (if drawn up) is laid down, the help to be offered is not. Decisions to refer children can lead to a variety of outcomes, giving rise to argument, concern and frustration. The decision-taking process is, therefore, a particularly fraught one for teachers who are faced with the consequences of doing nothing (carrying on trying to cope within the classroom) and the consequences of doing something (starting the referral process which may lead to some form of special educational provision).

With young children teachers are often more inclined to play a waiting game than to bring children's learning difficulties to the attention of head teachers or visiting professionals (for example, advisory staff or educational psychologists). They feel that, given time, difficulties will resolve themselves. This may be so, for children's development is open to many variations (Upton, 1981). But in some cases difficulties may become more pronounced or more entrenched over time. They become accepted as the child's normal functioning and any further deviations are explained as stemming from them. Research evidence (Richman et al., 1982) indicates that as far as behaviour difficulties in young children are concerned there is a tendency for them to persist over the years and for those problems which were considered quite mild in young children to give rise to difficulties later on. If children's response to the educational programme is inadequate in some way at the start of their school experience, the foundations for future learning may not be sound. There would seem to be a case for deciding to investigate learning difficulties sooner rather than later.

If this were to be done the possibility of overcoming the difficulties is likely to be increased and the extra help required could well be provided within the ordinary classroom. Programmes for young children are sufficiently flexible for this to be attempted in many cases. In later years decisions to segregate children from their peers in ordinary classes and provide them with separate special education do not then need to be taken and their implications for the children's future education, acceptance and employment can be avoided (Barton and Tomlinson, 1984).

Programme Planning

Whoever takes the decision that certain children have learning difficulties, whether teachers or others involved with them (as in local authority screening procedures – see Gipps and Gross, 1984), provision of extra help is an important issue. Classroom teachers are very much seen now as central to this provision. 'The pattern of LEA provision is apparently changing, away from withdrawal, towards working with the class teacher' (Gipps and Gross, 1984, p. 8). Withdrawing children formally to offer them remedial help from specialist peripatetic or even school-based teachers has never been seen as entirely appropriate to young children in the initial stages of acquiring the basic skills. More often, it has been the case that additional help has been offered informally to individuals or small groups of children by teachers or headteachers. The nature and quality of the help offered, however, has depended very much on the expertise of the staff concerned and the time available. A careful assessment of specific needs, followed by the devising of individually tailored programmes, has not always been carried out. Yet, such programmes are much more likely to be effective than simply repeating the normal classroom activities which have not been successfully tackled in the first place.

Failure to be precise about the extra help required may stem from the very flexibility and informality which should make it possible to give such help. Bolton (1985 p. 13) comments:

> The absence of clarity and agreement about what children should be capable of at various stages of their primary education leads to a distinct lack of information about standards of pupil achievement in individual primary schools and a consequent difficulty of establishing any standards of achievement as a basis for an assessment of performance.

Where there is no clear statement of what the children should be able to do, it is not easy to be precise about children's learning difficulties. The result is that, although special activities could be accommodated without undue upheaval, there is no pressure to devise them as the children's lack of progress is seen in general, not specific, terms. The hope is rather that somehow children will overcome their difficulties in the normal course of events and the full extent of the difficulties and their implications may not be realized. For young children, the way to learn is seen to be 'through play and through their presumed interests' (King, 1978) and intervention in learning difficulties may even be construed by some as interference. Current opinion (for example, Welsh Office, 1984) seems to be in favour of teachers being offered the advice and the resources they need to work out a programme for children with learning difficulties which will be classroom-based. Such a programme would aim at carefully 'matching' pupils' needs to the experiences provided. It might well draw on parental support as in the many schemes in various parts of the country which encourage parents to participate in their children's reading (see chapter 9).

Teachers can be helped to gather the information necessary to achieve a 'good match' in a number of ways, as will be discussed in the next section and in the next chapter. A brief consideration of ways of tackling difficulties in reading in the early years might be appropriate here to illustrate how such a 'match' might be translated into practical classroom terms (see, also, Clay, 1979).

1   From careful listening, questioning and recording, a tentative description of the difficulties in reading should be made. This will be tentative as often more difficulties appear when help is offered and the child's grasp of the early skills is found to be uncertain.

2   From this description, the areas to be tackled should be identified and, if possible, assessed (see section on Further Reading). In the early years, the main problems in reading may lie in word-recognition, knowledge of sounds, ability to hear sounds in words and to blend them, or in understanding what is involved in the reading process. Tape-recording attempts at reading and watching how the business of reading is handled can yield a great deal of information (Arnold, 1982).

3   Once the particular aspects to be tackled first have been pinpointed, the programme can then be devised. It might be better to implement such a programme in such a way that the children concerned do not miss the general class-work in reading, whether that is linked to a reading scheme or not. Rather they should be given appropriate books. Children who are not progressing as well as the others should not be unduly singled out. The special programme could take the place of some written activities when the class may well be absorbed in a variety of different tasks.

4   Ideas for programme activities can be thought up by teachers themselves, based on commercially available materials (for example, Stott Programmed Reading Kit; LDA materials) or adapted from suggestions to be found in a wide variety of books (for example, McNicholas and McEntee, 1973; Gregory, 1982; Ames, 1983). (A list of books which might prove helpful in devising programmes can be found in the section on Further Reading.)

5   Most importantly, all approaches should be devised with the aim of improving children's view of themselves as readers. If they find reading frustrating or unrewarding, they will continue to see it as something to be avoided, whereas to have fun with reading activities, or even more to be successful in them, can transform attitudes, expectations and performance.

Children's early response to number activities is also important, of course. In many ways the approach outlined above can be used, with a particular emphasis on sufficient practical experience being made available for those who seem to be slow to grasp the vocabulary of number (greater than, share, counting for instance) or have very poorly developed number concepts. Opportunities to talk about their practical activities, to play games to promote counting and to use basic skills in as many different contexts as possible can all help children in difficulties in this area (for further discussion, see Williams, 1970; for suggestions for games, see Williams and Sommerwill, 1982). As the Cockroft Report (DES, 1982b) states: 'Failure can only be compounded if efforts are made to build further on a foundation which does not exist' (para. 334).

SUPPORT AND RESOURCES

To educate almost all children together and at the same time differentiate their learning experiences sufficiently to meet their needs and abilities cannot be achieved without considerable financial outlay. In some cases, integration is seen as a way of saving on expenditure on expensive separate provision. Simply to disband special classes or to close special units or schools are recipes for disaster. The expertise which the separate sector has acquired should be made available to all teachers if integration is to be successfully accomplished.

Availability of Expertise

There are two main problems with regard to helping mainstream teachers to deal more precisely with learning difficulties. The first is that the teachers themselves do not often ask for advice (Croll and Moses, 1985). They willingly discuss children's progress in general terms with their colleagues or with parents; to find time, however, to make precise assessments is often considered impossible. Even when other professionals do so, teachers may be reluctant to accept their judgements. There was little whole-hearted enthusiasm for guidance from advisory staff or educational psychologists in a small-scale research project carried out with first-year junior school teachers (Chazan and Laing, 1985), a few of these teachers being reluctant even to seek help from their headteacher with regard to classroom situations. Others, of course, welcomed all the within-school help they could get. The second problem is that other professionals are scarce and often find all their time and energies absorbed in coping with the difficulties presented by older pupils. For whatever reason, it would seem that the main responsibility for programme planning for special educational needs in the early years, as for the ordinary programme, will usually fall on class teachers.

Support within the School

Many of the problems facing teachers of young children with special educational needs might well be eased if guidelines and general objectives could be agreed with regard to what all the children should be achieving at any stage. To say this is in no way to remove the flexibility which is essential in all teaching of young children. However, the existence of curricular guidelines and efficient records are also invaluable in monitoring progress. Children with special educational needs, especially when these take the form of intellectual limitations, seem to make little progress from day to day. Over a longer period of time the extent of change may be more obvious and, in addition, fluctuations in progress can be identified once the records have shown the children's usual rate of acquiring or consolidating skills. All this information ensures that the programmes offered to children, whether highly structured or less so, are what they need and contain a helpful balance between their weaknesses and their strengths. New teachers, too, would find agreed guidelines supportive.

To designate a member of staff as having a particular interest in and responsibility for children with special educational needs can also be helpful (Hodgson et al., 1984). While this should not detract from the responsibilities of the class teachers, it could make a source of expertise readily available and also identify someone within the school with whom children's progress or behaviour could be discussed when concern is first felt. Dessent (1985) recommends that any support offered to teachers should be easily accessible; should be based on the school's resources and organ-ization; and should be intended to reassure class teachers of their ability to respond adequately to children's needs. The staff member so designated would require specific expertise gained from appro-priate experience and attendance at courses (see McCabe, 1980; Sebba, 1985); he or she would then be able to provide real and immediate help to colleagues.

Mention has already been made of the separate special education sector. In some areas links of various kinds have been established between ordinary and special school staff (Fish, 1984; Moses, 1985), the latter providing the support and expertise for the ordinary classroom teacher as envisaged in the Warnock Report (DES, 1978b). The nature of the links vary from area to area and may involve the transfer of pupils from special education as well as staff. As far as special school staff are concerned, involvement in ordinary schools may involve teaching small groups of pupils with learning difficulties, or providing materials or advice.

It may now be clear why providing appropriate education for pupils with special educational needs in the ordinary school is expensive. There are also implications with regard to resources. In the infant school years requirements may be fairly light, as there is easy access to all the variety of materials suitable for children who are just beginning to acquire various skills. Where children move on to junior school provision at seven years of age, the resource implications are considerable and special allowances really need to be made to enable each school to build up a central store of useful, suitable equipment, books and learning aids.

In this chapter particular attention has been paid to pupils with learning difficulties, particularly difficulties in acquiring reading skills. Obviously, children's special educational needs are much wider than this. Although learning difficulties must be the school's major concern, the isolation of very withdrawn or silent children (who may be quite good readers) or the frustration of children with speech difficulties (see chapter 5) or problems in their relationships with adults or other children (see chapter 7) or the obstacles facing those who suffer from physical or sensory disabilities must not be overlooked. Even gifted children may have special educational needs, as was noted at the beginning of this chapter. In the early years at school, before children's views of themselves as learners, or indeed as people, have been fully formed, it is vitally important that they encounter skilled teaching and sensitive understanding.

9

Collaborating with Parents and Others

In recent years schools have increasingly come to recognize the importance of working closely with parents, the support services and the wider community rather than being isolated and closed institutions. This chapter will consider why parental involvement in education should be encouraged; the different roles and perceptions of parents and teachers in the early school years; informal and formal home–school relationships; and co-operation between schools and the various agencies concerned with the welfare of children.

PARENTAL INVOLVEMENT

Why Involve Parents in Education?

A series of reports on education have highlighted the crucial role of parents in the educational process. The Plowden Committee (CAC, 1967) stated in strong terms that one of the essentials for educational advance was a closer partnership between those two parties to every child's education. Although focusing attention on children, families and schools in 'educational priority areas', the Plowden Report considered that parental participation in education was vital in all types of primary school, pointing out that while it is not entirely clear whether performance is better it is likely that the positive association found between parental interest and children's attainments is the result of the continuous interaction between home and school. The Bullock Report on language learning and teaching (DES, 1975) supported this emphasis on parental involvement in education, drawing attention in particular to the importance of the child's parents in language development. Both the Plowden and Bullock Reports dealt mainly, though not wholly, with children who had no physical, mental or emotional disabilities. As mentioned in the previous chapter, the Warnock Report (DES, 1978b), *Special Educational Needs*, considered those children whose educational progress may be hampered by some form of developmental difficulty. Similarly to the two reports mentioned above the Warnock Report put special emphasis on the need for collaboration between parents and schools. The Report insisted, in a chapter devoted to the theme of 'Parents as Partners', that the successful education of children with special educational needs is dependent upon the full involvement of their parents and that parents should be seen as equal partners in the educational process. All three reports saw the relationship between parents and schools as mutually supportive, rather than one party being more dominant than the other.

The Plowden, Bullock and Warnock Committees all supported their views with references to the mass of research evidence which exists to confirm the links between children's home backgrounds and their performance at school (for reviews of this evidence, see Sharrock, 1970, 1980; Wolfendale, 1983). Research studies have particularly highlighted the relationship between parental interest in education and school achievement. 'Interested' parents are those, in particular, who believe that education is important, who give attention to their children's work and progress at school and who support their children's efforts in school by providing them with suitable facilities at home. Douglas (1964), for example, found in his survey that those children (aged eight and eleven) did best in attainment tests whose parents were the most interested in their education; and those who did worst were the ones with 'least interested' parents. This was partly a social-class effect, as the 'middle-class' parents tended to take more interest in their children's progress at school than 'working-class' parents, and they became relatively more interested as their children grew up; but the relation between school performance and parental interest persisted within each social class.

Douglas concluded, too, that those parents who made frequent visits to school and were seen most often by teachers also had high standards in, for example, the quality of the care which they gave their children at home. Although other factors (for example, the general condition of the home, size of family, quality of the school) are also important in school achievement, the advantages of children with interested parents are still considerable, even when adjustments are made to take account of these factors. The findings of the National Child Development Study confirm that the lower a child's achievement, the less likely are the parents to have shown interest in their child's education (Fogelman, 1983). Fontana (1981) considers that through their interest in their children's education, parents show the child both the importance they attach to him or her as a person and to his or her future. Teachers also benefit in that they get to know more about the child's background and can discuss learning problems where the parents may be able to help (for general consideration of parental involvement, see also Rutherford and Edgar, 1979; Craft et al., 1980; Pugh, 1981; Tizard et al., 1981).

Different Roles and Perceptions of Parents and Teachers

If parents and teachers are to co-operate constructively in the interests of the children with whom both parties are concerned, they need to understand each other's attitudes and perceptions of their roles. Although parents may legitimately take on a relatively formal teaching role at times, especially in the case of younger children (see pp. 169–71), it is necessary to recognize that parents and teachers have very different roles. It is the function both of parents and teachers of children in the early school years to ensure physical care and safety; to extend social awareness; to provide appropriate stimulation; to encourage positive attitudes to learning and exploration; and to exercise firm and consistent, but reasonable, control.

However, the parent–child relationship is inevitably a closer and more intimate one than the teacher–child relationship. The child looks to the parents to provide a secure home base and a continuous experience of warmth and affection. Teachers of young children do have to be warm and sympathetic in the classroom and even to act in a quasi-parental role at times, particularly when children are upset or disturbed at school; but, in their professional capacity, they are bound to be less intimate in their contacts with their pupils. As Taylor (1980) puts it, the orientation of teachers must necessarily be different from that of parents. The parental role emphasizes acceptance of the child, irrespective of standards of performance or of levels of attainment; the teacher's role demands a more objective, achievement-oriented approach. The essential differences in role between parents and teachers should not be overlooked whenever parents are encouraged to become involved in home-teaching schemes or the more formal aspects of school life or learning. The emotional relationship between individuals not infrequently gets in the way of the establishment of an effective teaching and learning situation.

Parental Views on Involvement in Education

Interviews carried out for the Plowden Committee (CAC, 1967) showed that parents of primary school children were, on the whole, satisfied with the opportunities for involvement provided by the schools. However, a considerable number of parents said that they would have liked more information about how their children were getting on at school; roughly a third thought that the teachers should have asked them more about their children. The Plowden Committee considered that the general satisfaction of parents may have been only evidence of their low expectations; when special efforts are made in a school, the response from parents is often beyond that when no demands are made upon them.

Chazan et al. (1976) sought the views of a sample of 116 parents of infant school children, living in different urban areas, on the opportunities which they had had for contact with the teachers and their impressions of their children's schooling. The overall picture gained indicated that there was a great deal of goodwill towards the infant schools on the part of parents, and a faith in the capability and effectiveness of the teachers. The parents put most emphasis on knowing more about their own child's individual progress. It was the parents living in the most disadvantaged conditions who were more inclined to feel that they should leave the child's education entirely to the school, and there were a few parents who were so completely overwhelmed by the problems of coping even at a minimal level with the demands of daily living that they could contribute little to their children's education. However, most of the parents in the sample were keen to help the school or their own child in any way possible.

Teachers' Perceptions of Parental Involvement

The Plowden Committee (CAC, 1967) found that primary school heads considered their relations with parents to be good, however rudimentary the arrangements for liaison with them actually were. Opportunities for parents to discuss school policy and practice or to talk about their children individually, were not provided to the extent that the Committee thought desirable. Chazan et al. (1976) report that most of the infant schools in their study were making efforts to reach the parents and that the schools' attitudes to parents were positive on the whole, but in practice parental involvement was limited and seen by schools in rather narrow terms. Urban infant schools showed little enthusiasm for formal contact with parents, for example, through parent–teacher associations, preferring informal contact when the children were collected. A wide range of attitudes to parental contact existed among school staffs. Some schools, especially those in 'middle-class' areas, seemed to regard parental help and interest as interference, while others felt the need for a closer link with parents, but, particularly in the 'deprived' areas, required more staff and support to enable them to achieve this. In general, few teachers were in favour of parents working in the classroom and, outside the deprived areas, most teachers felt that parents were already providing sufficient learning experiences in the home.

In summary, the studies referred to above indicate much individual variation in attitudes towards parental involvement in education among both parents and teachers of children in the early school years, as well as providing evidence of goodwill on both sides. As will be shown later in this chapter, some of the barriers which have prevented effective home–school partnership in the past are gradually breaking down. Nevertheless, it would seem that parents are still too often frustrated by a lack of positive response on the part of the school to their legitimate interest in their children's education and progress.

Changing Structure of the Family: Involving Fathers

In the past, professionals, including teachers, have tended to look upon mothers as their main point of contact in connection with the education and welfare of children neglecting the contribution fathers can make. The changes which have been taking place in the structure of the family as well as in the perception of parental roles make it both more necessary than ever that fathers should be fully involved in the educational process, and that it should also be easier to achieve this objective. These changes are: first, the trend towards more sharing of duties and responsibilities between mother and father. Second, that it can no longer be assumed that the father is the main breadwinner or that the mother is the main caretaker. The rising divorce rate, coupled with the increasing prevalence of single mothers, means far more children are living in one-parent families (Tizard et al., 1976; Rimmer and Wicks, 1984; Central Statistical

Office, 1986). In some areas the one-parent family rather than the nuclear two-parent family may be the norm. Third, rising unemployment has meant that more fathers are available in normal working-hours. Further, schools catering for ethnic-minority groups will know that in the case of immigrant families, traditional cultural and family patterns may dictate that only the mother, or only the father, deals with the school.

Supportive fathers can make all the difference to the physical and emotional state of mothers struggling to cope with running a home, often in difficult circumstances. Interested fathers can be of considerable help in fostering the development of their children. It is essential, therefore, that teachers and other professionals should do whatever they can to make contact with fathers as well as mothers.

Improving Home–School Relationships

Home–school relationships in the early school years are fostered in a variety of ways, both informal and formal. Most schools invite parents to watch their children performing in plays and concerts, or to Open Days when parents can look at children's work and discuss aspects of the school's activities. As mentioned above, many teachers and parents prefer contact by informal means. However, informal teacher–parent relationships can make only a limited contribution to the partnership between home and school, and in recent years a variety of developments has taken place to encourage more systematic and effective relationships between teachers and parents. In some cases, schools have gone beyond organizing functions at which parents and teachers can meet only briefly. Brind (1984), for example, gives an account of activities developed by a primary school for both mothers and children, which included the provision of children's story books to enhance the mothers' skills in reading, talking and listening; joint swimming sessions for mothers and children; various courses of interest to parents; and a monthly working lunch for the agencies involved with children and parents.

In Griffiths and Hamilton (1984), Wilkinshaw describes the efforts made by an infant school to involve the whole family in their work, as a part of the Inner London Education Authority's PACT scheme (Parents, Teachers and Children Project). In this school, the headteacher is freely available to see parents and the school is seen as a place for the entire family; a Parents, Teachers and Friends

Group has been organized; parents come in to read, tell stories and talk to children who speak their language; parents come into classrooms; and parents help to decorate the school, making it more attractive. Additionally, provision is made for toddlers and escorts on one afternoon a week, there are affiliations with a local playgroup and educational use is made of the resources of a nearby street market. PACT is particularly concerned to promote shared experiences between parents and children in connection with reading but, as Wilkinshaw states, the scheme in her school means much more than getting parents to help at home with reading – it means involving the staff with parents as a way of getting them to play a role in the life of the school and in their children's total education.

The path of progress in the attempts to improve home–school relationships has not been a smooth one. A large-scale national survey of parental involvement in primary schools, undertaken by the National Foundation for Educational Research, suggested that primary schools have progressed cautiously towards greater participation by parents in the educational process over the decade since the Plowden Report (Cyster and Clift, 1979, 1980). Nevertheless, the survey showed that teachers were still concerned to defend their professional teaching role from the intrusion of parental amateurs and to prevent an excessive ramification of their teaching role. As with any personal or professional partnership, relationships are fraught with potential difficulties – but this is no reason for resisting developments which are generally considered to be beneficial all round.

The main strategies for improving home–school contact which have been used in recent times include the expansion of parent–teacher associations or other types of joint group; involving parents more in the management of schools; increasing the participation of parents in the classroom and in tuition at home; home visits by teachers; and providing parents with more meaningful written information about both schools and the progress of their own children. These strategies will be discussed here, together with a consideration of how teachers might talk to parents.

Parent–teacher associations (PTAs) The Plowden Committee (CAC, 1967) found that only seventeen per cent of the national sample of primary schools surveyed had parent–teacher associations. The Committee recognized the value of these associations where good leadership is given by the headteacher but did not think that they were necessarily the best means of fostering close relationships between home and school, particularly as a smaller proportion of manual workers tend to go to PTA meetings than to any other type of function relating to school. In their sample of 116 parents, Chazan et al. (1976) reported that only nineteen out of thirty-one who had the opportunity belonged to a PTA. Some confusion seemed to exist in the mind of the parents interviewed in their study about what exactly constituted a parent–teacher association, especially in schools where occasional parents' meetings were arranged but no organized association had been established. The parents were divided in their responses to questions asking about their interest in belonging to a PTA if one were available to them:

'The schools do very well now. They can do better without parents pushing them.'

'I'm not pro PTAs – they just become social cliques.'

'It's enjoyable and it gives you a lot of information.'

'I've never thought about it. I don't know anything about them.'

'I wouldn't go – you've got to be like the Bingo people to go out like that.'

In the national survey reported by Cyster and Clift (1980), only thirty-five per cent of a sample of 1401 primary schools had a PTA, twenty-six per cent had a less formal parents' committee of some kind, and thirty-nine per cent were without any parent group as such. Some schools were of the opinion that formal parent–teacher associations were not attractive to many parents and, in fact, inhibited them from attendance.

Lynch and Pimlott (1980) give an account of new initiatives aimed at increasing parental concern, information and interaction in educational matters; increasing teacher interest in parental involvement; and assessing the impact of improvements in these areas. They formed, first, parents' and teachers' discussion groups separately and later teacher–parent discussion groups, with these objectives in mind and as a result found staff better informed and morale higher.

Parents as managers   In the past parents have been able to exercise very little influence on the management of schools, in spite of the fears of some headteachers that parents might interfere unduly with professional concerns. However, in recent years central authority has increasingly attempted to determine how schools should relate to parents (Thorp, 1985). The Report of the Taylor Committee (Taylor, 1977), established to make recommendations on school government, recommended strengthening school governing bodies, suggesting that a quarter of their membership should be elected by parents and another quarter should represent the staff of the school. In the subsequent 1980 Education Act it was specified only that there should be at least two parent governors and one elected teacher governor (two in the case of schools with over 300 pupils). The 1986 Education Act, however, does strengthen the parental representation on school governing bodies, as this will be increased to a quarter of the membership (the same as local authority representation). The 1986 Act also requires school governing bodies to prepare an annual report for parents.

Pollard (1985) observes that although accountability of schools to the community is gradually increasing and parents can seek to have an effect on school policies – for example, through PTAs or representation on boards of governors – they do so from a relatively powerless position, especially as they lack detailed information about the internal workings of schools (see also Golby, 1985). Kogan et al. (1984) found that in many cases the influence of governing bodies has been minimal, except where involved in staff appointments. Nevertheless there is potential for school governing bodies to provide the machinery for constructive collaboration between parents and schools (see Slater, 1985; and Thorp, 1985 for a discussion of the functions of school governors).

Participation of parents in classroom and tuition at home   Helping on school visits and outings, assisting at school functions, making equipment, fund-raising, sewing and doing minor repairs are all parental activities acceptable to many parents and schools (Plowden Report, CAC, 1967; Cyster and Clift, 1980). The study carried out by Chazan et al. (1976) found that the majority of infant schools encouraged parents to help their children at home but few were prepared to allow them to assist in the work of the classroom: only one school out of a sample of thirty-six had tried using parent help in the classroom. However, Cyster and Clift (1980) found that, in spite of widely expressed professional misgivings on the part of teachers, more than a quarter of primary schools had parents in to hear children read. They reported, too, that classroom-based involvement was generally more frequent in schools catering for the lower age-ranges. This was mainly because of the day-to-day contact between parents and teachers made possible when children were escorted to school; increasing organizational formality on the part of schools as the child grew older; and less of a feeling of ignorance about the curriculum in the case of parents with young children. Factors affecting school-based parental involvement included the openness and informality of the school (particularly marked for the infant age-group) and school size, but social class seemed to be the strongest influence.

The idea of parents going into the classroom to help the teacher was novel to most parents in the survey conducted by Chazan et al. (1976). Sixty out of 116 parents responded positively to questions about their willingness to be involved in the infant school classroom, but twenty-seven had reservations and twenty-nine said that they would be unwilling or unable to help in the classroom:

'I wanted to be a teacher. I'd love to help in any way.'

'I have no patience with other people's children.'

'It's not my cup of tea, but it's a good idea.'

Schemes involving parents in their children's reading   The extent to which parents should take an active role in teaching their children to read has been the subject of much debate. Some professionals are of the opinion that the teaching function should be left solely to them, and certainly not everyone will agree with the view expressed by Young and Tyre (1985) that parents should be the main educators of their children in reading, writing and spelling in the early years. However, during the past decade there has been a growing interest in encouraging parents to help their children read at home, stimulated by a number of studies and experimental projects.

Hewison and Tizard (1980), in a study of the relationship between home background and reading ability, found that the home-background factor which emerged as most strongly related to reading achievement was whether or not the mother regularly heard the child read. In a subsequent empirical study evaluating the effects of a sample of final-year infant school, inner-city children reading regularly to their parents from books sent home by the class teacher, it was reported that highly significant gains resulted from the extra reading practice. In this experiment, parents were given advice on 'good practice', but no specific training. Portsmouth et al.

(1985) also used a 'listening skills' approach with children with moderate learning difficulties adapted from a Home Tutorship procedure devised by Glynn et al. (1980). In this scheme, guidelines were provided to the parents advocating spending ten minutes with the child on at least three occasions a week, showing enthusiasm and giving plenty of praise, being calm and relaxed and discussing the meanings of new or difficult words and the content of pictures and stories.

A rather more structured technique of parental involvement known as Paired Reading has also proved popular with a number of parents and schools (Morgan, 1976; Morgan and Lyon, 1979; Bushell et al., 1982; Topping and McKnight, 1984). In this approach, children and parents are taught specific techniques of *simultaneous* and *independent* reading. In the initial stages, the parent and child read together *simultaneously*, with the main aim of avoiding any feeling of failure on the part of the child, who is helped by the parents to read any word that presents difficulty. The parent is encouraged to give a lot of praise. At a later stage, the child moves on to *independent* reading, stopping when meeting a word he or she cannot tackle. A simple signal leads the parent to join in and *simultaneous* reading is reverted to until the child feels ready to carry on alone again. Paired Reading schemes usually last for several months and seem to produce significant gains in reading (Topping and McKnight, 1984).

Lindsay et al. (1985) raise the question whether the gains obtained from Paired Reading are due specifically to the techniques employed, or rather to other factors, notably a general reduction in anxiety which has been reported in several studies. Lindsay et al. compare Paired Reading approaches with a simpler method called Relaxed Reading, which aims to encourage children reading with their parents in a way which is non-anxiety provoking. The focus in this approach is on showing parents and children how to read together in a warm, positive and rewarding atmosphere. The parents are also shown how parent–child endeavours can end up disastrously, with the parent being negative and critical and the child becoming upset and resistant. A small-scale comparison between Paired Reading and Relaxed Reading approaches suggests that both methods can lead to substantial improvement in reading ability.

Home-tuition schemes encouraging relaxed parent–child collaborative efforts have shown sufficiently promising results to justify further experiment, particularly as they usually involve the school as well as parents and children. Nevertheless it has to be recognized that there may be parents who are unable to adopt a relaxed attitude in any kind of teaching situation where their own child is concerned.

Home visits by teachers   The Plowden Committee (CAC, 1967) reported that some primary schools were undertaking home-visiting with success but did not recommend home visits by teachers as a universal recipe for success, at the same time stressing that if the parents did not come near the school some agency should go to them. Chazan et al. (1976) found that although some teachers had no objection to visiting homes on invitation, the majority were either reluctant to visit or opposed to it except in an emergency. Rural schools were somewhat more positive than urban schools towards home-visiting, probably because relationships between teachers and parents tend to be closer in small rural communities. In the same enquiry, the vast majority of parents (104 out of 116) said that they would be quite happy to welcome a teacher to their home. Even so, there was a considerable difference of opinion as to whether these visits were of real value, or whether they should be regarded as a 'last resort':

'I'd love to have the teacher here and be able to talk in private.'

'I wouldn't mind myself, but I think it might upset the child.'

'You should only expect teachers to do this if a serious problem arose.'

In their national survey, Cyster and Clift (1980) report that in twenty-two per cent of primary schools, predominantly nursery schools and schools with nursery classes, home-visiting was undertaken by the headteachers or assistant teachers. Home-visiting by educational welfare officers or home-liaison workers of various kinds was carried out in about a half of all primary schools.

Providing written information for parents   There is general agreement that parents should be provided with appropriate written information both on the school which their child is attending (or about to attend) and on the progress being made by the child at school. The national survey carried out by Cyster and Clift (1980) found that sixty-five per cent of primary schools sent written information about themselves to new parents, with ninety-two per cent inviting new parents to visit them before their child started school. Less than half of all primary schools sent written reports about the individual child's work or behaviour, those doing so being predominantly the schools for children older than seven years.

The Plowden Report (CAC, 1967) encouraged the use of informative booklets, giving parents the basic facts about such matters as the organization of the school, size of classes, grouping methods used and how to get in touch with teachers. Under the Education (School Information) Regulations 1981 (DES, 1981b), local education authorities are required to give parents access to information about local schools. The London Borough of Brent (1985), for example, fulfilling this requirement, publishes a booklet on 'Primary Schools and Under-Fives Facilities', which is available in three languages besides English. This booklet lists all the schools relevant to the age-group covered, explains nursery, primary and special educational provision, discusses the curriculum and achievement levels to be expected, encourages parental involvement and advises parents about their rights of appeal in connection with choice of school. The booklet is additional to published information provided by individual schools within the borough.

Much criticism has been directed at the kind of written reports which schools have given to parents in the past about individual pupils. The Plowden Committee considered that they were so conventional that they conveyed nothing to parents. Fontana (1981) observes that school reports are not specific enough in indicating how any aspect of the child's progress or behaviour which is unsatisfactory can be put right. Vague phrases such as 'could do better' succeed only in upsetting the parents and confusing the child. What is needed instead is practical guidance which can be put into effect by the child, if appropriate with the help of his or her parents. It is clear that schools need to give fresh consideration to the ways in which they report to parents on the progress of their children, ensuring that any written report serves the purpose of beginning a dialogue between parents and teacher.

Talking to parents   As Hurford and Stow (1985) underline, teachers have little formal or informal preparation for the delicate task of talking to parents. To help teachers in this task, they organized one-day workshops which emphasized: (a) the importance of listening to parents; (b) the need to avoid making overhasty judgements about causal factors or offering instant advice, while at the same time not appearing to be defensive in an uncaring way; (c) how to help parents to relax, by showing warmth, empathy and a genuine interest in them; and (d) ways of stating one's own viewpoint in a non-threatening way, in particular by taking responsibility for the part of the problem which affects the teacher and by avoiding attributing teachers' difficulties to the parents.

The content of their discussions with parents is often a cause for anxiety among teachers, who wonder what kind of questions they might ask and what questions they ought to avoid. Chazan et al. (1983) provide some guidance on talking to parents in their handbook for teachers of nursery groups concerned about behaviour difficulties, and much of this is applicable also to teachers of children between five and eight. The main aims of teachers' discussions with parents are considered to be: (a) to seek and to give information about the child's development; (b) if appropriate, to find out whether the family has had, or needs, contact with any of the support services; and (c) to see to what extent and in what ways teachers can work with parents in the interests of the child. It is suggested that initially only fairly straightforward and non-disturbing questions should be asked, for example about factual aspects of the family background; the child's physical attributes; intellectual and linguistic performance at home; general behaviour; interests; and activities. At a later stage, it may be appropriate to talk to parents at a deeper level but only if the parents seem to be receptive and willing to talk about a particular problem. At all times parents should be encouraged to express their ideas and should receive sympathetic attention. A checklist of possible questions to ask and topics to discuss is provided in Chazan et al.'s handbook.

THE SUPPORT SERVICES

A variety of support services is available to help schools in their work, particularly in relation to pupil welfare. Local educational authorities have a body of specialist advisors, closely involved in the functioning of schools. There are also medical, psychological and social services with statutory responsibilities for promoting physical and mental health in children. These services do not always work together as harmoniously and constructively as might be desired; teachers, especially of younger children, are sometimes over-reluctant to call upon them – and when they do invoke their help, schools are not always satisfied with the response they get. As teachers are sometimes uncertain about the roles and functions of the different support services, it will be useful to discuss them here. The part played by a wide range of voluntary agencies concerned with the care and welfare of children, particularly those with special needs, has expanded over the years and merits consideration too.

Educational Services

Advisers   Advisers and local inspectors are an important point of contact and communication with schools. They have a wide range of responsibilities, including personnel matters, curriculum development and in-service training, and are highly influential in matters of school policy and planning (Cohen and Mannion, 1981). They tend to be seen as relating particularly to the headteachers and class teachers may regard them as somewhat remote (Johnson et al., 1980).

Support teachers   In addition to a team of advisers with more general responsibilities in the education service, most authorities have a body of advisory and remedial teachers available to help with specific problems, especially reading failure and behaviour difficulties. Hannon and Mullins (1980) carried out a survey of the first year of operation in the setting up of a support-teacher service in an urban area as a part of provision to help ordinary schools cope with children with special educational needs. Most of the class teachers at the receiving end said that the support teacher had not only provided advice and support but had actually taught the children in question. There was general satisfaction with the help received, although some uncertainty was apparent about whether the support teacher should focus on giving advice or on actual teaching.

Croll and Moses (1985) report that, typically, remedial and advisory services wait for the headteacher to invite them into the school. In their survey, several authorities referred to recent changes in the organization and functioning of advisory and remedial services. Until recently, it had been common practice for peripatetic teachers to help individual children through withdrawal but to an increasing extent these teachers had expanded their advisory role in the hope of enabling class teachers to cope more efficiently with all the children in their classes. At the time of the survey, some authorities were aiming at having at least one teacher with some training in handling learning difficulties on the staff of a school.

Educational Welfare Officers The major work of Educational Welfare Officers in the educational service concerns the enforcement of compulsory school attendance. However, they have become increasingly involved in wider aspects of child and family welfare, such as child employment, neglect, the provision of clothing and meals and arrangements for school transport of handicapped children (MacMillan, 1977; Finch, 1984). As they frequently visit schools as well as homes they are readily accessible to teaching staffs and can act as a bridge between the school and the social services.

Medical and Related Services

The school health service, which was the responsibility of local education authorities until 1974, is now under the aegis of the National Health Service. As Finch (1984) points out, although the school health service is concerned with the health of all children, one of the major areas of its work has been the identification and assessment of handicapped children. Fitzherbert (1980) observed that the most favoured school health service model at the time of writing was for a single, detailed medical examination for all children at school entry, followed by the annual screening of particular functions (vision and hearing for instance) by a nurse or technician, backed up by regular meetings between doctors, nurses and teachers about children giving cause for concern. Although most serious sensory or physical defects are discovered at an early stage, the existence of previously undetected defects of vision or hearing at the age of seven demontrates the part which teachers in the first school can play in identifying and reporting any such problems which become apparent in the classroom (Ingram, 1973; Fogelman, 1983).

The role of the school nurse, because of her expertise and accessibility, has been recognized as increasingly important and her work is generally valued, as is the contribution of speech therapists, now employed by the National Health Service but often spending a great deal of time in schools. However, although the provision of speech therapy services has improved since the Quirk Report (DES, 1972) drew attention to the inadequacy of the supply of speech therapists to meet the demand, there is still a shortage of speech therapists in some areas. The current emphasis on the early identification of speech problems should encourage teachers of young children and speech therapists to work closely together (see also chapter 5, pp. 93–5).

School Psychological Services

Among their functions, local authority School Psychological Services have responsibilities relating to the identification and assessment of children considered to have special educational needs; ensuring that such children are suitably placed; and advising on appropriate management and intervention strategies. Educational psychologists are increasingly keen to collaborate with schools in the prevention of learning and behaviour difficulties and also to become more involved, both directly and indirectly, with children other than those presenting problems. They tend to work mainly in schools rather than in clinics or outside centres, preferring to use the school as the base for meeting both teachers and parents in connections with individual cases referred to them. Many School Psychological Services provide a range of in-service courses for teachers, as well as workshops for parents.

Educational psychologists are anxious to identify vulnerable children at as early a stage as possible, and many local education authorities carry out some kind of formal screening procedure at about the age of seven or eight, if not before, designed to identify pupils who are failing to make satisfactory progress at school. Screening can lead to constructive dialogue between psychologist and school, not only in relation to individual children considered to be 'at risk' but also over general policy and curriculum issues such as the teaching of reading in a school.

Teachers and educational psychologists, who themselves normally include a teachers' certificate and teaching experience among their qualifications, have a great deal in common and there is much scope for constructive collaboration between them. However, working relationships between teachers and educational psychologists are not always as good as they might be (see Muckley, 1981). Teachers of young children, although very conscious of the many-sided needs of the developing child, tend to refrain too often from calling on the educational psychologist, preferring on the whole to rely on their own internal resources for coping with learning or behaviour difficulties in their pupils, perhaps seeing referral to the School Psychological Service as a 'last resort'

(Chazan and Jackson, 1971). This may be because they are reluctant to admit that they cannot cope with a young child without outside help, or because they do not fully appreciate the nature of the support which psychologists can provide, or because they do not feel that psychologists can give them what they want. Lovejoy (1985), reviewing the literature concerned with the reactions of headteachers and teachers to the help provided by school psychological services, concludes that in many cases school staffs have expectations of the educational psychologist's role which are different from those expectations that the psychologist may have. This conflict of role-perception is likely to damage the relationship between the professions and affect the effectiveness of the services offered. In general, teachers tend to want practical help with children causing them difficulties, while psychologists tend to emphasize preventive work involving projects which will indirectly help larger numbers of children.

Conclusions such as these highlight the need for teachers and educational psychologists to engage in discussion about each other's roles, functions and expectations. It is unfortunate that in practice it is very unusual for a class teacher to be able to make individual contact with an educational psychologist, even if he or she visits the school regularly, since negotiations normally take place through the primary headteacher (Croll and Moses, 1985).

Social Services

Unlike the services discussed above, local authority Social Service Departments are 'community-based' rather than 'school-attached'. School-attached services, as Welton (1985) states, work mainly with and through schools, whereas community-based professions, such as social workers and police juvenile liaison officers, have school-age children as only part of their client group and see the school as just one of the several institutions with which their clients may have contact. Social workers have a wide range of statutory responsibilities relating to the welfare of families, particularly those faced with considerable stress, whatever the nature of that stress may be. They are concerned to help children who may be handicapped, or at risk of abuse or neglect. They share many common interests with teachers but are not always as closely involved with schools as might be desirable.

Davie (1977) points out that social workers and teachers rarely meet during training and that as a result their framework of professional concepts will differ quite markedly. Social workers and teachers work in services which have different organizational structures and different orientations. Social workers tend to develop a family-oriented or community perspective, whereas the teacher's orientation will usually be child-centred. M. Robinson (1980) discusses the overlapping perspectives of social work and education which have characterized the growth of both the services, while pointing to the inevitability that they should have developed so separately. Robinson stresses that both social workers and teachers alike need to acquire skills in relationship and communication, although they may use these skills differently according to the tasks which they undertake.

In spite of their different orientations every advantage is to be gained from close contact between social workers and schools catering for five to eight year-olds. At this stage, in particular, school staffs tend to know their pupils well and have easier contact with parents than is usually possible in the case of older children.

Voluntary Bodies

A variety of voluntary bodies exist which supplement the work of the statutory services and attempt to influence educational policy and provision, as well as filling gaps in information and, in some cases, facilities. They perform a particularly valuable function in relation to a wide range of children with special educational needs, offering advice, support and practical help to parents and others, particularly in the case of the mentally and physically disabled. (For information on relevant voluntary associations concerned with special needs, see Stone and Taylor, 1977; Lansdown, 1980; Male and Thompson, 1985.) There are also a number of national and local organizations which cover general educational matters, including parent–teacher relationships. Organizations such as the Advisory Centre for Education, the Confederation for the Advancement of State Education, the National Confederation of Parent–Teacher Associations, the Home and School Council and the Children's Legal Centre (to mention only a few) have greatly helped to raise the level of public understanding about educational issues and to make parents more aware of their rights (see Stone and Taylor, 1976; National Council for Voluntary Organizations, 1983). Although voluntary organizations sometimes serve as an outlet for the expression of frustration and dissatisafaction about the practice and policies of schools, it is to be hoped that they will be seen by teachers as helping the cause of education rather than in any threatening way.

Working Together

There is already a great deal of purposeful and constructive collaboration between teachers and the support services. Webb (1969) observes that the teaching staff would have been unable to help many of the infant school children with difficulties who are discussed in her book without the co-operation, support and treatment of various kinds offered by agencies on the fringe of, or completely outside, the educational system. Nevertheless, there is much room for improved communication between school and support services. Fitzherbert (1980) asserts that the lack of knowledge of and interest in the child-care services in education on the part of the teaching profession has for years proved to be an obstacle in their development. Considerable confusion is often evident in the attitudes of teachers towards intervening in family or personal problems and many teachers seem to find the combination of teaching and welfare roles difficult. Fitzherbert, highlighting inter-disciplinary co-operation as an important skill for all concerned with children, stresses the need for teachers to be constructively critical consumers of the other child-care services.

It is all too easy for schools to become isolated from the community they serve, or to erect a mere facade of co-operation with parents and others. In stressing the value of a genuine partnership between schools and both parents and the support services, this chapter has drawn attention to a variety of productive and imaginative ways in which such a partnership can be encouraged and fostered.

10

Change and Continuity

INTRODUCTION

Since the introduction of comprehensive secondary schooling in the early 1970s, for the first time it has been possible to view children's formal education as a continuous process from five to sixteen years of age. This long perspective of education is one the government is keen to foster and, over the last few years, a stream of curricular papers concerning five to sixteen year-olds (for example, DES 1979, 1980, 1981a, 1984), reports, surveys and discussion documents (DES, 1978–85) has emerged from official sources.

A recurrent theme in many of these documents has been a concern to establish more effective continuity both within and between successive stages of schooling. Educational continuity remains an area little researched, with the exception of studies which have focused on the primary–secondary transition (see Galton and Willcocks, 1983; Stillman and Maychell, 1984; Derricott, 1985; Gorwood, 1986). However, further down the age-range, two National Foundation for Educational Research projects have examined the problems surrounding children's earliest transitions from home to nursery or playgroup and, later, on first entry to school (Blatchford et al., 1982; Cleave et al., 1982). Although the importance of curriculum continuity and consistency is raised by HMI in the survey of primary schools (DES, 1978a), very few studies directly address the question of continuity of experience within a particular stage of schooling.

This chapter is an attempt to clarify some of the issues surrounding the concepts of change and continuity, concentrating particularly on the implications for curriculum planning and co-ordination, as well as assessment and record-keeping in the early stages of schooling. Consideration will also be given to the strategies teachers might adopt to ease the transition for children on both entering and leaving infant school.

CHANGE

There are many sound arguments for the education given to pupils to change as they grow up. These changes, or transitions, reflect the varying needs of the pupil and the increasing demands of society as the pupil nears adulthood (Stillman and Maychell, 1984, p. 1).

Children, like adults, enjoy and are stimulated by novelty and change. (Plowden Report, CAC, 1967, para. 427).

Throughout their education children have to accommodate to many changes. Perhaps the greatest and potentially most traumatic is the initial move from home to school. From five years of age onwards children inevitably have to adjust to a yearly change of class, usually of teacher and perhaps of friends and curriculum too. The majority of children will, at some point in their school career, change school, if not once then twice, as they progress to a more advanced stage of education and a minority will transfer more often, if their parents move to another area for example. Recent census figures indicate that over 600,000 children move house each year and, while not all these moves will entail a change of school, it is estimated that a large number of children – sufficient to populate a sizeable city – will transfer schools for this reason (Clift et al., 1981). Change of itself is not necessarily a bad thing, provided, of course, that it is adequately prepared for and not too sudden – points stressed by the Plowden Report – if the change is to stimulate and not dishearten.

Although the literature tends to dwell on the negative aspects of change, there can be advantages which should not be overlooked. Some children will welcome the opportunity of a fresh start that changing class or school can offer; not only those who have acquired a bad reputation or who are not progressing well, as many able children thrive in new environments (Gorwood, 1986). However, increased awareness of the emotional difficulties that can accompany changes in stages of schooling has meant that the pastoral aspects of transition have received more attention and, perhaps, have been more successfully dealt with than the thorny problem of curriculum continuity. This disparity was remarked upon by HMI in the survey of primary schools (DES, 1978a, p. 38): 'While considerable efforts were clearly made to ease children's transition from one school to the next, the importance of continuity in the curriculum of the schools was largely overlooked.'

CONTINUITY

Continuity has been defined as the degree to which curricular activities offered to children relate to and build on their previous experience (Richards, 1981). It is used in relation to children's experience in any one class during the course of a school year, or as they move from class to class within a school, or on transfer from one stage of schooling to the next. It is arguable whether complete continuity, both within and between schools, is educationally desirable or even attainable without a total reorganization of the education system around a centrally agreed curriculum. However, although the freedom that a devolved system allows is welcome, it seems reasonable to try to ensure that differences between classes and schools should not be so extreme that they become confusing or disturbing to children. Nor should the kinds of situations so graphically described by Dean (1980) be encouraged:

> situations in which teachers are critical of what has happened previously and miss the strengths of past experience. There are teachers who do not build on what has gone before, teachers who start their pupils all over again from the beginning without noting what has been done; teachers who mistrust their professional colleagues and are not interested in what they say. (p. 44)

As mentioned earlier, the concept and overall implications of curricular continuity are not so easily discussed as the more obvious and immediate problems surrounding transitions from school to school, where the 'emphasis is predominantly procedural, largely concerned with the induction of new pupils and parents, record keeping and transfer' (Findlay, 1984, p. 126). Continuity obviously includes such strategies but is a much wider issue which requires teachers to see their work with children in the context of the children's total educational experience and to be convinced of the need to improve continuity. It also means teachers relinquishing some of their much-prized autonomy so as better to understand and appreciate the work of colleagues in relation to their own, as well as developing a more collaborative style of planning and teaching. Although joint planning is important when providing a continuous education for young children, teachers should also consider carefully the kinds of record-keeping which will provide useful and accessible information about children and what they have been taught for the benefit of successive teachers and the classes in their care. As Dean (1980) comments: 'We have given lip-service to the idea of continuity for many years. Continuity will only happen when our commitment is sufficient to give it a high level of priority. There is a very real need to do so' (p. 52).

STARTING SCHOOL

Children starting school for the first time at about five years of age are likely to have had a variety of very different pre-school experiences. It is becoming increasingly unlikely nowdays that children will come into the reception class straight from home without ever having attended some form of pre-school provision. Cleave et al. (1982), in their study of continuity from pre-school to school, found only one such child in their sample of twenty-six. The range of pre-school facilities and settings is wide and diverse and some children are likely to have sampled more than one type before schooling begins. The majority of children are likely to have attended either a playgroup or a nursery school/class on a part-time basis for up to two years prior to school entry. Largely because nursery education is not mandatory, LEA provision of nursery schools and classes varies enormously from one part of the country to the next. Although some rural authorities attach importance to nursery education, provision is likely to be greater in urban areas, with a consequently larger proportion of children entering school from a nursery background, than rural areas where the majority of children may have had playgroup experience only; pre-school services are also unevenly distributed according to social class, in favour of professional and managerial families (Osborn et al., 1984). Children attending playgroup may have spent as little as two hours a week away from home whereas children in nursery schools/classes may have attended for as many as twelve or more hours a week. A few children beginning school may have been in the care of a child-minder or placed in a day nursery from an early age (other possibilities include community nurseries, combined nursery centres or even work-place crèches).

Thus, on the first morning at school the reception-class teacher is faced not only with children of different temperament, abilities and home circumstances but also with possibly equally divergent pre-school experiences encountered in a variety of settings. How can teachers build on such a range of experiences in order to minimize the potentially distressing effects that starting school can have on children?

Cleave et al. (1982) found that three 'ingredients' were essential if children were to settle happily into school. First, sudden changes were to be avoided and new experiences introduced only gradually. Second, it was helpful if children were to some extent familiar with the school and staff rather than everyone and everywhere being totally alien. Third, children needed to have a sense of security in order to cope adequately with this quite momentous change in their lives. This study also revealed some of the strategies employed by teachers and schools to help ease the transition into full-time schooling. The next part of the chapter will be devoted to a consideration of these, together with suggestions from other sources (Palmer, 1971; Basham, 1982; Pre-School Playgroups Association, 1983). It is evident that a stress-free start at school requires (a) careful preparation some weeks or months ahead; (b) sensitive handling on the first day; and (c) judicious monitoring at least until half-term.

Preparation for Starting School

The majority of infant schools arrange for parents and children to visit the school at least once before term begins. The format of these visits can vary enormously from school to school but usually they are seen as an opportunity for the headteacher and parents to exchange information and for the new entrants to be introduced to their teachers and classroom. Children who have brothers or sisters in the school or who attend a nursery class attached to the school may be, to some extent, already familiar with the building and some of the teachers. 'One-off' visits of this kind, although better than nothing, do have major drawbacks. They are usually too brief to be satisfactory either as an information-gathering exercise or for teachers and children even to begin to get to know one another, particularly if the groups are large. (Some teachers in the NFER study failed to recognize a single child after a visit of this kind.) It is also usual for these visits to take place in the term prior to entry, which in the case of September entrants may mean a lapse of perhaps two months or more over the summer holidays.

Although more difficult to arrange, a possibly better alternative would be an initial introductory meeting for all parents and prospective pupils, followed by a series of visits spaced over a few weeks for groups of half a dozen children and parents at a time. Coming into the class to listen to a story at story-time, for example, can be a pleasant introduction to school and is not perhaps so daunting a prospect for a newcomer as being thrust into an integrated session in full swing. Regular visits to the reception class should be easy to arrange for children attending a nursery class in the same school. However, Cleave et al. (1982) found that liaison between infant and nursery departments was not always good and was often hampered by the physical isolation of the nurseries. These were commonly housed in separate buildings fenced off from the main part of the school or at the end of a long spur of corridor with separate entrances and exits. If bringing children from the nursery into school proves difficult, it might be possible for the reception teacher(s) to visit them in the nursery – perhaps during the infants' morning assembly. In this way teachers can observe their prospective charges in an environment in which they feel confident and at ease and may be able to have contact with their future pupils in a much more relaxed manner than in the new and possibly threatening situation of the reception class.

Nursery teachers usually send some kind of information to the infant school about new entrants, although this can vary from verbal reports, to folders of children's work, to official LEA record cards where these begin at nursery age. Cleave et al. (1982) comment that quite detailed records were often ignored by reception teachers, who preferred to make their own judgements about a child without being influenced by the opinions of others. There seems to be a definite case here for nursery and reception teachers to get together and discuss the kinds of information which can usefully be passed on and the form these records should take. It may well be that the records a nursery teacher passes on might need to be different from those she keeps for her own benefit.

If liaison between nursery and reception teachers in the same schools is not always good, it is not surprising that Cleave et al. discovered that liaison with other forms of pre-school provision was often non-existent. Playgroup leaders and matrons of day nurseries were usually more than willing to provide schools with information about children or to have teachers visit but there was often reluctance on the part of schools to initiate any contact. What little contact there was between schools and playgroups, for instance, seemed more likely to have arisen through informal chance meetings than by design. However, if a large proportion of children entering the reception class are coming from playgroups it would surely be worthwhile to forge links with the playgroup leaders. It might be difficult for infant teachers to be freed from the classroom to visit playgroups but there is no reason why playgroup leaders and a group of children should not come to school for a short series of visits. Indeed, the Pre-School Playgroups Association to which many playgroups are affiliated, is very aware of the difficulties that can arise when children begin school. A conference held by the northern region in 1983 came up with a list of recommendations urging closer co-operation between school, parents and playgroups as well as an appraisal of pre-entry practices with a view to standardizing the approaches used by schools (PPA, 1983).

There seem to be powerful barriers of professional suspicion which prevent schools from developing a good liaison system with the pre-school facilities in their area. Thus, for a variety of reasons, some children arrive at school with little preparation and are met by teachers who know very little, if anything, about them — circumstances which are not conducive to instilling a sense of security in children. To summarize, several suggestions have been made for preparing children adequately for starting school:

1 children should be given the opportunity to visit the school on several occasions before entry;
2 teachers should forge links with all the pre-school facilities in the area, perhaps by exchanging visits;
3 teachers should discuss with pre-school staff and parents the kinds of records/information they find useful to have prior to entry.

The First Day at School

First impressions can be critical and it is vital that teachers handle the arrival of new children with care and sensitivity if they are to settle successfully. Admitting large numbers of children together is not to be recommended, as the noise, bustle and lack of individual attention can be very bewildering and distressing. It would be much better to adopt a staggered system of admission with children and parents arriving at intervals throughout the day or, as some schools do, extend this period over a few days or even weeks. When deciding upon an admission procedure, staff will have to take into account the type of class the children are entering — it may be an established vertically grouped class, for example, or consist of entirely new entrants, dependent, perhaps, on whether it is LEA policy to admit annually, termly or twice yearly. Cleave et al. (1982) found that children were less likely to become upset when they were welcomed personally one at a time and when parents were allowed time to chat with the teacher and then with the child for a while if they wished. Having a coat-peg and drawer ready with the child's name on it or a name badge to wear helped the child's self-esteem. Again, having a variety of toys and activities set out made it easy for the child either to become involved, watch what others were doing or explore.

One of the major differences children have to accommodate to when entering school is the length of time they are away from home. The school day is much longer than short playgroup sessions or the half-days of nursery class, and many young children find it extremely tiring, not least because the time is filled with unfamiliar sights, sounds and activities. Some schools solve this problem by allowing reception children to attend mornings only for a few weeks, or shortening the day by curtailing the lunch break and omitting the afternoon break altogether. It needs to be borne in mind, however, that shortening the length of the school day can make things difficult for parents who are collecting older children or for reception children who are escorted home by older brothers or sisters in the same school.

Another big difference and potential source of stress for newcomers is the size of the school building and the much greater range of territory to which they will have access. Typically, playgroups and nurseries are housed in large single rooms with integral toilet and cloakroom facilities and an outside play area immediately adjacent. In comparison, infant or primary schools are much bigger, often with long corridors, perhaps on several levels connected by staircases, with a hall, dining room and possibly several toilets, cloakrooms and playgrounds. This confusing building will also be filled with large numbers of older, bigger children and a bewildering range of adults. For the first few days it is probably wise to confine new children to the immediate vicinity of their classroom, gradually extending their range and introducing them to the wider geography of the remainder of the school as and when necessary or when it is felt they can cope. A guided tour of the route to the toilets, cloakrooms and the playground, together with introductions to any member of staff met on the way, would be a natural way to begin this exploration on the first day. Where toilet facilities are distant from the classroom, having an older child accompany new entrants for the first few days will prevent them from getting lost or, indeed, being afraid to ask to go because of this uncertainty. Organizing class toileting expeditions is generally not a good idea, as they take up a lot of time and can be very off-putting to children who may not need to go at that moment.

Both Cleave et al. (1982) and the PPA (1983) highlight playtimes and mealtimes as periods likely to be a source of continuing difficulty, even for children who otherwise appear to have settled in school well. The idea of a fixed compulsory time for going outside to play is likely to be completely new for children who may have experienced little or no outside play, depending on the type of pre-school they attended (if indeed they did attend any). Certainly, nearly all nursery classes have a fenced-off outdoor play space complete with a range of toys and equipment, as do some playgroups, but children would rarely be compelled to go out if they did not want to do so. The problem with most school playgrounds for young children is their comparatively large size, their general lack of amenities, apart from the odd bench or climbing frame, and the overwhelming numbers of boisterous older children rushing about.

Several strategies have proved effective in making playtime more enjoyable for new children, all or some of which could be adopted by schools wishing to make improvements in this area. First, having a familiar adult outside on duty helps and so perhaps the reception teacher could re-arrange the duty rota so that her playground supervisions all fall in the first few weeks of term. Having a separate playtime for younger children is another possibility. This does cut down the numbers but has the disadvantage of preventing children from playing with older brothers and sisters or friends, which can be a comfort in the early days. A much better idea is to pair off new entrants with older children, who are given responsibility for looking after them. In this way first or only children in a family can be made to feel more secure by the presence of an older child who is wise in the ways of the school. A final suggestion, and one which many schools are already beginning to implement, is to make playgrounds more inviting places, perhaps creating quiet corners using low walls and seating or providing more equipment made of vandal-proof materials such as large concrete drain pipes.

For newcomers staying at school for a mid-day meal, the long break at that time can be particularly trying. It can mean spending as much as an hour out in the playground being supervised by ancillary helpers generally known as 'dinner ladies'. Often children are not allowed inside unless it is actually raining, which can mean a cold miserable introduction to dinnertimes for children who begin school in January. Schools in the NFER study did very little to mitigate the distressing effects of long, cold dinner breaks but the researchers did make some suggestions that are worth considering. Where schools have two sittings for dinner the new children could go to the second sitting, thus breaking the long play period into two more manageable periods, one of which could, perhaps, be spent indoors. Providing portable play equipment, especially for younger children (such as bean bags, hoops, skittles and skipping ropes), could help to alleviate boredom, particularly if parent volunteers were encouraged to come and help out in the early days. They could help to organize ring games or join in games of catch or skittles, making the dinner hour a much more enjoyable experience.

Staying to dinner can in itself be an ordeal for new children, involving complex new routines of toileting and hand-washing and being marshalled from one part of the building to another in company with many other children. Dining rooms, particularly in larger primary schools, must seem very noisy, confusing places to small children unused to eating under such bustling crowded conditions. In the NFER study newcomers fared better when they had some control over the content and amount of what they ate and so cafeteria systems or family service, which offer children some choice, are obviously to be favoured over systems where complete plated meals are presented to children. Other helpful measures adopted by some schools include allowing new entrants to sit with older brothers and sisters, providing chairs and tables of suitable height and, most importantly, allowing children plenty of time to eat without coercion. This latter point is particularly important, as some children may choose not to eat at all rather than be hurried or forced to eat something which they do not like. One of the problems posed by school meals is that children often do not recognize the food as anything they have been used to at home and therefore refuse to eat it. Bringing a packed lunch from home is a sensible alternative for children who do not like or cannot get used to school cooking.

While teachers, parents and children alike may view the first day as something of a hurdle and all are relieved when it is over, if children are to make a successful adjustment to school life then the same care and attention accorded to their first day needs to be extended over their next few weeks in school.

The First Weeks in School

Basham (1982) points out that there are likely to be children who, at first, appear to settle well into school but who later become distressed and start crying sometime during these first weeks, perhaps as a result of the dawning realization that attendance is compulsory and very long-term! There may also be children who do not settle at all and whose insecurity causes regressive behaviour such as thumb-sucking, rocking, wetting or tantrums. All these symptoms will be very evident to the teacher, who will need to be extremely patient and reassuring if children are to overcome their fears and happily join in classroom life. It is for the benefit of children like these – and others whose insecurity may not be so apparent – that the reception teacher needs to take things very slowly at first.

Strange rituals such as school assembly, and activities such as PE which children will not have encountered before starting school, are probably best not attempted during the first few weeks. Small assemblies held in the classroom (perhaps held jointly when there is more than one reception class or where newcomers are in vertically grouped classes) allow children to become familiar with the words of hymns and prayers, as well as the pattern of the service, so they will be able to join the whole school assembly with some confidence later in the term. Seating arrangements for assembly in the hall can make all the difference as to how children cope at first. Rather than placing the children class by class in rows facing the front, if they are ranged around three sides of a square then the reception children can take their cue from the older children because they will be able to see clearly what is happening.

Physical education often poses problems because of children's reluctance to undress, either because of shyness or fears of not being able to get clothes back on properly afterwards. It is a good idea to take the class along as spectators when an older group is having a PE lesson in the hall in order to give them an idea of what to expect. Extra helpers, parents perhaps, who come in to lend a hand at changing times are very useful. Otherwise teachers may find half the lesson is taken up by getting the children ready and an even longer period may be spent after the lesson hauling on tights, putting shoes on the right feet and fastening them. There is little point in attempting to force or cajole reluctant children to join in. It is far better to let them watch from the sidelines, if need be for several weeks, until they pluck up the necessary courage for active participation.

If by half-term there are children still showing signs of distress persisting beyond their immediate arrival in the morning, then it is likely that other factors apart from school are involved, such as the death of a grandparent, or a parent being in hospital (Basham, 1982). In cases like these, teachers need to involve parents so that they can be better informed about home difficulties in order to provide extra support for the child in school. Fortunately for teachers, parents and children, starting school is now rarely the traumatic experience it was until relatively recently, with sobbing children being prised from their mothers' grasp at the school door. The employment of some, or all, of the strategies mentioned above might reduce even further the difficulties often experienced during this transitional period.

CURRICULUM CONTINUITY

Once embarked upon their school career children will spend a varying number of years in their first school, depending on whether it is an infant, first or primary school. Increasing numbers of infant and junior or first and middle schools are being amalgamated to form single units under one headteacher (sometimes with nursery classes attached), so that it is possible for some children to be spending up to eight or nine years in one primary school. However, whether children are attending a large primary school which they attend for a number of years, or a small infant school, the need to provide for curriculum continuity is equally great in both cases and it is an issue that can only be successfully tackled by the commitment of the whole staff.

Continuity from Nursery/Playgroup to Reception Class

The curricular aims of the reception class are likely to be different in many ways from those of playgroups and nursery classes. Most forms of pre-school provision place a great deal of emphasis on fostering independence and developing social skills; once in school, it is the cognitive skills associated with reading, writing and number work which are emphasized. Because of this change in emphasis reception classes tend to be equipped and organized for 'work' rather than play, although most will retain some items familiar to the child from pre-school days, such as a Wendy house or sand and water trays. Apart from the introduction of 'work', the most striking differences felt by children used to the routines of playgroup or nursery will be restriction of movement and the diminished freedom of choice – the first usually partly dictated by lack of space and the latter by the increasing predominance of teacher-directed activities related to the basic skills. Freedom to choose will usually be dependent on successful completion of a work activity (Cleave et al., 1982). Also, because the adult/child ratio is generally less favourable in infant schools than in nurseries (about 1:30 instead of about 1:12) children spend more time waiting around or queuing for adult attention.

There are several things that can be done to ease children into their new classroom so that the change will not be too abrupt. Nursery teachers/playgroup leaders could introduce their 'rising fives' to more school-type activities and routines in the term before they move on, in a systematic attempt to prepare them for school. Reception-class teachers could organize their classrooms more along nursery lines by giving children choices from a wide range of play-oriented activities and introducing them to the concept of 'work' very gradually. The reception class should act as a kind of half-way house, offering some kind of continuity of experience for children and providing a bridge to the later stages of infant education.

Planning for Continuity

Traditionally, teaching in an infant and primary school has been an isolated activity dictated in part by the class teacher system and by the typical architectural style of individual, box-like classrooms ranged around a central hall. Because of the British decentralized system of education, which imposes few constraints, heads and teachers in Britain have had a degree of autonomy concerning the curriculum which is found nowhere else. Benyon (1981) argues that this much-prized autonomy is the prime reason why curriculum continuity 'has largely been ignored, gone unrecognized as a problem, been left to chance or at best only been partly tackled'. The publication of several surveys (DES, 1978a, 1982a, 1983) highlights the lack of consistency and continuity in many parts of first and primary school curricula and has led to a serious questioning of the desirability of LEAs, heads and teachers continuing to have so much organizational freedom. Added to this, several years of economic recession have increased calls for accountability from our education system which means that, in future, schools may have to provide regular reviews of their policies including accounts of the way in which they ensure continuity and consistency in the curriculum they offer. It would seem that the sacrifice of some professional autonomy is inevitable if curriculum continuity is to be attempted.

The most usual route schools have taken in aiming to promote curriculum continuity has been through the adoption of curricular guidelines. The HMI survey of first schools (DES, 1982a), however, found that more than half the schools visited had no guidelines at all, other than for mathematics, language, physical and religious education – and even these were not exemplary. Alexander (1984) warns against overestimating the impact of guidelines, as a 'paper' curriculum does not guarantee the adoption of common policies in the classroom. The gap between words and deeds can be very wide. Alexander (1984) also feels it unwise for heads in collusion with senior staff to try to impose definitive, prescriptive schemes on teachers, suggesting instead that all curricular documents should be the 'product of substantial collective discussion and subjected to regular review and modification in the light of both the experience of implementing them and of changing circumstances'. This idea of a set of curriculum guidelines being working documents more similiar to a draft than a perfectly honed scheme and subject to frequent scrutiny and modification, should help prevent them gathering dust in cupboards. It should also allow new teachers to the school to feel able to make their contribution to curricular documents, rather than being expected to work from a set of ready-made schemes of work which, like a pair of second-hand shoes, may fit very badly. It cannot be over-emphasized that if teachers are to use guidelines with a collective sense of purpose, they must also have a sense of involvement in them which can only be achieved through discussion and a shared analysis of problems.

This raises the question of when such meetings can best take place, as infant/primary teachers, unlike their secondary colleagues, have no free periods other than contrived ones, such as assembly or school hymn practice, usually taken by the head to allow the staff some preparation time. Most infant headteachers rely upon the goodwill and professional attitude of staff in giving up their lunch hours and spending time after school to conduct these essential curricular planning and review sessions. Many schools have been involved in GRIDS (Guidelines for Review and Internal Development in Schools), a joint project of the Schools Council and Bristol University, one of the aims of which has been to produce and evaluate a framework and set of strategies which will enable schools to develop and review areas of the curriculum in a more systematic and effective way than has formerly been the case. The success of the GRIDS approach is heavily dependent upon the involvement and consultation of staff at every stage of the process – a considerable commitment of time.

Liaison between Infant and Junior Schools

Where infant and junior schools are separate, each with their own headteacher, more effort will be required to ensure that major discontinuities do not occur. For example, the Schools Council Working Paper 75, *Primary Practice* (1983), cites the difficulties experienced by seven year-olds starting in junior schools which entirely reject the mathematics or reading scheme or style of handwriting adopted by their feeder infant schools. A shared site can facilitate visits and exchanges between teachers from the two schools enabling junior teachers to be introduced to the children who are soon to move on to them and helping staff to get to know something of each other's aims and methods of teaching. Such links need not entail complete uniformity of teaching methods. It is nevertheless important that teachers do not adopt radically different approaches to teaching mathematics or reading which serve only to confuse and bewilder children.

Neighbouring infant and junior schools will also find it relatively convenient to arrange joint activities such as concerts and assemblies, or even embark upon a shared project, such as developing a 'nature trail' within the school grounds. Frequent social contact of this kind may serve to bring down the invisible barriers which often hamper more formal attempts at professional collaboration. A recent report on primary schools in the ILEA (ILEA, 1984) goes even further, recommending that contact should be for a variety of purposes and embedded in a coherent programme of work and methodology. It gives several examples of what could be considered to be good practice, including junior children visiting infant classes to read stories they have written, to play musical instruments or to sing, and infant school children going next door to the 'big school' to show their work or join in assembly. These shared experiences allow infant school children to become familiar with the neighbouring school as well as to build up confidence for their eventual transfer.

Good liaison between schools may be difficult to achieve but this is no reason why it should not be attempted. Creasey et al. (1983) offer the following good advice on the subject: 'make the effort, be tactful, be patient, make sound relationships, be specific, start with the children, aim for a two-way exchange and *persevere*'.

The Importance of Assessment and Record-Keeping

Assessment, taken in the broadest sense, lies at the heart of good teaching and is as important in the early years, if not more so, than in later schooling, for a variety of reasons, many of which are directly related to overcoming problems of a possible lack of continuity. It is to these reasons, rather than the more specialized purposes of assessment in the diagnosis and remediation of learning difficulties, that this section is addressed. (For a fuller account of assessment and learning difficulties see chapter 8.)

A group of children arriving in the reception class will vary enormously in terms not only of physical characteristics but also of temperament and general ability. Some account will already have been taken of these differences by nursery/playgroup staff, if the children have attended pre-school. It is likely that teachers in LEA-run nurseries will keep some form of assessment or record sheet which will be passed on to the receiving school. Some nursery teachers devise their own records, based on judgements about children's social, emotional and cognitive development; others adopt or adapt published checklists, of which the Keele Pre-School Assessment Guide (Tyler, 1980) is among the most popular. Therefore, teachers in the reception class may not always have to start from scratch when making decisions about where to begin with individual children.

For children starting school from home or playgroup there may be little or no information available and teachers will have to begin an extensive process of assessment in order to provide appropriate classroom activities. Formal methods of assessment are unlikely to prove useful in this context; systematic observation, grounded in a sound knowledge of developmental stages, would yield more valuable information about children's skills and abilities. Every opportunity should be taken to monitor children across the entire spectrum of activities in the infant school day. This monitoring should be a continuous process as the value of these appraisals lies in their ability to inform teaching across the curriculum. Assessment of this kind should begin in the reception class and carry on throughout the infant school, as it is vital in ensuring that activities and work are presented at the right level of difficulty for children. Comments in the survey of primary education (DES, 1978a) indicate clearly that HMI were concerned about the suitable match of tasks to children, reporting that even experienced teachers found it difficult to judge the appropriate level of work. With the exception of reading and mathematics – in which the match was reasonably accurate – they found that in most other areas of the curriculum children's abilities were seriously underestimated, with the result that they were neither stretched nor stimulated by the tasks they were set.

Checklists and rating scales can be helpful in this context as they provide a structure and framework for teachers' observations. Although such assessment schedules for reading, language and mathematical skills are readily available, other curricular areas are not as well catered for. It may be more beneficial in the long run for teachers in a school either to design their own checklists or make adaptations and additions to existing ones. In this way the checklists can be closely linked to the aims and teaching method ology of the school and therefore are more likely to be used by teachers. School-devised checklists and rating-scales can greatly facilitate continuity as teachers will have a common frame of reference for appraising pupils.

The Schools Council Working Paper 75 (Schools Council, 1983) suggests that assessment should also contribute to planning the next stage of work. However, the *Education 5 to 9* survey (DES, 1982a) found little evidence that this was actually happening and HMI comment that individual differences revealed by assessments were sometimes disregarded and previously planned programmes or assignments were not adjusted to take account of them.

Teachers generally collect an enormous amount of information about their pupils over the course of a year, the bulk of which may have come from assessment of one kind or another. Effective record-keeping is essential if this information is to be readily accessible either as a guide to teaching or for the benefit of staff further up the school. Clift et al. (1981) surveyed around 200 primary schools which were said by their local authorities to keep very good records. The Schools Council (1983) warned against the temptation of using these findings as a basis for a record-keeping system to fit all primary schools. They endorsed the view that a school staff should collaborate in producing their own records. If these are intended to be passed on to teachers at the next stage of schooling, then they too should contribute. Clift et al. (1981) offer a list of criteria which could serve as a useful starting point for any school intending to design or update their record-keeping system. Included are guidelines for both layout and content, as well as instructions for users concerning abbreviations and symbols, and criteria for the assessment of pupils.

There is no doubt that, if carried out effectively, record-keeping can overcome some of the difficulties of maintaining progression and continuity in children's education but it is also an extremely time-consuming activity. Whenever possible, therefore, children should be encouraged to keep their own records of activities tackled and completed, either on a personal card or on a wall-chart in the classroom. Children could also select items of work they are pleased with, to be retained in a folder and then passed on to the next class or school when the child moves on. Similarly it would also seem sensible and time-saving to hand over to the next teacher the set of exercise books that the children were working in prior to their change of class or school. By looking through these books the receiving teacher will gain a good idea of the standard of individual children's work and their rate of progress.

Clift et al. (1981) were also concerned about the time factor and felt that much valuable information about pupils and their learning habits is lost because primary teachers have insufficient time to keep detailed notes. They conclude, somewhat gloomily:

> without time being made available, the inter-school visiting and collaboration so important in ensuring continuity in the curriculum between stages of education and the creation of a system of records which communicate meaningfully across the 'transition barrier' cannot be achieved. (Clift et al,. 1981 p. 242)

Ensuring that children have a good introduction to their school career and a coherent, consistent education thereafter is by no means an easy task, the responsibility for which does not, of course, reside exclusively with infant school teachers. However, these teachers are ideally placed to initiate and pursue from the outset many of the processes outlined in this chapter. Establishing links with nurseries/playgroups at one end of the school and with junior schools at the other is essential in mitigating the traumatic effects of change on children. Co-operation between schools leads to improved transition procedures and co-ordination of curriculum matters. Good intentions need to be realized for the benefit of all children as they set out on their school careers.

References

Alexander, R. J. 1984: *Primary Teaching*. London: Holt, Rinehart and Winston.

Ames, T. 1983: *40 Remedial Games to Make and Play*. London: Macmillan Education.

Anderson, E. M. 1973: *The Disabled Schoolchild: a study of integration in primary schools*. London: Methuen.

Andrew, P. and Provis, W. M. 1983: One school's experience in setting up a scheme to involve parents in listening to their child read. *Links*, 9 (1), 26–9.

Anthony, W. S. 1977: Activity in the learning of Piagetian operational thinking. *British Journal of Educational Psychology*, 47, 18–24.

Archer, J. and Lloyd, B. 1982: *Sex and Gender*. Harmondsworth: Penguin Books.

Argyle, M. 1973: *Social Interaction*. London: Tavistock.

Arnold, H. 1982: *Listening to Children Reading*. Sevenoaks: Hodder and Stoughton.

Ashton, P., Keen, P., Davies, F. and Holley, B. J. 1975: *The Aims of Primary Education: a study of teachers' opinions*. London: Macmillan Educational.

Ausubel, D. 1963: *The Psychology of Meaningful Verbal Learning*. New York: Grune and Stratton.

Axline, V. 1971: *Dibs: In Search of Self*. Harmondsworth: Penguin Books.

Baetens Beardsmore, H. 1982: *Bilingualism: Basic Principles*. Clevedon: Tieto Ltd.

Bandura, A. 1977: *Social Learning Theory*. New York: General Learning Press.

Barton, L. and Tomlison, S. (eds) 1984: *Special Education and Social Interests*. Beckenham: Croom Helm.

Basham, M. 1982: *Getting Ready for School*. London: Longman.

Bassey, M. 1978: *Nine Hundred Primary School Teachers*. Windsor: NFER.

Bate, M., Smith, M. and James, J. 1981: *Review of Tests and Assessments in Early Education (3–5 years)*. Windsor: NFER–Nelson.

Bax, M. 1977: Man the player. In B. Tizard and D. Harvey (eds), *The Biology of Play*, London: Spastics International Medical Publications/ Heinemann Medical Books.

Becker, W. C. 1978: The national evaluation of Follow Through. *Education and Urban Society*, 10, 431–58.

Bee, H. 1975: *The Developing Child*. New York: Harper and Row.

Bell, P. 1970: *Basic Teaching for Slow Learners*. London: Muller.

Bennett, N. 1976: *Teaching Styles and Pupil Progress*. London: Open Books.

Benyon, L. 1981: Curriculum continuity. *Education 3–13*, 9 (2), 39–41.

Bereiter, C. and Engelmann, S. 1966: *Teaching Disadvantaged Children in the Pre-school*. Englewood Cliffs, NJ: Prentice-Hall.

Bernstein, B. 1960: Language and social class. *British Journal of Sociology*, 11, 271–6.

    1970: Education cannot compensate for society. *New Society*, 26 February.

    1971: *Class, Codes and Control, Volume I*. London: Routledge and Kegan Paul.

    1973: *Class, Codes and Control, Volume II*. London: Routledge and Kegan Paul.

Bigge, M. L. 1982: *Learning Theories for Teachers*. (4th edn) New York: Harper and Row.

Bijou, S. W. and Baer, D. M. 1961: *Child Development, Volume I*. New York: Appleton.

Blatchford, P., Battle, S. and Mays, J. 1982: *The First Transition*. Windsor: NFER–Nelson.

Bloom, B. S. 1964: *Stability and Change in Human Characteristics*. New York: John Wiley.

    1976: *Human Characteristics and School Learning*. New York: McGraw-Hill.

Blyth, J. 1979: Teaching young children about the past. *Education 3–13*. 7 (2), 42–7.

    1984: *Place and Time with Children 5–9*. Beckenham: Croom Helm.

Blyth, W. A. L. 1965: *English Primary Education: a sociological description*. (Vols I and II) London: Routledge and Kegan Paul.

    1984: *Development, Experience and Curriculum in Primary Education*. Beckenham: Croom Helm.

Bolton, E. 1985: Assessment: putting the cart before the horse. *Times Education Supplement* 22 November, 13.

Bower, T. G. R. 1974: *Development in Infancy*. San Francisco: W. H. Freeman.

    1977: *A Primer of Infant Development*. San Francisco: W. H. Freeman.

Bowker, G. 1968: *Education of Coloured Immigrants*. London: Longman.

Boxall, M. 1976: The nurture group in the primary school. *Therapeutic Education*, 4 (2), 13–18.

Brainerd, C. J. 1978: Learning research and Piagetian theory. In L. S. Siegel and C. J. Brainerd (eds), *Alternatives to Piaget*, New York: Academic Press.

Brandis, B. and Henderson, D. 1970: *Social Class, Language and Communication*. London: Routledge and Kegan Paul.

Brearley, M. and Hitchfield, E. 1966: *A Teacher's Guide to Reading Piaget*. London: Routledge and Kegan Paul.

Brind, R. J. 1984: Home/School liaison project. *Links*, 10 (1), 17–18.

Brittan, E. 1976: Multiracial Education 2, teacher opinion on aspects of school life. Part 2: pupils and teachers. *Education Research*, 18, 182–91.

Bronfenbrenner, U. 1970: *Two Worlds of Childhood: US and USSR*. New York: Russell Sage Foundation.

— 1974: *A Report on Longitudinal Evaluation of Pre-school Programmes. Volume 2: Is Early Education Effective?* Washington: US Children's Bureau.

Brown, D. 1979: *Mother-tongue to English: the young child in the multicultural school*. London: Cambridge University Press.

Brown, G. and Harris, T. 1978: *Social Origins of Depression*. London: Tavistock Publications.

Bruner, J. S. 1960: *The Process of Education*. Cambridge, MA: Harvard University Press.

— 1973: Organisation of early skilled action. *Child Development*, 44, 1–11.

— 1981: Child's Play. In R. D. Strom, *Growing Through Play: readings for parents and teachers*, Monterey, CA: Brooks/Cole Pub. Co.

Jolly, A., and Sylva, K. (eds) 1976: *Play: its role in development and evaluation*. Harmondsworth: Penguin.

— and Sherwood, V. 1976: Peekaboo and the learning of role structure. In J. S. Bruner, A. Jolly and Sylva, K. *Play: its role in development and evaluation*, Harmondsworth: Penguin Books.

Bryant, P. 1974: *Perception and Understanding in Young Children*. London: Methuen.

Burden, R. 1981: Systems theory and its relevance to schools. In B. Gillham (ed.), *Problem Behaviour in the Secondary School*, London: Croom Helm.

Burns, R. B. 1979: *The Self Concept-theory, measurement, development and behaviour*. London: Longman.

— 1982: *Self-Concept, Development and Education*. London: Holt Rinehart and Winston.

Bushell, R., Miller, A. and Robson, D. 1982: Parents as remedial teachers. *Association of Educational Psychologists Journal*, 5 (9), 7–13.

Butler, N. R., Peckham, C. S. and Sheridan, M. D. 1973: Speech defects in children aged 7 years. *British Medical Journal*, 1, 253–7.

Calderhead, J. 1984: *Teachers' Classroom Decision Making*. London: Holt, Rinehart and Winston.

Case, R. 1974: Structures and strictures: some functional limitations on the course of cognitive growth. *Cognitive Psychology*, 6, 544–73.

— 1975: Gearing the demands of instruction to the developmental capacities of the learner. *Review of Educational Research*, 45, 59–87.

Central Advisory Council for Education (England) (CAC) 1967: *Children and their Primary Schools* (The Plowden Report). London: HMSO.

Central Statistical Office 1986: *Social Trends*. London: HMSO.

Chalk, J. 1975: Sanctuary units in primary schools. *Special Education/ Forward Trends*, 2 (4), 18–20.

Charlesworth, W. R. 1983: An ethological approach to cognitive development. In C. J. Brainerd (ed.), *Recent Advances in Cognitive–Developmental Theory*, New York: Springer-Verlag.

Chazan, M. 1973: Strategies for helping poorly adjusted children in the infant school. *Therapeutic Education*, 1 (2), 5–13.

—— 1985: Behavioral aspects of educational difficulties. In D. D. Duane and C. K. Leong, (eds), *Understanding Learning Disabilities: International and Multidisciplinary Views*, New York: Plenum Press.

—— Cox, T., Jackson, S. and Laing, A. F. 1977: *Studies of Infant School Children: 2 – Deprivation and Development*. Oxford: Basil Blackwell.

—— and Jackson, S. 1971: Behaviour problems in the infant school. *Journal of Child Psychology and Psychiatry*, 12, 191–210.

—— and Jackson, S. 1974: Behaviour problems in the infant school: changes over two years. *Journal of Child Psychology and Psychiatry*, 15, 33–46.

—— and Laing, A. F. 1985: Teachers' strategies in coping with behaviour difficulties in young children. *Maladjustment and Therapeutic Education*, 3 (3), 11–20.

—— Laing, A. F., Cox, T., Jackson, S. and Lloyd, G. 1976: *Studies of Infant School Children: 1 – Deprivation and School Progress*. Oxford: Basil Blackwell.

—— Laing, A. F., Jones, J., Harper, G. C. and Bolton, J. 1983: *Helping Young Children with Behaviour Difficulties*. Beckenham: Croom Helm.

—— Laing, A. F., Shackleton Bailey, M. and Jones, G. 1980: *Some of Our Children*. London: Open Books.

Cherry, L. 1975: Teacher–child verbal interaction: an approach to the study of sex differences. In B. Thorne and N. Henley (eds), *Language and Sex: difference and dominance*, Rowley, MA: Newbury House.

Choat, E. 1984: The Cockcroft Report on Mathematics in the Primary School. *Journal of the Association of Educational Psychologists*, 6 (3), 6–18.

Chomsky, C. S. 1969: *The Acquisition of Syntax in Children from Five to Ten*. Cambridge, MA: MIT Press.

—— 1972: Stages in language development and reading exposure. *Harvard Educational Review*, 42, 1–33.

Clay, M. M. 1972: *Reading: the patterning of complex behaviour*. Auckland: Heinemann.

—— 1979: *Early Detection of Reading Difficulties*. London: Heinemann.

Cleave, S., Jowett, S. and Bate, M. 1982: *And So To School.* Windsor. NFER–Nelson.

Clift, P., Weiner, G., and Wilson, E. 1981: *Record-Keeping in Primary Schools (Schools Council Research Studies).* London: Macmillan Educational.

Cohen, D. 1983: *Piaget: Critique and Reassessment.* London: Croom Helm.

Cohen, L. and Mannion, L. 1981: *Perspectives on Classrooms and Schools.* London: Holt, Rinehart and Winston.

Coleman, J. S. 1967: Learning through games. In J. S. Bruner, A. Jolly and K. Sylva (eds.); *Play: its role in development and education* Harmondsworth: Penguin Books.

Cooke, T. P. and Apolloni, T. 1976: Developing positive social-emotional behaviours: a study of training and generalisation effects. *Journal of applied Behavioural Analysis,* 9, 65–78.

Coopersmith, S. 1967: *The Antecedents of Self-Esteem.* San Francisco W. H. Freeman.

Cope, A. and Anderson, E. M. 1975: *Special Units in Ordinary Schools* Windsor: NFER.

Cox, C. B. and Dyson, A. E. (eds) 1969: *Fight for Education: A Black Paper.* London: Critical Quarterly Society.

(eds) 1971: *The Black Papers on Education.* London: Davis Poynter.

Craft, M., Raynor, J. and Cohen, L. 1980: *Linking Home and School: a new review.* (3rd edn) London: Longman.

Creasey, M., Findlay, F. and Walsh, B. 1983: *Language across the Transition: Primary/Secondary Continuity and Liaison in English* (Schools Council Programme Pamphlets). London: Longman.

Croll, P. and Moses, D. 1985: *One in Five.* London: Routledge and Kegan Paul.

Cronbach, L. J. 1957: The two disciplines of scientific psychology *American Psychologist,* 12, 671–84.

Crystal, D. 1976: *Child Language, Learning and Lingustics: an overview for the teaching and therapeutic professions.* London: Edward Arnold

1980: *Introduction to Language Pathology.* London: Edward Arnold.

Cummins, J. 1979: Linguistic interdependence and the educational development of bilingual children. *Review of Educational Research* 49, 2, 221–251.

Cyster, R. and Clift, P. 1979: *Parental Involvement in Primary Schools* Slough: NFER–Nelson.

1980: Parental Involvement in Primary Schools: the NFER Survey. In M Craft, J. Raynor and L. Cohen (eds), *Linking Home and School: a new review,* (3rd edn) London: Harper and Row.

Dale, P. S. 1976: *Language Development: structure and function.* New York: Holt, Rinehart and Winston.

Davie, R. 1977: The interface between education and social services. In

DHSS Development Group Social Work Service/Welsh Office, *Working Together for Children and their Families*, London: HMSO.

Butler, N. and Goldstein, H. 1972: *From Birth to Seven*. London: Longman.

Dean, J. 1980 Continuity. In C. Richards (ed.), *Primary Education: issues for the eighties*, London: A. and C. Black.

1983: *Organising Learning in the Primary School Classroom*. Beckenham: Croom Helm.

de Bono, E. 1976: *Teaching Thinking*. London: Temple Smith.

Delamont, S. 1980: *Sex Roles and the School*. London: Methuen.

Demaine, J. 1980: Compensatory education and social policy. In M. Craft, J. Raynor and L. Cohen (eds), *Linking Home and School: a new review* (3rd ed), London: Longman.

Department of Education and Science (DES) 1972: *Speech Therapy Services* (The Quirk Report). London: HMSO.

1975: *A Language for Life (Report of the Committee of Inquiry appointed by the Secretary of State for Education and Science)* (The Bullock Report). London: HMSO.

1978a: *Primary Education in England: a survey by HM Inspectors of Schools*. London: HMSO.

1978b: *Special Educational Needs* (The Warnock Report). London: HMSO.

1979: *Mathematics 5–11*. London: HMSO.

1980: *A View of the Curriculum* (HMI series: Matters for Discussion). London: HMSO.

1981a: *The School Curriculum* (guidance by the Secretaries of State). London: HMSO.

Department of Education and Science (1981b): *The Education (School Information) Regulations 1981*. London: HMSO.

1982a: *Education 5 to 9: an illustrative survey of 80 first schools in England*. London: HMSO.

1982b: *Mathematics Counts* (The Cockcroft Report). London: HMSO.

1983: *9–13 Middle Schools: an illustrative survey*. London: HMSO.

1984: *The Organisation and Content of the 5–16 Curriculum*. London: HMSO.

1985: *Education for All* (The Swann Report). London: HMSO.

Derrick, J. 1966: *Teaching English to Immigrants*. London: Longman.

Derricott, R. (ed.) 1985: *Curriculum Continuity: primary to secondary*. Windsor: NFER–Nelson.

Dessent, T. 1985: Supporting the mainstream: do we know how? *Educational and Child Psychology*, 2 (3), 52–9.

de Villiers, P. A. and de Villiers, J. G. 1979: *Early Language*. London: Fontana/Open Books.

Dodds, D. 1984: Computers in the primary classroom. In A. V. Kelly (ed.), *Microcomputers and the Curriculum*, London: Harper and Row.

Donaldson, M. 1978: *Children's Minds*. London: Fontana.

and Reid, J. 1985: Language Skills and Reading: a developmental perspective. In M. M. Clark (ed.) *New Directions in the Study of Reading*, London: Falmer Press.

Douglas, J. W. B. 1964: *The Home and the School*. London: McGibbon and Kee.

Dowling, M. and Dauncey, E. 1984: *Teaching 3–9 year olds: theory into practice*. London: Ward Lock Educational.

Downey, M. and Kelly, A. V. 1978: *Moral Education: theory and practice*. London: Harper and Row.

Education Act 1981: London: HMSO.

Education Act 1986: London: HMSO.

Elliot, A. J. 1981: *Child Language*. London: Cambridge University Press.

Ennever, L. and Harlen, W. 1972: *With Objectives in Mind: guide to science 5–13*. London: Macmillan Educational (for the Schools Council).

Entwistle, D. R. and Frasure, N. E. 1974: A contradiction resolved: children's processing of syntactic cues. *Developing Psychology*, 10, 852–57.

Erikson, E. H. 1950: *Childhood and Society*. New York: W. W. Norton and Co.

Evans, K. M. 1962: *Sociometry and Education*. London: Routledge and Kegan Paul.

Eysenck, H. J. 1972: The development of aesthetic sensitivity in children. *Journal of Child Psychology and Psychiatry*, 13, 1–10.

Fein, G. G. 1981: Pretend Play in Childhood: an integrative review. *Child Development*, 52, 1095–118.

Feuerstein, R. 1981: Mediated learning experience in the acquisition of kinesics. In B. L. Hoffer and R. N. St Clair (eds), *Developmental Kinesics*, Baltimore: University Park Press.

Rand, Y., Hoffman, M. and Miller, R. 1980: *Instrumental Enrichment*. Baltimore: University Park Press.

Finch, J. 1984: *Education as Social Policy*. London: Longman.

Findlay, F. 1984: Continuity and liaison: primary–secondary practices. In C. Richards (ed.), *The Study of Primary Education: a source book. Vol. 2: Curriculum and Teaching*. London: Falmer Press.

Fischer, K. W. 1980: A theory of cognitive development: the control and construction of hierarchies of skills. *Psychology Review*, 87, 477–531.

Fish, J. 1984: The future of the special school. In T. Bowers (ed.), *Management and the Special School*. Beckenham: Croom Helm.

Fitzherbert, K. 1980: Strategies for prevention. In M. Craft, J. Raynor and L. Cohen (eds), *Linking Home and School*. London: Longman.

Flavell, J. H. 1962: *The Developmental Psychology of Jean Piaget*. New York: van Nostrand.

Botkin, P. T., Fry, C. C., Wright, J. W. and Jarvis, P. E. 1968: *The Development of Role-Taking and Communication Skills in Children*. New York: John Wiley.

Fogelman, K. 1970: *Piagetian Tests for the Primary School*. Slough: NFER.

(ed.) 1983: *Growing Up in Great Britain* (papers from the National Child Development Study). London: Macmillan (for National Children's Bureau).

Ford, J., Mongon, D. and Whelan, M. 1982: *Special Education and Social Control*. London: Routledge and Kegan Paul.

Francis, H. 1974: Social background, speech and learning to read. *British Journal of Educational Psychology*, 44, 290–9.

1977: *Language in Teaching and Learning*. London: Allen and Unwin.

1982: Language teaching research and its effect on teachers in early education. In A. Davies (ed.), *Language and Learning in Home and School*, London: Heinemann Educational Books.

Fries, M. E. and Woolf, P. J. 1953: Some hypotheses on the role of the congenital activity type in personality development. *Psychoanalytic Study of Children* (vol. 8). New York: International Universities, 48–62.

Fundudis, T., Kolvin, I. and Garside, R. F. 1980: A follow-up of speech retarded children. In L. A. Hersov and M. Berger (eds), *Language and Language Disorders in Childhood*, Oxford: Pergamon Pres.

Furth, H. G. and Wachs, H. 1974: *Thinking Goes to School*. New York: Oxford University Press.

Gagné, R. M. 1974: *Essentials of Learning and Instruction*. Hinsdale, Ill: The Dryden Press.

1977: *The Conditions of Learning*. (3rd edn.) New York: Holt, Rinehart and Winston.

Galloway, D. 1985: Meeting special educational needs in the ordinary school? Or creating them? *Maladjustment and Therapeutic Education*, 3 (3), 3–10.

and Goodwin, C. 1979: *Educating Slow-learning and Maladjusted Children: integration or segregation?* London: Longman.

Galton, M. and Simon, B. (eds) 1980: *Progress and Performance in the Primary Classroom*. London: Routledge and Kegan Paul.

Galton, M., Simon, B. and Croll, P. 1980: *Inside the Primary Classroom*. London: Routledge and Kegan Paul.

Galton, M. and Willcocks, J. (eds) 1983: *Moving from the Primary Classroom*. London: Routledge and Kegan Paul.

Garvey, C. 1977: *Play*. London Fontana/Open Books.

Geber, B. A. (ed.) 1977: *Piaget and Knowing*. London: Routledge and Kegan Paul.

Gelman, R. 1969: Conservation acquisition: a problem of learning to attend to relevant attributes. *Journal of Experimental Child Psychology*, 7, 167–87.

Gesell, A. and Ilg, F. 1965: *The Child from Five to Ten*. London: Hamish Hamilton.

Gillham, B. (ed.) 1986: *Handicapping Conditions in Children*. Beckenham: Croom Helm.

Gipps, C. and Gross, H. 1984: *Local Educational Authority Policies in Identification and Provision for Children with Special Educational Needs* (Occasional Paper No. 3: Screening and Special Educational Provision in Schools Project). London: University of London Institute of Education.

Glynn, E. L., McNaughton, S. S., Robinson, V. M. J. and Quinn, M. 1980: *Remedial Reading at Home: helping you to help your child.* Wellington: New Zealand Council for Educational Research.

Golby, M. 1982: The 'progressive' 'elementary' and 'technological' traditions. In C. Richards (ed.), *A Study of Primary Education: a source book, vol. 1.* London: Falmer Press.

(ed.) 1985: *Caught in the Act: teachers and governors after 1980.* (Perspectives 21). School of Education, University of Exeter.

Goodacre, E. J. 1967: *Reading in Infant Classes.* Slough: NFER.

1968: *Teachers and their Pupils' Home Background.* Slough: NFER.

Goodman, K. S. 1967: Reading, a psycholinguistic guessing game. In H. Singer and R. Ruddell (eds), *Theoretical Models and Processes of Reading.* Newark, DE: International Reading Association.

Gorwood, B. T. 1986: *School Transfer and Curriculum Continuity.* Beckenham: Croom Helm.

Gould, R. 1972: *Child Studies through Fantasy.* New York: Quadrangle.

Gregory, J. 1982: *Phonics: a resource bank and teachers' guide.* London: John Murray.

Griffiths, A. and Hamilton, D. 1984: *Parent, Teacher, Child–Working together in children's learning.* London: Methuen.

Gulbenkian Foundation (1982): *The Arts in Schools: Principles, Practice and Provision.*

Gulliford, R. 1971: *Special Educational Needs.* London: Routledge and Kegan Paul.

1985: *Teaching Children with Learning Difficulties.* Windsor: NFER–Nelson.

Hagedorn, J. 1986: Early years: less formal the better. *Times Educational Supplement*, 31 October, 8.

Halford, G. S. 1980: Towards a redefinition of cognitive developmental stages. In J. R. Kirby and J. B. Biggs, *Cognition, Development and Instruction*, New York: Academic Press.

Hall, C. S. 1954: *A Primer of Freudian Psychology.* New York: Mentor Books.

Halliday, M. A. K. 1969: Relevant models of language. *Educational Review*, 22, 26–37.

Halliday, M. A. K. 1975: *Learning How to Mean – explorations in the development of language.* London: Arnold.

Halsey, A. H. 1972: *Educational Priority. Vol. 1: EPA Problems and Policies.* London: HMSO.

Hannon, P. W. and Cuckle, P. 1984: Involving parents in the teaching of reading: a study of current school practice. *Educational Research*, 26, 7–13.

Hannon, P. and Mullins, S. 1980: Support teachers in Sheffield. *British Journal of Special Education*, 7 (4), 11–13.

Hare, B. A. and Hare, J. 1977: *Teaching Young Handicapped Children*. New York: Grune and Stratton.

Hargreaves, D. 1980: A sociological critique of individualism in education. *British Journal of Educational Studies*, 28, 187–98.

Hartup, W. W. 1970: Peer Interaction and social organisation. In P. Mussen (ed.), *Carmichael's Manual of Child Psychology* (3rd edn.), New York: John Wiley.

Havighurst, R. 1972: *Developmental Tasks and Education*. (Rev. edn.) New York: McKay.

Haystead, J., Howarth, V. and Strachan, A. 1980: *Pre-school Education and Care*. Sevenoaks: Hodder and Stoughton for SCRE.

Hegarty, S. and Lucas, D. 1978: *Able to Learn? The Pursuit of Culture-Fair Assessment*. Windsor: NFER.

Herriot, P. 1971: *Language and Teaching: a psychological view*. London: Methuen.

Hewison, J. and Tizard, J. 1980: Parental involvement and reading attainment. *British Journal of educational Psychology*, 50, 209–15.

Hodgson, A., Clunies-Ross, L. and Hegarty, S. 1984: *Learning Together*. Windsor: NFER–Nelson.

Hubbard, G. 1984: Social and educational effects of technological change. *British Journal of Educational Studies*, 32, 108–17.

Hughes, E. R. 1979: *Conceptual Powers of Children: an approach through mathematics and science*. London: Macmillan Educational.

Hughes, M., Pinkerton, G. and Plewis, I. 1979: Children's difficulties on starting infant school. *Journal of Child Psychology and Psychiatry*, 20, 187–96.

Hunt, J. McV. 1961: *Intelligence and Experience*. New York: The Ronald Press.

Hurford, A. and Stow, L. 1985: Talking to Parents – a skill-based course for teachers. *Educational Psychology in Practice*, 1 (2), 59–62.

Hutt, C. 1979: Exploration and play. In B. Sutton-Smith, *Play and Learning*, London: Gardner Press.

Ingram, R. H. 1973: Role of the school eye clinic in modern ophthalmology. *British Medical Journal*, 1, 278–80.

Inhelder, B. Sinclair, H. and Bovet, M. 1974: *Learning and the Development of Cognition*. London: Routledge and Kegan Paul.

Inner London Education Authority (ILEA) 1984: *Education in a Multi-ethnic Society: the primary school*. London: ILEA Centre for Learning Resources.

1985: Improving Primary Schools (Report of the Committee on Primary Education). London: ILEA.

Jackson, A. and Hannon, P. 1981: *The Belfield Reading Project*. Rochdale: Belfield Community Council.

Jahoda, S. 1963: Children's concept of time and history. *Educational Review*, 15, 90–101.

Johnson, D., Ransom, E., Packwood, T., Bowden, K. and Rog, M. 1980: *Secondary Schools and the Welfare Network*. London: Allen and Unwin.

Jones, R. (ed.) 1984: *Micros in the Primary Classroom*. London: Edward Arnold.

Joyce, B. and Weil, M. 1980: *Models of Teaching*. (2nd edn.) New Jersey: Prentice Hall Inc.

Kagan, J. and Moss, H. A. 1962: *Birth to Maturity: a study in psychological development*. New York: Wiley.

Kamii, C. K. 1971: Evaluation of learning in pre-school education: social-emotional, perceptual-motor and cognitive development. In B. S. Bloom, J. T. Hastings and G. F. Madaus, *Handbook on Formative and Summative Evaluation of Student Learning*, New York: McGraw-Hill.

  1974: Pedagogical principles derived from Piaget's theory. In M. Schwebel and J. Raph (eds), *Piaget in the Classroom*, London: Routledge and Kegan Paul.

Karmiloff-Smith, A. 1979: Language development after five. In P. Fletcher and M. Garman (eds), *Language Acquisition*, London: Cambridge University Press.

Kerr, J. and Engel, E. 1980: Can science be taught in primary schools? *Education 3–13*, 8 (1), 4–8.

King, R. A. 1978: *All Things Bright and Beautiful*. Chichester: Wiley.

Kogan, M., Johnson, D. Packwood, T. and Whitaker, T. 1984: *School Governing Bodies*. London: Heinemann.

Kohlberg, L. 1964: Development of moral character and moral ideology. *Review of Child Development Research*, 1, 383–431.

Kolvin, I., Garside, R. E., Nicol, A. R., MacMillan, A., Wolstenholme, E. and Leitch, I. F. 1977: Familial and social correlates of behavioural and sociometric deviance in 8 year old children. In P. J. Graham (ed.), *Epidemiological Approaches in Child Psychiatry*. London: Academic Press.

Kolvin, I., Garside, R. E., Nicol, A. R., MacMillan, A., Wolstenholme, E. and Leitch, I. F. 1981: *Help Starts Here*. London: Tavistock Pubs.

Kounin, J. S. 1970: *Discipline and Group Management in Classrooms*. New York: Holt, Rinehart and Winston.

Labon, D. 1973: Helping maladjusted children in primary schools. *Therapeutic Education*, 1 (2), 14–22.

Laing, A. F. and Chazan, M. 1987: *Teachers' Strategies in Coping with Behaviour Difficulties in First Year Junior School Children*. Birmingham: Association of Workers for Maladjusted Children.

Lambert, W. A. 1977: The effects of bilingualism on the individual:

cognitive and socio-cultural consequences. In P. A. Hornby (ed.), *Bilingualism: psychological, social and educational implications*, New York: Academic Press.

Lansdown, R. 1980: *More than Sympathy: the everyday needs of sick and handicapped children and their families*. London: Tavistock Publications.

Lawrence, E. (ed.) 1952: *Friedrich Froebel and English Education*. London: University of London Press.

Lawton, D. 1968: *Social Class, Language and Education*. London: Routledge and Kegan Paul.

Lazar, I. and Darlington, R. 1979: *Lasting Effects after Preschool*. Washington: US Dept. of Health and Human Services.

Leach, D. J. and Raybould, E. C. 1977: *Learning and Behaviour Difficulties in School*. London: Open Books.

Leinhardt, G., Seewald, A. M. and Engel, M. 1979: Learning what's taught: sex differences in instruction. *Journal of Educational Psychology*, 71, 432–9.

Lewis, E. G. 1981: *Bilingualism and Bilingual Education*. Oxford: Pergamon Press.

Leyden, S. 1985: *Helping the Child of Exceptional Ability*. Beckenham: Croom Helm.

Lindsay, G. A. 1980: The Infant Rating Scale. *British Journal of Educational Psychology* 50, 97–104.

Lindsay, G., Evans, A. and Jones, B. 1985: Paired reading versus relaxed reading, *British Journal of Educational Psychology*, 55, 304–9.

Lindsay, G. A. and Wedell, K. 1982: The early identification of educationally 'at risk' children re-visited. *Journal of Learning Disabilities*, 15 (4), 212–17.

Lloyd, G. 1977: *Studies of Infant School Children. Vol. 3 – Deprivation and the Bilingual Child*. Oxford: Basil Blackwell.

London Borough of Brent 1985: *Primary Schools and Under-Fives Facilities 1986/87 (Parents' Handbook)*. Obtainable from Director of Education, PO Box No. 1, Chesterfield House, 9 Park Lane, Wembley, Middesex, HA9 7RW.

Lovejoy, S. 1985: What do they expect? – headteacher, teacher and social worker expectations of EPs. *Educational Psychology in Practice*, 1 (3), 108–11.

Lovitt, T. C. 1982: *Because of my Persistence, I've Learned from Children*. Columbus: Charles E. Merrill Publishing Co.

Luria, A. R. 1961: *The Role of Speech in the Regulation of Normal and Abnormal Behaviour*. New York: Pergamon Press.

Lynch, J. and Pimlott, J. 1980: Parents and teachers: an action-research project. In M. Craft, J. Raynor and L. Cohen (eds), *Linking Home and School*, London: Longman.

McCabe, C. (ed.) 1980: *Evaluating In-service Training for Teachers*. Windsor: NFER–Nelson.

McCarthy, D. 1954: Language development in children. In L. Carmichael (ed.), *Manual of Child Psychology*, (2nd edn) New York: John Wiley.

McGee, R., Silva, P. A. and Williams, S. 1984: Perinatal, neurological, environmental and developmental characteristics of seven-year-old children with stable behaviour problems. *Journal of Child Psychology and Psychiatry*. 25 (4), 573–86.

McInnes, J. A. 1973: Language pre-requisites for reading. In M. M. Clark and A. Milne (eds), *Reading and Related Skills*. London: Ward Lock.

McMichael, P. 1977: Self-esteem, behaviour and reading skills in infant school children. In J. Reid and H. Donaldson (eds), *Reading Problems and Practices*, London: Ward Lock.

—— 1979: The hen or the egg? Which comes first – antisocial emotional disorders or reading disability? *British Journal of Educational Psychology*, 49, 226–38.

McNicholas, J. and McEntee, J. 1973: *Games to develop Reading Skills*. London: NARE.

Mabey, C. 1981: Black British literacy. *Educational Research* 23, 83–95.

MacMillan, K. 1977: *Education Welfare*. London: Longman.

MacNamara, J. 1966: *Bilingualism and Primary Education: a study of Irish experience*. Edinburgh: Edinburgh University Press.

Maccoby, E. E. 1980: *Social Development: psychological growth and the parent-child relationship*. New York: Harcourt Brace Jovanovich.

—— and Jacklin, C. N. 1974: *The Psychology of Sex Differences*. Stanford, CA: Stanford University Press.

Male, J. and Thompson, C. 1985: *The Educational Implications of Disability*. London: Royal Association for Disability and Rehabilitation.

Manning, K. and Sharp, A. 1977: *Structuring Play in the Early Years at School*. London: Ward Lock Educational.

Manning, M., Heron, J. and Marshall, T. 1978: Styles of hostility and social interactions at nursery, at school and at home: an extended study of children. In L. A. Hersov, M. Berger and D. Shaffer, *Aggression and Anti-social Behaviour in Childhood and Adolescence*, Oxford: Pergamon Press.

Marshall, S. 1963: *An Experiment in Education*. London: Cambridge University Press.

Marston, N. and Stott, D. H. 1970: Inconsequence as a primary type of behaviour disturbance in children. *British Journal of Educational Psychology*, 40 (1), 15–20.

Matthews, G. 1984: Learning and teaching mathematic skills. In D. Fontana (ed.), *The Education of the Young Child*, Oxford: Basil Blackwell.

Meadows, S. (ed.) 1983: *Developing Thinking*. London: Methuen.

Merrett, F. and Wheldall, K. 1984: Classroom behaviour problems which junior school teachers find most troublesome. *Educational Studies*, 10 (2), 87–91.

Moore, T. 1966: Difficulties of the ordinary child in adjusting to primary school. *Journal of Child Psychology and Psychiatry*, 7, 17–38.

Moore, T. 1969: Stress in normal childhood. *Human Relations*, 22 (3), 235–50.

Morgan, R. T. T. 1976: Paired-reading tuition: a preliminary report on a technique for cases of reading deficit. *Child: Care, Health and Development*, 2, 13–28.

 and Lyon, E. 1979: Paired Reading – a preliminary report on a technique for parental tuition of reading retarded children. *Journal of Child Psychology and Psychiatry*, 20, 151–60.

Morley, M. 1972: *The Development and Disorders of Speech in Childhood*. (3rd edn) Edinburgh: Churchill Livingstone.

Moses, D. 1985: The end of isolation: link schemes between ordinary and special schools. *Educational and Child Psychology*, 2 (3), 96–101.

Muckley, A. 1981: Some experienced teachers' perceptions of the psychologist. *Association of Educational Psychologists Journal*, 5, 6.

Murray, F. B. 1980: The generation of educational practice from developmental theory. In S. Modgil and C. Modgil (eds), *Toward a Theory of Psychological Development*. Windsor: NFER.

Mussen, P. H., Conger, J. J. and Kagan, J. 1979: *Child Development and Personality*. New York: Harper and Row.

National Council for Voluntary Organisations 1983: *Voluntary Organisations – an NCVO directory 1983/84*. London: Bedford Square Press.

Newson, E. 1976: Parents as a resource in diagnosis and assessment. In T. E. Oppé and P. Woodford (eds), *Early Management of Handicapping Disorders*, London: IRMMH Review of Research and Practice No. 19.

Newson, J. and Newson, E. 1979: *Toys and Playthings in Development and Remediation*. Harmondsworth: Penguin Books.

Nisbet, J. and Shucksmith, J. 1984: *The Seventh Sense*. Edinburgh: Scottish Council for Research in Education.

Obrist, A. J. 1983: *The Microcomputer and the Primary School*. Sevenoaks: Hodder and Stoughton.

Oden, S. and Asher, S. 1977: Coaching children in social skills for friendship making. *Child Development*, 48, 495–506.

Ogilvie, E. 1973: *Gifted Children in Primary Schools: the report of the Schools Council Enquiry into the teaching of gifted children of primary age 1970–71*. London: Macmillan.

O'Leary, K. D. and O'Leary, S. G. 1977: *Classroom Management: the successful use of behaviour modification*. (2nd edn.). New York: Pergamon Press.

Olson, D. R. and Torrance, N. G. 1983: Literacy and cognitive development: a conceptual transformation in the early school years. In W. S. Meadows (ed.), *Developing Thinking*, London: Methuen.

Osborn, A. F., Butler, N. R. and Morris, A. C. 1984: *The Social Life of Britain's Five-year-olds.* London: Routledge and Kegan Paul.

Palmer, R. 1971: *Starting School.* London: University of London Press.

Piaget, J. 1932: *The Moral Judgement of the Child.* London: Routledge and Kegan Paul.

   1951: *Play, Dreams and Imitation in Childhood.* London: Routledge and Kegan Paul.

   1959: *Language and Thought of the Child.* (Originally published in French, 1926.) London: Routledge and Kegan Paul.

   and Inhelder, B. 1969: *The Psychology of the Child.* London: Routledge and Kegan Paul.

Phillips, J. L. 1981: *Piaget's Theory: a primer.* San Francisco: W. H. Freeman.

Pollard, A. 1985: *The Social World of the Primary School.* London: Holt, Rinehart and Winston.

Portsmouth, R., Wilkins, J. and Airey, J. 1985: Home-based reading for special school pupils. *Educational Psychology in Practice*, 1 (2), 52–8.

Povey, R. M. and Hill, E. 1975: Can pre-school children form concepts? *Educational Research* 17, 180–92.

PPA (Pre-School Playgroups Association) 1983: *Easing the Transition from Home to School.* Newcastle: Northern Region PPA.

Pringle, M. L. Kellmer, Butler, N. R. and Davie, R. 1966: *11,000 Seven-year-olds.* London: Longman.

   1970: *Able Misfits.* London: Longman.

Pugh, G. 1981: *Partnership with Parents.* London: National Children's Bureau.

Pulaski, M. A. 1973: In J. L. Singer (ed.), *The Child's World of Make-believe: experimental studies of imaginative play,* New York: Academic Press.

Quicke, J. 1982: *The Cautious Expert.* Milton Keynes: Open University Press.

Quigley, H. 1971: Nursery teachers' reactions to the Peabody Language Development Kit. *British Journal of Educational Psychology*, 41, 155–62.

Reilly, M. (ed.) 1974: *Play as Exploratory Learning.* Beverly Hills, CA: Sage Publications.

Rhine, W. R. 1981: *Making Schools More Effective.* New York: Academic Press.

Richards, C. 1981: The primary curriculum: perennial questions and current issues. *Primary Education Review*, 12, 5–9.

   (ed.) 1982: *New Directions in Primary Education.* Lewes: The Falmer Press.

Richards, R., Collis, M. and Kincaid, D. 1980: *Learning through Science: Formulating a School Policy.* London: Macmillan Educational (for Schools Council).

Richman, N., Stevenson, J. and Graham, P. J. 1982: *Pre-school to School: a behavioural study*. London: Academic Press.

Richmond, P. G. 1970: *An Introduction to Piaget*. London: Routledge and Kegan Paul.

Rimmer, L. and Wicks, L. 1984: The family today. In E. Butterworth and D. Weir (eds), *The New Sociology of Modern Britain*, London: Fontana.

Robeck, M. C. and Wilson, J. A. R. 1974: *Psychology of Reading: foundations of instruction*. New York: John Wiley.

Roberts, A. and Ewan, R. T. A. 1984: A case study of educational micro-computer use in upper schools. *Research in Education*, 32, 67–85.

Roberts, K. 1980: School, parents and social class. In M. Craft, J. Raynor and L. Cohen (eds), *Linking Home and School: a new review*, (3rd edn.), London: Longman.

Roberts, T. 1979: The hidden curriculum in the infants school. *Durham and Newcastle Research Review*, 8 (42), 29–33.

Robinson, E. 1983: Metacognitive development. In S. Meadows (ed.), *Developing Thinking*, London: Methuen.

Robinson, M. 1980: The overlapping perspectives of education and social work. In M. Craft, J. Raynor and L. Cohen (eds), *Linking Home and School: a new review*, (3rd edn.), London: Longman.

Robinson, W. P. 1980: Language management, socio-economic status and educational progress. In L. A. Hersov and A. R. Nicol (eds) *Language and Language Disorders in Childhood*, Oxford: Pergamon Press.

Rogers, C. 1982: *A Social Psychology of Schooling*, London: Routledge and Kegan Paul.

Rosen, C. and Rosen, H. 1973: *The Language of Primary School Children*. Harmondsworth: Penguin Books.

Rushby, N. J. 1979: *An Introduction to Educational Computing*. London: Croom Helm.

Rutherford, R. and Edgar, E. 1979: *Teachers and Parents*. London: Allyn and Bacon.

Rutter, M. 1972: *Maternal Deprivation Reassessed*. Harmondsworth: Penguin Books.

   1977: Brain damage syndromes in childhood: concepts and findings. *Journal of Child Psychology and Psychiatry*, 18, 1–21.

   Tizard, J. and Whitmore, K. (eds) 1970: *Education, Health and Behaviour*. London: Longman.

   and Yule, W. 1975: The concept of specific reading retardation. *Journal of Child Psychology and Psychiatry*, 16, 181–97.

Safran, S. P. and Safran, J. S. 1985a: Classroom context and teachers' perceptions of problem behaviours. *Journal of Educational Psychology*, 77, 20–8.

   1985b: Special and regular educators' judgements of problem behaviours as influenced by classroom disruptiveness. Paper presented at the International Special Education Congress, Nottingham, July 1985.

Saunders, G. 1982: *Bilingual Children: Guidance for the Family*. Clevedon: Multilingual Matters.

Saunders, M. 1982: *Multicultural Teaching: a guide for the classroom*. Maidenhead: McGraw-Hill.

Schools Council 1972: *Teaching English to West Indian Children (Concept 7–9)*. London: Longman.

—— 1983: *Primary Practice: a sequel to the practical curriculum* (Schools Council Working Paper 75). London: Methuen Educational.

Sears, R. R., Maccoby, E. E. and Levin, H. 1957: *Patterns of Child Rearing*. Evanston, Ill: Row Peterson.

Sebba, J. 1985: The development and evaluation of short school-focused courses on special educational needs. *Educational and Child Psychology*, 2 (3), 130–7.

Sharp, J. D. and Stott, D. H. 1976: *Effectiveness Motivation Scale* (manual). Windsor: NFER.

Sharrock, A. 1970: *Home/School Relations*. London: Macmillan.

—— 1980: Research on home-school relations. In M. Craft, J. Raynor and L. Cohen (eds), *Linking Home and School*, London: Longman.

Shaw, K. 1984: Enter the six-year-olds. *Times Educational Supplement*, 14 September, 22.

Sheppard, J. L. 1974: Compensation and combinatorial systems in the acquisition and generalisation of conservation. *Child Development*, 45, 717–30.

Sheridan, M. D. and Peckham, C. S. 1973: Hearing and speech at 7. *Special Education*, 62, 16–20.

Simon, B. 1981: The Primary School revolution: myth or reality? In B. Simon and J. Willcocks (eds), *Research and Practice in the Classroom*, London: Routledge and Kegan Paul.

—— and Willcocks, S. J. (eds) 1981: *Research and Practice in the Primary Classroom*. London: Routledge and Kegan Paul.

Singer, J. L. (ed) 1973: *The Child's World of Make-Believe: experimental studies of imaginative play*. New York: Academic Press.

—— 1977: Imagination and make-believe in early childhood: some educational implications. *Journal of Mental Imagery*, 1, 127–44.

Slater, D. 1985: The education sub-government: structure and context. In M. Hughes, P. Ribbins and H. Thomas (eds), *Managing Education: the system and the institution*, London: Holt, Rinehart and Winston.

Sleap, M. 1983: Is Physical Education needed in the Primary Skill Curriculum? In M. Mawer and M. Sleap (eds), *Physical Education within Primary Education*, London: Physical Education Association of Great Britain and N. Ireland.

Smedslund, J. 1977: Piaget's psychology in practice. *British Journal of Educational Psychology*, 47, 1–6.

Smith, F. 1971: *Understanding Reading: a psycholinguistic analysis of reading and learning to read*. New York: Holt, Rinehart and Winston.

Smith, P. K. 1977: *Social and Fantasy Play in Young Children*. In B.

Tizard, and D. Harvey (eds), *The Biology of Play*, London: Spastics International Medical Publications/Heinemann Medical Books.

1984: *Play in Animals and Humans*. Oxford: Basil Blackwell.

and Simon, T. 1984: Object play, problem-solving and creativity in children. In P. K. Smith, *Play in Animals and Humans*, Oxford: Basil Blackwell.

Sonquist, H. D. and Kamii, K. 1967: Applying some Piagetian concepts in the classroom for the disadvantaged. *Young Children*, 22, 231–40.

Southgate, V., Arnold, H. and Johnson, S. 1981: *Extending Beginning Reading*. London: Schools Council/Heinemann Educational Books.

Spence, S. H. 1983: Teaching social skills to children. *Journal of Child Psychology and Psychiatry*, 24, 621–7.

Spivack, G. and Shure, M. B. 1974: *Social Adjustment of Young Children*. San Francisco, CA: Jersey Press.

Spivack, G., Platt, J. and Shure, M. B. 1978: *The Problem-Solving Approach to Adjustment*. San Francisco, CA: Jersey Press.

Staines, J. W. 1958: The self-picture as a factor in the classroom. *British Journal of Educational Psychology*, 28, 97–111.

Stephens, L. S. 1974: *The Teacher's guide to Open Education*. New York: Holt, Rinehart and Winston.

Stillman, A. and Maychell, K. 1984: *School to School: LEA and teacher involvement in educational continuity*. Windsor: NFER–Nelson.

Stone, J. and Taylor, F. 1976: *The Parents' Schoolbook*. Harmondsworth: Penguin Books.

1977: *Handbook for Parents with a Handicapped Child*. London: Arrow Books.

Stone, M. 1981: *The Education of the Black Child in Britain: the myth of multiracial education*. London: Fontana.

Stonier, T. 1982: Changes in Western society: educational implications. In C. Richards (ed.), *New Directions in Primary Education*, Lewes: Falmer Press.

Strom, R. D. 1981: *Growing through play: readings for parents and teachers*. Monterey, CA: Brooks/Cole Pub. Co.

Strommen, E. A., McKinney, J. P. and Fitzgerald, H. E. 1977: *Developmental Psychology: the School-Aged Child*. Homewood, Ill: The Dorsey Press.

Sutton-Smith, B. 1977: Play as adaptive potentiation. In P. Stevens (ed.), *Studies in the Anthropology of Play*, Cornwall, NY: Leisure Press.

1979: *Play and Learning*. New York: Gardner Press.

Sylva, K., Roy, C. and Painter, M. 1980: *Childwatching at Playgroup and Nursery School*. London: Grant McIntyre.

Tamburrini, J. 1982: New directions in nursery school education. In C. Richards (ed.), *New Directions in Primary Education*, Lewes: The Falmer Press.

Tanner, J. M. 1962: *Growth at Adolescence*. (2nd edn.) Oxford: Basil Blackwell.

1984: Physical development. In D. Fontana (ed.), *The Education of the Young Child*, Oxford: Basil Blackwell.

Taylor Parker, S. 1984: Playing for Keeps: an evolutionary perspective on human games. In P. K. Smith *Play in Animals and Humans*, Oxford: Basil Blackwell.

Taylor, P. H., Exon, G. and Holley, B. J. 1972: *A Study of Nursery Education* (Schools Council Working Paper No. 41). London: Evans/ Methuen Educational.

Taylor, T. 1977: *A New Partnership for our Schools*. London: HMSO.

Taylor, W. 1980: Family, School and Society. In M. Craft, J. Raynor and L. Cohen (eds), *Linking Home and School*, London: Longman.

Templin, M. 1957: *Certain Language Skills in Children*. London: Oxford University Press.

Thomas, A. and Chess, S. 1977: *Temperament and Development*. New York: Brunner/Mazel.

Thomas, A., Chess, S. and Birch, H. G. 1968: *Temperament and Behaviour Disorders in Children*. New York: University Press.

Thomas, B. 1986: Schools in Ethnic Minorities: Wales. *Journal of Multilingual and Multicultural Development*, 7, 2 and 3, 169–86.

Thomas, D. 1978: *The Social Psychology of Childhood Disability*. London: Methuen.

1985: The dynamics of teacher opposition to integration. *Remedial Education*, 20 (2), 53–8.

Thomas, J. B. 1973: *Self-Concept in Psychology and Education: a review of research*. Windsor: NFER Publishing Company.

Thorp, J. 1985: Accountability versus participation? In M. Hughes, P. Ribbins and H. Thomas (eds), *Managing Education: the system and the institution*, London: Holt, Rinehart and Winston.

Tizard, B. and Harvey, D. 1977: *Biology of Play*. London: Spastics International Medical Publications/Heinemann Medical Books.

Tizard, B. and Hughes, M. 1984: *Young Children Learning: talking and thinking at home and at school*. London: Fontana.

Tizard, B., Mortimore, J. and Burchell, B. 1981: *Involving Parents in Nursery and Infant Schools: a source book for teachers*. London: Grant McIntyre.

Tizard, J., Moss, P. and Perry, J. 1976: *All Our Children*. London: Temple Smith.

Tizard, J., Schofield, W. N. and Hewison, J. 1982: Collaboration between teachers and parents in assisting children's reading. *British Journal of educational Psychology*, 52, 1–15.

Tomlinson, P. 1981: *Understanding Teaching: interactive educational psychology*. London: McGraw-Hill.

Tomlinson, S. 1982: *A Sociology of Special Education*. London: Routledge and Kegan Paul.

1983: *Ethnic Minorities in British Schools*. London: Heinemann.

Topping, K. 1984: Paired reading. *Child Education*, December 10–11.

1985: Paired reading. *Child Education*, January, 10–11.

and McKnight, G. 1984: Paired Reading – and parent power. *Special Education: Forward Trends*, 11 (3), 12–14.

Tough, J. 1973a: *Focus on Meaning*. London: Allen and Unwin.

1973b: The language of young children: the implications for the education of the young disadvantaged child. In M. Chazan (ed.), *Education in the Early Years*, Faculty of Education, University College of Swansea and Aberfan Disaster Fund.

1977a: *Talking and Learning: a guide to fostering communication skills in nursery and infants schools*. London: Ward Lock Educational.

1977b: *The Development of Meaning*. London: Allen and Unwin.

1984: How young children develop and use language. In D. Fontana (ed.), *The Education of the Young Child* (2nd edn), Oxford: Basil Blackwell.

Townsend, H. E. R. and Brittan, E. M. 1972: *Organisation in Multi-Racial Schools*. Slough: NFER.

Trasler, G. 1962: *The Explanation of Criminality*. London: Routledge and Kegan Paul.

Trickey, G. and Crispin, L. 1982: A reading project in Barking. *Special Education Forward Trends*, 9 (4) 6–9.

Turner, J. 1984: *Cognitive Development and Education*. London: Methuen.

Tyler, S. 1980: *Keele Pre-School Assessment Guide*. Windsor: NFER.

1984: Assessment with young children. In D. Fontana (ed.), *The Education of the Young Child*, (2nd edn.) Oxford: Blackwell.

Ungoed-Thomas, J. R. 1978: *The Moral Situation of Children*. London: Macmillan.

Upton, G. 1981: The Early Years controversy and its implications for teaching maladjusted children. *New Growth*, 1 (2), 11–20.

van der Eyken, W. 1982: *The Education of Three to Eight Year-Olds in Europe in the Eighties*. Windsor: NFER–Nelson.

Vernon, P. E., Adamson, G. and Vernon, D. F. 1977: *The Psychology and Education of Gifted Children*. London: Methuen.

Voyat, G. 1974: The development of operations. In M. Schwebel and J. Raph, (eds), *Piaget in the Classroom*, London: Routledge and Kegan Paul.

Vuyk, R. 1981: *Overview and Critique of Piaget's Genetic Epistemology 1965–1980, Vols. 1 and 2*. London: Academic Press.

Vygotsky, L. S. 1962: *Thought and Language*. Cambridge, MA: MIT Press.

1967: Play and its role in the mental development of the child. *Soviet Psychology*, 5, 6–18.

Ward, G. W. S. 1977: *Deciding What to Teach*. London: National Association for Multiracial Education.

Webb, L. 1969: *Children with Special Needs in the Infants' School*. London: Collins/Fontana Books.

Weikart, D. P., Epstein, A. S., Schweinhart, L. and Bond, J. T. 1978: The Ypsilanti Preschool Demonstration Project No. 4: *Preschool Years and Longitudinal Results*. Ypsilanti: High Scope.

Weitz, S. 1977: *Sex Roles: biological, psychological and social foundations*. New York: Oxford University Press.

Weller, K. and Craft, A. 1983: *Making Up Our Minds: an exploratory study of Instrumental Enrichment*. London: Schools Council.

Wells, G. 1979: Variation in Child Language. In P. Fletcher and M. Garman (eds), *Language Acquisition*, London: Cambridge University Press.

—— 1981: *Learning Through Interaction*. London: Cambridge University Press.

—— 1982: Influences of the home on language development. In A. Davies (ed.), *Language and Learning in Home and School*, London: Heinemann Educational Books.

—— 1984: Success and failure in language learning: some findings from the Bristol Study. *British Association for Applied Linguistics*, Newsletter 21, Summer 1–24.

—— 1985: *Language Development in the Pre-School Years*. London: Cambridge University Press.

Welsh Office 1984: *A Survey of Provision for Special Education Needs in the Ordinary School (Primary)*. Cardiff: Welsh Office.

Welton, J. 1985: School and a multi-professional approach to welfare. In P. Ribbins (ed.), *Schooling and Welfare*, London: Falmer Press.

Werry, J. S. 1972: Organic factors in childhood psychopathology. In H. C. Quay, and J. S. Werry, (eds), *Psychopathological Disorders in Childhood*, New York: John Wiley.

Westwood, P. 1979: *The Remedial Teacher's Handbook*. Edinburgh: Oliver and Boyd.

Wheldall, K. and Merrett, F. 1984: *Positive Teaching: the behavioural approach*. London: Allen and Unwin.

Williams, A. A. 1970: *Basic Subjects for the Slow Learner*. London: Methuen.

Williams, J. 1979: Perspectives on the multi-cultural curriculum. *The Social Science Teacher*, 8, 126–33.

Williams, M. K. R. and Sommerwill, H. 1982: *Early Mathematic Language*. London: Macmillan Educational.

—— 1982: *40 Maths Games to Make and Play*. London: Macmillan Educational.

Williams, P. (ed.) 1984: *Special Education in Minority Communities*. Milton Keynes: Open University Press.

Winchester, S. 1985: Learning through talk – classroom applications. In *Talking to Some Purpose*, Educational Review Occasional Publication, No. 12, University of Birmingham.

Wolfendale, S. 1983: *Parental Participation in Children's Development and Education*. New York: Gordon and Breach.

Wolff, S. 1973: *Children under Stress*. (Rev. edn.). Harmondsworth: Pelican Books.

Woodhead, M. 1984: Pre-school education has long-term effects: but can they be generalised? *Oxford Review of Education*, 11, 133–55.

Young, P. and Tyre, C. 1985: *Teach Your Child to Read*. London: Fontana.

Zaichkowsky, O. O., Zaichkowsky, L. B., and Martiner, T. J. 1980: *Growth and Development: the Child and Physical Activity*. St Louis, Missouri: C. V. Mosby.

Further Reading

DEVELOPMENT OF FIVE TO EIGHT YEAR-OLDS

Bee, H. 1975: *The Developing Child*. New York: Harper and Row.
Child, D. 1986: *Psychology and the Teacher*. (4th edn.) London: Holt, Rinehart and Winston.
Donaldson, M. 1978: *Children's Minds*. London: Fontana.
Fontana, D. 1981: *Psychology for Teachers*. London: British Psychological Society and Macmillan Press.
Meadows, S. 1986: *Understanding Child Development*. London: Hutchinson.

GENERAL APPROACHES TO READING

Clark, M. M. 1985: *New Directions in the Study of Reading*. London: Falmer Press.
Hornsby, B. and Shear, F. 1974: *Alpha to Omega: the A–Z of teaching reading, writing and spelling*. London: Heinemann.
Hunter, E. 1977: *Reading Skills: a systematic approach*. London: Council for Educational Technology.
Smith, F. 1985: *Reading*. (2nd edn.) London: Cambridge University Press.
Somerfield, M., Torbe, M. and Ward, C. 1983: *A Framework for Reading*. London: Heinemann.
Southgate, V. Planning for Reading Success Series. London: Macmillan Educational.
  1983: Vol. 1. *Children Who Do Read*.
  1984: Vol. 2. *Reading: Teaching and Learning*.
  1986: Vol. 3. *Reading for Information*.
Southgate, V., Arnold, H. and Johnson, S. 1981: *Extending Beginning Reading*. London: Heinemann Educational (for Schools Council).
Wade, B. 1984: *Story at Home and School*. Educational Review Occasional Publications, No. 10, University of Birmingham.
Wade, B. (ed.) 1985: *Talking to Some Purpose*. Educational Review Occasional Publications, No. 12, University of Birmingham.

ACTIVITIES FOR HELPING WITH READING DIFFICULTIES

Ames, T. 1983: *40 Remedial Games to Make and Play*. London: Macmillan Educational.

Gregory, J. 1982: *Phonics: a resource bank and teachers' guide*. London: John Murray.

Hughes, J. 1979: *Using Phonics*. London: Macmillan.

McNicholas, J. and McEntee, J. 1973: *Games to Develop Reading Skills*. London: NARE.

Reason, R. and Lindsay, G. 1986: *Learning Difficulties in Reading and Writing*. Windsor: NFER–Nelson.

Root, B. 1982: *40 Reading Games to Make and Play*. London: Macmillan Educational.

Stott Programmed Reading Kit. Obtainable from Holmes-McDougall Ltd, Leith Walk, Edinburgh, EH6 8NS.

ASSESSMENT OF READING DIFFICULTIES

Ames, T. 1985: *The Macmillan Diagnostic Reading Pack*. London: Macmillan Educational.

Bradley, L. 1980: *Assessing Reading Difficulties*. London: Macmillan Educational.

Daniels, J. C. and Diack, H. 1970: *The Standard Reading Tests*. London: Chatto and Windus.

Edwards, P. 1976: *Reading Problems: Identification and Treatment*. London: Heinemann.

Hegarty, S. and Lucas, D. 1978: *Able to Learn? The Pursuit of Culture-fair Assessment*. Windsor: NFER.

Neale, M. D. 1958: *The Neale Analysis of Reading Ability*. (Rev. edn 1976) London: Macmillan Educational.

Raban, B. 1983: *Reading*. London: Macmillan Educational.

Vincent, D., Green, L., Francis, J. and Powney, J. 1983: *Review of Reading Tests*. Windsor: NFER–Nelson.

MATHEMATICS TEACHING

Burton, L. 1984: *Thinking Things Through: problem solving in mathematics*. Oxford: Basil Blackwell.

Department of Education and Science 1979: *Mathematics 5–11: a handbook of suggestions*. London: HMSO.

Department of Education and Science 1982: *Mathematics Counts* (The Cockcroft Report). London: HMSO.

ILEA 1976: *Primary School Mathematics: mathematical content*. ILEA Cenre for Learning Resources.

ILEA 1978: *Primary School Mathematics: checkpoints*. ILEA Centre for Learning Resources.

ILEA 1985: *Mathematics Counts: looking for bias and insensitivity in mathematics materials.* ILEA Centre for Learning Resources.

Schenk, C. 1986: *Hands on: Hands off – a computer activity book for schools.* London: A. and C. Black.

Williams, M. K. R. and Somerwill, H. J. 1982: *Early Mathematical Language.* London: Macmillan Educational.

Williams, M. K. R. and Somerwill, H. J. 1982: *40 Maths Games to Make and Play.* London: Macmillan Educational.

SCIENCE TEACHING

Blyth, J. E. 1984: *Place and Time with Children 5–9.* Beckenham: Croom Helm.

Department of Education and Science 1983: *Science in Primary Schools.* London: HMSO.

Gunning, S., Gunning, D., and Wilson, J. 1981: *Topic Teaching in the Primary School.* Beckenham: Croom Helm.

Mays, P. 1985: *Teaching Children through the Environment.* London: Hodder and Stoughton.

Schools Council 1973: *Environmental Studies 5–13: The use of historical resources (Working Paper 48).* London: Evans/Methuen Educational.

Richards, C. and Holford, D. 1983: *The Teaching of Primary Science: Policy and Practice.* London: Falmer Press.

CREATIVE ACTIVITIES

Davies, G. 1983: *Practical Primary Drama.* London: Heinemann Educational Books.

Demmery, S. (undated) *Drama in a Multicultural Society. Part 1. The Early Years, 4–12.* London: Educational Drama Association.

Department of Education and Science 1972: *Movement: physical education in the primary years.* London: HMSO.

Gentle, K. 1985: *Children and Art Education.* Beckenham: Croom Helm.

Gulbenkian Foundation 1982: *The Arts in Schools: principles, practice and provision.*

Hope–Brown, M. 1973: *Music with Everything.* London: Frederick Warne.

Learmouth, J. 1982: *Small Apparatus in Practice.* London: Schofield and Sims.

Schweitzer, P. 1980: *Theatre in Education – 5 Infant Programmes.* London: Methuen.

Walker, R. 1976: *Sound Projects.* London: Oxford University Press.

Werner, P. H. and Burton, E. C. 1979: *Learning through Movement: teaching cognitive content through physical activities.* St Louis, Missouri: C. V. Mosby.

Whittaker, K. 1976: *Movement in Practice.* London: Schofield and Sims.

Ethnographic Resources for Art Education: Resource packs exploring the art and craft traditions and techniques of different countries. Suitable for older age groups. Available from: ERAE c/o Department of Art, City of Birmingham Polytechnic, Margaret Street, Birmingham, BC 3BX.

RELIGIOUS EDUCATION

Holm, J. 1975: *Teaching Religion in School.* London: Oxford University Press.
Schools Council 1977: *Discovering an Approach.* London: Macmillan Educational.

HELPING LANGUAGE DEVELOPMENT

General

Crystal, D. 1976: *Child Language, Learning and Linguistics.* London: Arnold.
Durkin, R. (ed.) 1986: *Language Development in the School Years.* Beckenham: Croom Helm.
Francis, H. 1977: *Language in Teaching and Learning.* London: Allen and Unwin.

Language schemes

Chazan, M. and Cox, T. 1976: Language programmes for disadvantaged children. In V. P. Varma and P. Williams (eds), *Piaget, Psychology and Education,* London: Hodder and Stoughton.
Downes, G. 1978: *Language Development and the Disadvantaged Child.* Edinburgh: Holmes-McDougall.
Gahagan, D. M. and Gahagan, G. A. 1970: *Talk Reform.* London: Routledge and Kegan Paul.
Tough, J. 1977: *Talking and Learning: a guide to fostering communication skills in the nursery and infant school.* London: Ward Lock Educational.
Moyle, D. and Skyes, E. 1986: *Games for Language and Reading Development.* Eastbourne: Holt, Rinehart and Winston.

PROMOTING SOCIAL AND EMOTIONAL DEVELOPMENT

Behaviour modification strategies

Axelrod, S. 1977: *Behaviour Modification for the Classroom Teacher.* New York: McGraw–Hill.
Herbert, M. 1981: *Behavioural Treatment of Problem Children: a Practice Manual.* London: Academic Press.

Walker, J. E. and Shea, T. M. 1976: *Behaviour Modification: a practical approach for educators*. St Louis, Missouri: C. V. Mosby.

Westmacott, E. V. S. and Cameron, R. J. 1981: *Behaviour Can Change*. Basingstoke, Hampshire: Globe Education.

Social skills training

Canfield, J. and Wells, H. 1976: *100 Ways to Enhance Self-Concept in the Classroom*. Englewood, NJ: Prentice–Hall.

Cartledge, G. and Milburn, J. E. 1980: *Teaching Social Skills to Children*. Oxford: Pergamon Press.

Spence, S. H. 1980: *Social Skills Training with Children and Adolescents: a counsellor's manual:* Windsor: NFER.

Spence, S. H. and Shepherd, G. (eds) 1983: *Developments in Social Skills Training*. London: Academic Press.

Spivack, G., Platt, J. and Shure, M. B. 1978: *The Problem-Solving Approach to Adjustment*. San Francisco, CA: Jossey–Bass.

Index